GRANTS,
ETC.

Dedication

To *Morah* Rickie, an *Eshet Chayil*

GRANTS, ETC.

SECOND EDITION

Originally Published as Grantsmanship and Fund Raising

ARMAND LAUFFER

SAGE Publications
International Educational and Professional Publisher
Thousand Oaks   London   New Delhi

For information address:

 SAGE Publications, Inc.
2455 Teller Road
Thousand Oaks, California 91320
E-mail: order@sagepub.com

SAGE Publications Ltd.
6 Bonhill Street
London EC2A 4PU
United Kingdom

SAGE Publications India Pvt. Ltd.
M-32 Market
Greater Kailash I
New Delhi 110 048 India

Printed in the United States of America

Library of Congress Cataloging-in-Publication Data

Lauffer, Armand.
      Grants, Etc. / author, Armand Lauffer. — 2nd ed.
          p.   cm.
      "Originally published as Grantsmanship and fund raising."
      Includes bibliographical references and index.
      ISBN 0-8039-5468-9 (acid-free paper). — ISBN 0-8039-5469-7 (pbk.:
acid-free paper)
      1. Fund raising. 2. Proposal writing in the social sciences.
3. Proposal writing for grants. I. Lauffer, Armand. Grantsmanship
and fund raising. II. Title.
HG177.L375 1997
36107'068'1—dc21   97-4597

This book is printed on acid-free paper.

      05 06 07 08 10 9 8 7

Acquiring Editor:	Jim Nageotte
Editorial Assistant:	Kathleen Derby
Production Editor:	Sanford Robinson
Production Assistant:	Karen Wiley
Book Designer/Typesetter:	Janelle LeMaster
Cover Designer:	Candice Harman
Print Buyer:	Anna Chin

Contents

PART III: FUND-RAISING FUNDAMENTALS

Preface

There is a great deal of good news for grant seekers and fund-raisers. More and more Americans have larger and larger chunks of disposable income. Individual donations to charity have increased by approximately 10% a year since 1994. New configurations of interests between the public, private, and voluntary sectors result in shared fund-raising and funding efforts and more targeted allocation patterns. These changes may mean that there is more money available to your organization to do its business. New or redirected dollars, however, may also require that your current patterns of doing business will have to change to accommodate emerging funding requirements.

Parts I and II of this volume are about changes in the funding environment and how best to respond to them. Part III addresses the tools and techniques that successful fund-raisers use to get the resources they need to do business.

The past 20 years have not been encouraging for many practitioners and administrators in the human services and other nonprofit organizations. Some have lost their positions through cutbacks. Others are carrying especially heavy loads in an effort to maintain the quality of services in the context of shrinking resources. The picture has been especially bleak in certain service sectors, and the situation has had a disproportionate impact on vulnerable client populations: ethnic and racial minorities, the disabled, new immigrants, those who are among the structurally unemployed, and those who have been defined by society as deviants rather than as the victims of circumstances. The arts and the environment have also been severely cut. Education has been hurt by reduced levels of support from local, state, and federal sources.

The largesse of the 1960s and early 1970s seems to have been replaced by a niggardliness of spirit and resource. Perhaps, perhaps not. Certainly the distribution of resources has changed considerably. Also, the balance of responsibility for funding service and cause-oriented programs has shifted back and forth between the public, private, and voluntary sectors. The redistribution of resources and responsibilities has caused strains virtually everywhere in the human services and in many other quasi-public and nonprofit settings. Private philanthropy has been unable to fill the gaps caused by government withdrawal.

This is not exactly an upbeat way to begin a book on fund-raising. The truth is that there is much to be optimistic about. Individual agencies, even consortia of agencies, may not be able to do much to affect the larger societal forces that have caused this redistribution. They can, however, assure that they and their constituents get their proper share of the resource pie. It is not an unlimited pie. It is probably a good deal larger than it seems (or at least the pie dish can be replenished), even though it may not be as deep as many of us would like it to be. Unfortunately, we do not all have equal or adequate access to the pie.

That is what this book is all about—increasing your access and increasing the likelihood that you and those you represent can re-plenish needed resources to stay in business and to do that business better.

Previous versions (*Grantsmanship* [1977, 1983] and *Grantsmanship and Fund Raising* [1984]) addressed twentieth-century challenges— challenges faced by organizations created in this century to address the public's interests under voluntary auspices. We are entering a new century in which the paradigms of an earlier time may not be in place for too long. The privatization of public services has made the fund-raising process much more competitive. This not only requires more sophistication in resource procurement but it also means that we must harness those resources more carefully so as to do the most good (and to assure that we will continue to get the resources we need). That is the reason readers familiar with earlier editions of this book will find this edition to be much different. Many of the chapter headings may be the same, but you will discover that more than 80% of the content is new! Why a single volume on gifts, contracts, and grants? Why so much content on program design, marketing, and the context within which fund-raising takes place? Could not these topics be treated separately in different volumes? Certainly, and, as the many references at the end of each chapter suggest, they have been. I have chosen to treat them together so as to go beyond instruction in technique to an exploration of the forces that are likely to shape the success of the fund-raising strategies you choose to employ. In other words, there are many fine cookbooks: Some focus on desserts, others on soups. There are also excellent books on the promotion of family health through proper nutrition. This volume attempts a bit of both, prescribing how to do things, while describing the context within which it is done.

The book is written primarily with fund-raisers in the nonprofit sector in mind. Many of the principles and processes described, however, are likely to be of equal interest to those working in the private and public sectors for whom getting contracts, grants, or gifts is of central import. Although I use the word *agency* to refer to the organization seeking support from others, and although many of my examples are drawn from human service agencies, I use this term generically. By "your agency," I also mean your school, library, recreation program, museum, concert hall, health service, or public park.

In each chapter, you will find many excellent suggestions for how to make your fund-raising efforts more productive. For the most part, they are not my own. They come from both new and seasoned fund-raisers—some of them volunteers, others professional fund-raisers, and still others responsible for making the decisions about who to fund and for how much. Wherever possible, I quote those whose work is described. They can say it much better than I.

Acknowledgments

I learned about grantsmanship and fund-raising the way most people do—by doing it. It was not without encouragement, however, first and foremost from five deans at the University of Michigan School of Social Work. Fedele Fauri, whose spirit continues to infuse the school with social commitment and intellectual honesty, told me when I first arrived at Michigan to "take a few months, get to know the state, and then start building a program, but make sure that the faculty are behind you." He knew well that professional and career interests, when supportive of institutional directions, are a strong combination. He said, "To win at horse racing, you not only have to have horses that can, but will run." To maintain the institution of horse racing, you need consumer publics (race fans and others who have interests in supporting the institution), suppliers (of horses and goods), and collateral service providers.

To win at fund-raising, you also need access to knowledge about the programs for which you are seeking support and technical competence in planning and design. I gained a good deal of both from Bob Vinter, who taught me to be rigorous in program design and meticulous in budgeting. Phil Fellin continued in the traditions of his

xvi - GRANTS, ETC.

predecessors, knowing when to rein in a feisty colt and when to let
him have his head. Harold Johnson permitted me the freedom to
write when he might have preferred to have me out there hustling—
practicing what I teach. Paula Allen-Meares gave me the license to
put some of my writing aside for a few years while building relationships with community institutions to make it possible for a new
academic program to succeed.

I continue to owe a debt to Wyatt Jones, Professor Emeritus of
Brandeis University, who taught me that to write effectively you have
to think more about who will be reading or using your material than
about the material itself. The dozens of community leaders and
human service practitioners and nonprofit administrators whose
words and experiences are related in these pages are its real authors.
I have tried to provide them with a way to communicate directly to
you. I am referring to government and foundation officials, nonprofit
agency board members, industrialists, planners and administrators,
community activists, direct service practitioners, professional fund-
raisers, and others whose knowledge and skill I have tried to include
in each chapter.

I owe a personal debt of gratitude to two consummate professionals—Marty Kraar, chief executive officer of the Council of Jewish
Federations, and Bob Aronson, executive of the Jewish Federation of
Metropolitan Detroit. Each taught me that successful fund-raising
requires genuine respect for donors. Stanley Frankel, Larry Jackier,
and Conrad Giles—an attorney, a developer, and a physician, respec-
tively—taught me that donors are often the best fund-raisers, especially when helping peers articulate their deepest aspirations.

I also acknowledge the contributions of several former students.
Deborah Lynn Kroopkin searched an often fugitive literature for
examples of innovations in grant seeking and fund-raising. You will
find her work reflected throughout each chapter. Anita Morse, a
professional librarian (often a fund-raiser's best friend), searched the
Internet for information on funding sources. You will find her work
summarized in Appendix A and in the Michigan Web site:
http://www.umich.edu/~socwk/alauffer/grantetc.html. Finally, a
special thanks to the students at Michigan and UCLA who read and
commented on a first draft of this book. Their honest and critical
comments saved you all from some painful moments.

I

Philanthropic Resources

1

Doing Well so as to Do Good

The Business of Grant Getting, Contracting, and Fund-Raising

Imagination is more important than knowledge. Knowledge is limited. Imagination encircles the world.
—Albert Einstein (Source: Einstein and Relativity exhibit at the Israel Museum, June/July, 1996)

THE BUSINESS OF RAISING MONEY

Let's talk business—the business of raising money and putting it to good use. You may not generally think of yourself as being in the fund-raising business, but if you are not, you probably should be. It is an important business. If you do not do it well, you and your organization may not be in the business of doing good for very long. Although the resource base for many nonprofit organizations has expanded rapidly during the past few decades, it is an unsteady base for most.

That base draws from funding sources in the public, private, and voluntary sectors—each of which is undergoing major changes as

3

government agencies embrace privatization strategies. The three funding mechanisms that are treated most extensively in this book—grants, gifts, and contracts—are also introduced. The news, we will find, is not all bad, and for those who understand what is going on it can be quite good. To understand why, we will take a brief look at the

- sources of supply (of money and other resources);
- mechanisms of distribution;
- competition.

In the second half of this chapter, approaches to increasing the likelihood of getting the resources to stay in business and to do good on behalf of your constituencies will be addressed.

Sources of Supply

The sources of supply have both expanded and shrunk. The bad news is that government cutbacks have put the squeeze on agencies that provide social services, health care, education, the arts, and the environment. The American appetite for using nongovernmental organizations to carry out public business, however, appears unabated. Governments at all levels use such mechanisms as grants, contracting out, and coproduction to engage the private and voluntary sectors in performing good work.

There is good and bad news on the philanthropic front as well. There has been rapid growth of new foundations, some of them with start-up endowments in the tens of millions. For example, the Packard Foundation, with a posthumous gift from its founder in 1996, is likely to rival the Ford Foundation's $6 billion dollar endowment. The bad news is that foundations account for only $6 of every $100 philanthropic dollars (approximately $4 comes from corporate gifts and $90 is donated by individuals). The surprising news is that, when one totals all private contributions to museums, libraries, social service agencies, church-sponsored charitable activities, and other charities, it is under 3% of the national income. The total is dwarfed by government expenditures.

Brian O'Connell, president of the Independent Sector, estimates that voluntary organizations are about one-tenth of the (economic) size of all government organizations in the United States. This represents an enormous set of undertakings and a significant economic force, but it is not a substitute for government nor can it be expected to shoulder the responsibilities that are properly those of government. Approximately 45% of all charitable giving goes to religious organizations or for religious purposes, followed by education, social services, health, culture, the arts, and the environment. This could be good news for some, if the total percentage of the national income allocated to philanthropy were growing. It does not appear to be, however. For example, United Way and many sectarian federation campaigns are flat or dropping precipitously. The adult children of many wealthy donors are not likely to continue in their parents' philanthropic footsteps. Younger adults are much less apt to donate money to charities and to "good causes" than were their counterparts in earlier generations.

As might be expected, at least 90¢ of every dollar donated by individuals for religious purposes goes to congregational and church-sponsored charities (i.e., from the voluntary sector to the voluntary sector). One might expect other funds, from the private and public sectors, also to go into the voluntary sector, but this is not always the case. For example, most government expenditures for health services go to other governmental institutions (such as the Veterans Administration and county or municipal hospitals) or to private institutions or individuals (such as multihospital corporations, health management organizations [HMOs], nursing homes, and private medical practices). Perhaps more surprising is that roughly 30% of all private, foundation, and corporate donations for education, culture, and the environment go to public institutions. These included state universities, public school districts, municipal libraries, state and national parks, and even state highways.

Mechanisms of Distribution:
Gifts, Contracts, and Grants

When the first edition of this book was published in 1977, the focus was exclusively on grant getting. Today, that would no longer suffice. Chasing grants when the bulk of your funds are more likely to come from fees-for-service, third-party payments, service contracts, gifts, and sales would not make much sense. In this edition, comparable attention is paid to gifts, contracts, and grants and to the strategies that produce income through all three.

Gifts

For the purposes of this book, a *gift* is defined as a contribution made to a nonprofit or public body, generally for philanthropic purposes. Gifts can be made with or without stipulating how they must be used. They are contributed by individuals, foundations, corporations, or voluntary associations. They can be

* in the present or deferred (as when they are put into a will or payment pledged at some future date);
* in cash or in-kind (e.g., equipment or volunteer time);
* to be spent now or invested with only the proceeds to be spent.

In-kind gifts are discussed in Chapter 9. Foundation and corporate gifts are described in Chapters 5 and 6, whereas gifts from religious and civic associations and individuals are discussed in Chapters 8 and 10.

Contracts

A *contract* (see Chapter 4) is an award to perform a specific task or service. The organization making the award generally specifies what is to be done, by whom to whom or to what, within what time frame, following what standards, and at what cost. Purchase-of-service contracts (POSCs) are the principle mechanisms by which government agencies fund services provided by voluntary (nonprofit) or proprietary (private or for-profit) organizations. In other words, they are used by government to buy the services of others to do its business. Contracts and subcontracts are also used to purchase the services of their own vendors by those who receive POSCs from government. Even more complicated, some private institutions purchase services from government. For example, one state may purchase the services of a proprietary firm to build and manage prisons.

That firm, however, because it may be tight on space, may temporarily or permanently purchase jail space from jurisdiction in another state.

Grants

Grants are awards, often to nonprofit institutions, that allow the recipient to do something of its own design but that also addresses the interests of the funding agency. Grants are the principal mechanism by which the federal government reallocates funds to states and local government units for domestic programs. Block grants are usually awarded in large sums to states for some designated purpose (housing, welfare, and medical assistance). State governments may then use the funds to cover their own costs of providing the service or reallocate the federal dollars via grants and POSCs. Some grants are *categorical*—that is, intended for specific services to targeted populations. These may be awarded to other government units or to nonprofit and proprietary (for-profit) organizations (see Chapter 3). These categorical program or project grants (shorter in duration) are the ones for which your organization may qualify.

Grants are also the primary mechanism used by foundations and corporations to make philanthropic awards to individuals, organizations, or consortiums of organizations involved in some collaborative enterprise (Chapters 5 and 6).

Increasingly Complex Exchanges

Gifts, contracts, and grants are part of a very complex and little understood system of exchanges in which cash and noncash resources are transferred from one party to another. In a simple voluntary exchange, A might pay dollars to B for a service provided in a noncoercive environment. At first glance, that appears to be what happens when

- a state agency purchases the services of a contractor to open a child-care center;
- a corporation provides a gift of equipment to the center;
- a foundation provides the center with a grant to cover costs of a parent education program.

Presumably, each of the donor organizations meets some of its own needs via the transfer. The center benefits by having the resource to open and then stay in business. Clients benefit by being served, and the field of early childhood education may benefit if the center is innovative in its service approaches. Few exchange processes, however, are likely to be that simple. There are many stakeholders in each of these exchanges:

- other service providers who may collaborate with the center or compete with it for funds and clients;
- the direct beneficiaries of service—children and their families;
- advocacy groups (for the minority or handicapped children being served);
- employers (of the parents) or job training programs that depend on the center's availability;
- the welfare department that pays for parent job training and part of the operating costs of the center and so on.

Relationships become even more complicated when the center is part of a complex of interdependent programs that are linked together in consortium arrangements aimed at community renewal, such as Empowerment Zones (discussed in Chapter 5). These include employees, developers, health and mental health providers, schools, banks, churches, civic associations, and grassroots organizations.

Competition

The United States is a three-sector society that includes

- a public sector, with its national, state, regional, local, and even neighborhood jurisdictions;
- a private sector composed of individuals and for-profit business enterprises that can range from one-person operations to multinational conglomerates;
- a voluntary sector (sometimes referred to as the nonprofit, independent, or third sector) composed of such varied entities as social agencies, cultural institutions, civic associations, mutual benefit organizations, religious congregations, cause-oriented coalitions, and so on.

Although examples of overlapping and collaboration have been noted, there are many situations in which funding exchanges lead to competition between or within sectors. One of the stated intentions of using POSC mechanisms is to foster competition and thereby (presumably) increase creativity and productivity. These assumptions will be examined in Chapter 4. Competition is further fostered when the private sector is invited to bid on contracts that, a decade or two ago, might have been targeted to the voluntary sector. This movement toward privatization (in which the private sector assumes responsibility for providing public services) received a major boost from relatively recent changes in federal programs.

For example, Medicaid (1965) stimulated a major expansion of the nursing home industry, and the Health Maintenance Act of 1973, when combined with subsequent regulations and inducements, spurred an enormous growth in for-profit HMOs. Privatization is sometimes referred to as "corporate welfare" for two reasons: It involves the business world in the management and delivery of services, and it often benefits the needs of private capital (to expand and find new markets) rather than the needs of the disadvantaged. As the proprietary sector expands, it often dominates sections of the human services market and other services previously identified with public and voluntary agencies.

Corporate behavior is often more aggressive. Because many for-profit service providers have become regional and national entities, they often can dominate and even shape the market in ways that the voluntary sector cannot. Corporations can also use business mechanisms that may not be as readily available to the voluntary sector and may unavailable to the public sector. For example, corporations can finance their investments (e.g., building needed facilities or financing start-up costs) through commercial loans and stock offerings. Ongoing expenses are then covered via fees charged to clients and insurance companies or secured via contracts and grants. For-profit corporations are often less inhibited by either traditions influencing practices in the voluntary sector or by regulations imposed on the public sector. This has made them more effective competitors and changed the ways in which voluntary organizations operate (or should, if they are to be effective competitors) (Table 1.1).

75osta pre

Table 1.1 Some Examples of Corporate Conglomerates That Compete With Voluntary-Sector Organizations

Nursing homes:	Beverly Enterprises, ARA Services, and National Medical Enterprises (each of which manage more than 1,000 nursing homes)
Hospitals:	Humana, Hospital Corporation of America, American Medical International, and others that own eight or more hospitals and have a budget of upwards of $100 million per year
HMOs:	HealthAmerica and others are expected to serve 60 million members by the year 2000
Child Care (residential treatment, group homes, and day care):	Kinder-Care manages or franchises more than 1,000 child care centers
Home care:	Home Health Care of America and Health Force provide alternatives to nursing home care
Corrections:	Corrections Corporation of America builds and manages prisons or arranges for prisoner housing

The negative consequences of creating such huge enterprises include standardization and bureaucratization that may be unresponsive to regional or other differences and to professional standards. Another consequence is that it may knock voluntary agencies out of the arena. There appear to be a number of strategies that nonprofits and smaller proprietary for-profits can pursue in light of the competition, including downsizing, developing alternative and much needed services (i.e., staking a claim for and occupying a secure niche in the market), changing their domain (who is served, where, and how), or expanding the range and size of their income sources.

In addition, nonprofit agencies can capitalize on a distinct advantage of their own. Most are perceived as being public regarding rather than profit oriented. They have voluntary boards that represent community interests and whose members are not paid for their participation (unlike many corporate boards) and whose rewards are perceived to be intangible. In contrast, the investments of shareholders in corporations are financial, and their rewards are perceived to be in monetary dividends. Because voluntary agencies' surplus income, if any, is likely to be reinvested in service rather than distributed to owners and shareholders, they are perceived to be more trustworthy.

GETTING THE SUPPORT YOU NEED

If you ask, "What are our chances of getting the support we need to do our business?," the reply during the first 10 years of the next century is likely to be "Not very good." If you ask, however, "What are our chances of getting the support needed to do business?," the answer is "Not bad." In fact, the chances are probably pretty good—if you are clear about whose business you are doing.

Human service and other nonprofit organizations are in the business of doing the public's business. The support you are going to be able to muster will depend on the extent to which your organization's various publics perceive its activities as being in their interests. In the narrow sense, this is a book about fund-raising. In a broader sense, it is about program and resource development and about articulating your organization's interests with those of suppliers, consumers, and other publics. Without them, your organization would have no resources and no business.

The Resourceful Way to Raise Money

In everyday language, the term *resources* is usually understood to mean money. It can refer to money, of course, but the term is not limited to that usage. Resources are all those means and commodities needed to achieve an objective, produce a service, or distribute a product. Some resources, such as facilities, equipment, and supplies, may be purchased with money or can be used in lieu of cash. Other resources, such as legitimacy, expertise, and commitment, may or may not be related to money. Nevertheless, they are indispensable to the conduct of organizational affairs. Without them, fund-raising and grantsmanship are hardly likely to be successful.

Close attention to resource development and orchestration and a concern with programs and the various publics they serve distinguishes this book from a number of others that deal more narrowly with the "how to" of getting grants, contracts, or gifts. Many of these other books are excellent, and I recommend a number of them throughout the text. Their step-by-step directions for proposal writing or for organizing campaigns and their myriad tips on where to look for potential sources of support will themselves become an important resource for you. In this book, however, the approach is slightly different. The techniques of fund-raising will be presented within the context of an organization's overall fiscal strategies, and those strategies will be discussed within the context of its program and administrative policies.

Fund-Raising Within the Agency's
Overall Program and Fiscal Strategies

In many human service organizations, funds from contracts, gifts, and grants are still a small and sometimes insignificant element in the organization's overall income picture. Other sources of financial support include (a) general fund allocations, (b) fees or tuition, (c) sales and royalties, (d) investments, (e) reserve funds, and (f) in-kind materials and services. During the next decade, all these sources of funds will require effective orchestration.

Allocations come from the organization that sponsors your program. For example, a state department of public health will get its allocation from the governor's office as appropriated by a legislative committee. A school of social work will receive its general fund allocation from the university of which it is a part. A voluntary welfare agency may get its support from the United Way or its own board of directors. A research organization may get its support from a federal agency or through contributions from several local government units. Allocations are generally made on an annual basis. Until recently, an organization could assume that the funds allocated each year would be based on the total amount allocated the previous year with inflation and rising costs taken into account. As competitive forces become more significant, this is no longer likely to be the case.

Fees may be paid by individuals who seek services or by organizations that contract for services with your organization. They may also be paid by another organization in payment for services conducted by your agency. Many fees are paid by third parties. Third-party payments include client fees paid fully or in part by insurance companies or such government programs as Medicare and Medicaid. Tuition payments are fees paid by individuals who enroll in instructional programs. In some cases, a government body or employing organizations may cover the tuition of a client or staff member. Unlike allocations, contracts, or grants, the income from individual fees or from tuition need not be expended within a given fiscal year. Your organization's bylaws or regulations may permit banking any net gain over your expenses toward some future program or service.

The same is true of sales and royalties. Many research organizations sell their reports or collect royalties on their sales through commercial firms. This is also the case for educational institutions and, to a lesser extent, service agencies. The resulting income may also be used for investing in the development of other publications. With some limitations, non-profit organizations are permitted to sponsor commercial enterprises. There are two limitations to securing this income without having to pay taxes on it. First, it has to meet the "test of relatedness," which means that the activity (not the income alone) must contribute importantly to the performance of the organization's tax-exempt purpose. Second, if the activity is not financially sound in its own right, a tax benefit is not likely to turn it into a money machine. In effect, contrary to the cash cow myth, there are not likely to be very many surefire money-makers that will obviate the need for a broader fund-raising strategy.

Investments are of many types. For example, universities regularly invest in land and in stock portfolios. Several manage major businesses. Although this is less often true of social agencies, the use of stock portfolios and trust funds is taking on increasing importance.

Where permitted, reserve funds are generated through the accumulation of income from investments and from particular activities. They may be used only for specified activities or may be used generally for deficits when and where they occur. In fat years, the reserves may bulge considerably. In lean years, they may be quickly depleted.

As you and your organization reexamine your current sources of revenue, you may need to rethink the sources of supply you wish to tap—the government, the voluntary sector, the private sector, individual donors, or the persons who pay a fee for service. The wider the net you cast and the more varied the waters in which to troll, the less dependent you will be on a single source and the greater the likelihood that when one source dries up others will be available from which to draw.

Do not, however, think of fund-raising in the same way that you usually think of a fishing expedition. The objective is not to drop a line in the water to see what you can hook; the objective is to get the resources you need and to put them to effective use. A better analogy might be the marketplace, where people buy and sell and engage in other forms of bartering and values are set by supply and demand.

Staffing and Managing the Fund-Raising Efforts

The success of many program development or fund-raising efforts is determined by the relationships that are built and managed throughout the process. Successful fund-raising is rarely a onetime activity—or a one-person task. The day of the "Lone Ranger" fund-raiser who rides in on his white horse, cleans up the mess, locates the treasure, and rides off is long gone, if it ever existed at all. Successful fund-raising is not measured by a one-time contract or grant or by a single major gift. As many of the scores of fund-raising efforts described in this book suggest, the probability of success may be affected by the following:

- ongoing relationships between key stakeholders—grant and contract seekers, sponsors (grant and contract makers) and donors (individual and corporate), community volunteers, consumers, and others;
- involvement of many agency staffers, board members, and volunteers in addition to the executive or other administrators;
- building the fund-raising effort into the organization's strategic planning, marketing, and management processes;
- using proven fund-raising methods, including those associated with campaigns, securing endowments, writing proposals, preparing bids, and building long-term relationships with donors.

The most important factor, however, may be imagination, without which no amount of knowledge and know-how gained from this book and elsewhere is likely to be sufficient.

In the pages that follow, I will share with you what I think are among the most imaginative fund-raising approaches in practice today. Some of these have been developed by innovative newcomers who have grown into the fund-raising role. Others reflect the work of seasoned professionals and competent volunteers. Many of them are women, and this represents a breakthrough. During the past 10 to 20 years, an increasing number of women have entered fundraising practice as professionals. A community foundation executive stated, "My volunteering experience has prepared me well for this role. Donors are all volunteers and they need to be nurtured, appreciated, and listened to." She continues: "Women fund-raisers are less apt to hide their feelings, and are more detail oriented. We get excited when we build up small victories. We don't need a big score to know we're doing well." I do not have data to confirm these observations, but there is considerable evidence that women are increasingly playing key roles in the management of foundations, United Way and other federated funds, and so forth. The growth of minority-oriented foundations and the increased interest in multicultural programs has also resulted in a steady increase of fund-raisers representing various minority populations.

REVIEW

Fund-raising and other forms of resource development are integral to an organization's program and fiscal strategies. This suggests that they are more effective when not treated as separate and detached functions. Many members of the organization—its paid staff, its board and committee members, and its volunteers—and representatives of other organizations with which it interacts can all play key roles in the process. Dollars are a major resource for any agency, but the term resources should not be limited to money. It also includes facilities, equipment, expertise, commitment, energy, and all the other means and commodities needed to achieve an objective, produce a service, or distribute a product. Three distribution mechanisms—gifts, contracts, and grants—were discussed in some detail and an examination was begun of the three sectors—public, private, and voluntary—within which fund-raising and allocations take place. These will be revisited throughout the remaining chapters.

HOW THE BOOK IS ORGANIZED

Chapter 2 provides a conceptual underpinning for much of what is to follow. It describes the marketing imagination. Marketing is a way of designing programs so as to respond to the interests of various publics—providers, funders, consumers, and other stakeholders. It envisions the fund-raising process as a win-win situation rather than a contest in which two or more parties in an exchange try to get the best deal by focusing on their own narrow interests.

Each of the following chapters begins with a description of a program development, grant-making, contracting, or fund-raising approach. Frequently, the person responsible is quoted directly. The first six chapters of Part II describe the institutional sources of contracts, grants, and gifts—government, foundations, federated funds, religious bodies, civic associations, and mutual-benefit organizations. Each of these chapters begins by examining the history of philanthropic and social spending in each arena. The concluding part of each chapter describes winning techniques that you may wish to borrow or adapt to your own situation. The last two chapters follow a similar format, but the content areas are slightly different.

Chapter 9 addresses noncash contributions—both concrete gifts, such as equipment, property, and resalable items, and volunteer time—because of their increasing importance to both the recipient and the donor. Chapter 10 examines the motivations of individual donors and the many new approaches to the design of giving opportunities that meet donor needs as well as those of recipient agencies.

Although Part II is loaded with tips and techniques, only Part III could be thought of as a fund-raising manual. Chapter 11 deals with the management of specific types of campaigns, drawing on the previous chapter. What goes into a winning proposal and how to prepare and edit each section of a proposal is treated in Chapters 12 through 14. Chapter 15 is a review of what is already known about how to find out where the resources are and build relationships with key stakeholders, and it also discusses what to do while you are waiting to hear how your proposal fared and how to respond, whether you get funded or not.

SUGGESTIONS FOR FURTHER READING

Akerman, S. O. (Ed.). (1996). *The economics of nonprofit institutions: Studies in structure and policy.* New York: Oxford University Press.

Burlingame, D. F., & Hulse, L. J. (Eds.). (1991). *Taking fund raising seriously: Advancing the profession and practice of raising money.* San Francisco: Jossey-Bass.

Chess, H. (Ed.). (1990). *Resources for your nonprofit organization: A how to do it handbook.* Los Angeles: California Community Foundation.

Conry, J. C. (1991). The feminization of fund raising. In D. F. Burlingame & L. J. Hulse (Eds.), *Taking fund raising seriously: Advancing the profession and practice of raising money.* San Francisco: Jossey-Bass.

Dobkin, P. (1992). *Inventing the nonprofit sector and other essays on philanthropy, volunteerism, and nonprofit organizations.* Baltimore, MD: Johns Hopkins University Press.

Harvey, J. W., & McCroban, K. F. (1992). Changing conditions for fund raising and philanthropy. In P. Dobkin (Ed.), *Inventing the nonprofit sector and other essays on philanthropy, volunteerism, and nonprofit organizations.* Baltimore, MD: Johns Hopkins University Press.

Hopkins, B. R. (1991). *The law of fund-raising.* New York: John Wiley.

Jeavons, T. H. (1991). A historical and moral analysis of religious fund raising. In D. F. Burlingame & L. J. Hulse (Eds.), *Taking fund raising seriously: Advancing the profession and practice of raising money.* San Francisco: Jossey-Bass.

Kalas, J. W. (1987). *The grant system.* Albany, NY: State University of New York Press.

Kramer, R. (1981). *Voluntary agencies in a welfare state.* Berkeley: University of California Press.

Layton, D. N. (1989). *Philanthropy and voluntarism: An annotated bibliography.* New York: Foundation Center.

Lindahl, W. E. (1992). *Strategic planning for fund raising: How to bring in more money using strategic resource allocation.* San Francisco: Jossey-Bass.

McKinney, J. (1986). *Effective financial management in public and nonprofit agencies.* New York: Quorum.

Moynihan, D. P. (1990, January). Towards a post-industrial social policy. *Families in Society: The Journal of Contemporary Social Services, 71*(1), 51-56.

Nonprofit almanac, dimensions of the independent sector. (1995). San Francisco: Jossey-Bass/Independent Sector.

O'Connell, B. (1989, September/October). What voluntary activity can and cannot do for America. *Public Administration Review, 34*(4), 486-491.

Segal, U. A. (1991, Summer). Marketing and social welfare. *Administration in Social Work, 15*(4), 19-34.

Stern, L. W., & Gibelman, M. (1990, January). Voluntary social welfare agencies: Trends, issues, prospects. *Families in Society: The Journal of Contemporary Social Services, 71*(1), 13-23.

Stoesz, D. (1986, July/August). Corporate welfare: The third stage of welfare in the United States. *Social Work, 31*(4), 245-249.

Taft Group, The. (1997). *Foundation and corporate giving annual review.* Rockville, MD: Author.

Taylor, J., Austin, M. J., & Caputo, R. K. (1992, January/February). Managing mergers of human service agencies: People, programs and procedures. *Child Welfare, 71*(1), 37-51.

Van Til, J., & Associates. (1990). *Critical issues in American philanthropy*. San Francisco: Jossey-Bass.

Young, D. R., Hollister, R. M., Hodgkinson, V. A., & Finch, S. J. (with Gonsweig, D.). (1993). *Governing, leading, and managing nonprofit organizations*. San Francisco: Jossey-Bass.

2

Publics and Programs

A Marketing Orientation to Program Development and Fund-Raising

What Do You Want More of?

As I finished making my pitch for a much-needed extension to the shelter, I had the feeling that I'd said all the right things, but pushed all the wrong buttons. The more I talked about the shelter part of the Women's Crisis Center operations, the less interested the three corporate execs seemed. They had listened politely enough, but I knew I'd bombed out. As she walked me to the door, the vice president for marketing held me back a moment.

"Look," she said, "I understand where you are coming from, but you have to understand how we look at the world, too. Let me tell you a story, and if you find some meaning in it, give me a call.

"In the early seventies Black and Decker redefined the corporation's primary business as making household, in contrast to workshop, tools. This freed Black and Decker to explore creating a whole new line of tools for the kitchen. To find out what might make Black and Decker products more attractive than those distributed by those better identified with that market—like GE, Phillips, Hamilton-Beach, and Oster

—Black and Decker asked potential consumers a simple question: What do you need more of in the kitchen?

"The answer was equally simple: More counter space. Black and Decker accommodated by building toaster ovens, coffee makers, and can openers that could be hung from the upper cabinets rather than taking up counter space. Now, for $30, a consumer could buy $300 worth of counter space and receive a new appliance as a bonus!"

I got the point. I had been so intent on getting support for the Women's Crisis Center and our clients that it never occurred to me to find out what the corporation was interested in.

THE MARKETING IMAGINATION

Are there parallels to the Black and Decker story in the nonprofit world? If so, what does all this have to do with grant seeking and fund-raising? I will explain using three other examples and then return to the crisis center example.

Example 1

Jewish Experiences for Families (JEFF), a sectarian agency serving suburban Detroit communities, was created when philanthropist Mandell Berman became aware that many young Jewish families were unprepared to pass their heritage on to their children. JEFF's first director, Harlene Appelman, stated, "Many of the parents we wanted to reach were not about to take time away from work or family activity to study Jewish customs. What they were interested in [was] quality family time—of which there is precious little in many two-career families."

By developing camp weekends and holiday workshops in collaboration with synagogues and social agencies, JEFF responded to both consumer interests and the needs of other organizations to serve their members better.

Example 2

A former welfare administrator for the state of Washington explained, "Problem was, clients weren't being helped much by seeing a social worker for an hour a week. When families were in real crisis, there wasn't enough staff to see them through. That's why we were ready to experiment with a plan suggested by Homebuilders, one of our contractors."

The Homebuilders proposal had suggested that if the average family receives 50 to 100 hours of service during the course of a year, it could be better helped by receiving intensive services for concentrated periods—for example, 20 hours per week for a month or so when the family was in crisis. The experiment worked! Families got help when needed. Collateral providers (schools, mental health and substance abuse clinics, courts, and others) reported reduced client pressure during crisis periods.

Peter Forsythe, vice president of the Edna McConnel Clark Foundation, recalls, "We'd been on the look-out for innovative ways of serving vulnerable children and families. Here was a program that seemed worth learning more about. We later shared what we learned with other child and family care providers around the country, and offered some training and financial assistance to local organizations that were interested in adapting the Homebuilder model to their communities."

Example 3

The Campaign for Michigan set out to raise $1 billion in new dollars for the university. It raised twice as much. "I don't try to sell anyone on a particular program—be it athletics or academics," explains David Hermelin, one of the university's most successful alumni fund-raisers. Hermelin gets to know the person not as a prospect but as a peer who values his or her experiences at Michigan. He uncovers what a prospect cares about, personally and professionally, and then tries to match that interest with the appropriate university program. Like many committed fund-raisers, Hermelin is certain that he is doing the right thing—not just because he raises money for good works but because he makes it possible for others to do good and to feel fulfilled by their gift-giving.

Each of these vignettes exemplifies an approach to program design and fund-raising that is marketing oriented rather than sales oriented. The sales orientation focuses on your own organization's interests; the marketing focus is on the interests of consumers, donors, and others. The corporate executive who told the Black and Decker story explains, "The problem with the women's shelter proposal is that we were being pitched something we could not easily identify with. Fortunately, the shelter's director got my point and called me a few days later. By the end of our first meeting, I knew a bit more about what they do over there.

"But that's not what turned me around. It's when she told me that one out of five women in her shelter had a husband or boyfriend who work at my plant that I got interested. I saw that *we* were the ones with a problem. There had to be something wrong if so many of our employees are involved in abusing relationships. By our third meeting, we'd decided to contract with the Center to experiment with one or two family violence workshops to be conducted in the plant. And yes, we did eventually give the Center a grant to expand the shelter."

Finding out what others are interested in and then designing an affordable product to satisfy that interest requires a marketing imagination. Social and not-for-profit marketing focuses on promoting social improvements rather than profit making. Many marketing concepts, however, apply to both for- and not-for-profit. For example, most business marketing texts speak about "4 P's"—products, price, place, and promotions. Social marketers add a fifth "P": publics. This chapter examines how each P influences grant seeking and other approaches to fund-raising, and then ways in which you might address each public around its own interests are discussed. The chapter concludes by exploring how your organization might build a marketing strategy that targets funder interests on the basis of geography, demographics, psychographics, and function.

A word about jargon: This chapter is dripping with it. Although I normally prefer to write in plain English, sometimes the use of unfamiliar terminology is necessary—for two reasons. First, I believe that new concepts can lead to new ways of thinking and to more effective practice. Second, jargon is a short-hand way of communicating between colleagues. Because funders and other fund-raisers may use some jargon, so should we.

Tip: If a funder's promotional literature is written in plain English, follow the leader!

THE FIVE P's OF SOCIAL MARKETING

Publics and Resources

Publics means all those individuals, groups, and organizations on which an organization is dependent or with which it is interdependent. All organizations must be able to manage relationships with the following three kinds of publics:

- those that provide inputs;
- those that transform inputs into products or services;
- those that consume those outputs.

Input publics include all those that supply an organization with needed resources and with the legitimacy to do something with those resources. Resources include concrete items such as money, facilities, and equipment and such ephemerals as expertise, political influence, energy, and legitimacy.

When it comes to dollar inputs, Black and Decker (B&D), a private-sector organization, appears to have an easier time of it than many nonprofits. If B&D can get enough customers to buy their products and can keep costs down to a reasonable level, the company is likely to turn a profit. The same is not necessarily true of nonprofits. In nonprofit organizations, money may be supplied by consumers who pay fees to cover part of the cost of service, but the bulk of it is likely to come from government agencies, voluntary-sector fund-raising and allocating bodies, philanthropic foundations, corporations, and individual donors.

For example, JEFF has to satisfy donors who help underwrite their programs, congregations who contract for its services, and families who pay fees to participate. Homebuilders may get most of its funds through purchase-of-service contracts with state agencies, but it is also dependent on the endorsement of collateral providers, the support of philanthropic foundations, and the satisfaction of client populations. Nonprofits, it appears, may be dependent on a wider variety of input publics than many for-profits. Unlike for-profit organizations, however, nonprofits are more likely to be able to substitute noncash for monetary resources.

For example, although facilities and equipment can be purchased with money, they can also be contributed by outside suppliers, as when a congregation makes its facilities available to JEFF for programming or a corporation provides computers and (expert) volunteer time to help a charter school create a teaching lab. Professional and technical expertise can also be found in a wide variety of public- or voluntary-sector organizations such as universities, libraries, and professional journals or books. Sometimes, the same organization that provides financial support through grants, contracts, or purchase-of-service agreements also contributes expertise through technical assistance.

Political influence may be generated through association with powerful publics and through their involvement in program development and design. The same corporate executives who find it in their interest to support a shelter for battered women may also be energized to support the shelter's efforts to get city council appropriations. Energy also comes from multiple publics. It requires a commitment and a willingness to invest time and creativity in the program and resource development processes. For legitimacy, nonprofit agencies are dependent on a variety of sources. Foremost among these are their own boards of trustees, the licensing organizations that certify that an organization is fit to practice, and the direct beneficiaries of its services. If an organization's legitimacy is suspect, it is less likely to get the funding it seeks.

For example, in the early 1980s, the Detroit Public Library attempted to decentralize its services by locating branches in lower-income minority neighborhoods. There appeared to be two motivations—to make services more acceptable and relevant and to convince public authorities to increase the organization's funding. Parents and neighborhood leaders, however, had not initially been involved in decisions about where to locate services or what kinds of books to include. The new branches were poorly attended. The budget was cut.

INVENTORY OF INPUT PUBLICS

1. Look over the Input Publics Matrix. Think of an organization with which you are familiar: a social agency, a school, a hospital, and so on. Begin by identifying all the suppliers of financial resources and list these next to the appropriate row in the first column. Now complete the matrix for each of the other resource categories: facilities and equipment, expertise, political influence, energy, and legitimacy. You may find that some organizations or groups appear more than once, under several headings or in several rows. What does this suggest to you? Be as complete as you can. Check with others if your information is limited.
2. Now go back to each supplier you identified. If you think that it could be tapped for a significant increase in allocations, circle it using a different color pen or pencil.
3. Go back to the matrix again. In a second color, add new supplier publics that the organization is not currently tapping but that are potentially significant contributors.
4. What might be done to increase contributions of needed resources from those suppliers identified in the Input Publics Worksheet? Jot down some preliminary ideas on a separate sheet of paper. You will have occasion to refer back to both worksheets in completing exercises in subsequent chapters.

An organization's output publics are composed of the consumers of its products or services. This is what is often referred to as the organization's market. Black and Decker customers are output publics. Black and Decker could hardly stay in business if it did not consider their interests, nor would it have instituted a new line of kitchen tools if management was not aware of those interests. The individuals and families who partake in JEFF programs and the clients of Homebuilder services are also output publics, as are the congregations that both contract for (provide inputs to) and benefit from (receive the outputs of) JEFF's services and the corporations that benefit directly from the shelter's consultation on how to prevent

Exercise 2.1
INPUT PUBLICS MATRIX

Publics	Resources					
	Money	Equipment/ Facilities	Expertise	Political Influence	Time/ Energy	Legitimacy
Government Agencies						
Voluntary Organizations						
Foundations						
Private Sector Organizations						
Individual Donors						
Consumers						

family violence or indirectly by the shelter's work with their employees. Thus, it is possible for the same publics to perform both output and input functions at the same time. Sometimes, output publics become input publics at some later time—for example, when former students become alumni and then major donors to a university.

Input and output publics are external to the organization. Throughput publics are internal; they transform resources into products that are consumed by output publics. They include paid and volunteer staff, members of advisory committees, task groups, and boards. Throughput publics may also be consumers involved in the provision of their own services, such as members of self-help groups affiliated with a family service agency. Some consumers or providers may be organized—for example, unions or other collective bargaining units, professional associations, and consumer-advocacy groups.

The extent to which your organization will be able to attract resources from its input publics is likely to be influenced by the reputation, the competence, and the energy of these internal publics. The extent to which they will be able to turn resources into products will depend on how they are organized, the kinds of knowledge and skill they possess, and their perspectives of what should be done and their commitments to doing it. Peter Forsyth cautions, "It wasn't all that easy to replicate Homebuilders in other locales. . . . Staff had to be committed to intensive relationships to clients and to being available, almost round the clock in times of crisis." They also had to be open to the possibility of failure and all the uncertainties that come with trying out the radically new.

"When I first broached the possibility of conducting workshops in the plant, my staff was enthusiastic," explains the Women's Crisis Center Director. "But when it became clear that we would be working with many perpetrators of violence, several staffers balked. Things turned around when three men at the plant volunteered to be the nucleus of a support group for batterers. As one of the men put it, 'I love my family and I don't want to drive them away. When my wife first took off for the shelter, I cursed you women as lesbos and home wreckers. But I knew deep down that the problem was me, and when I saw you folks come into the plant, I figured if you made the first step, we should make the second.' "

In this example, corporate support became available when a program was developed that addressed the interests of the (a) center's staff (to prevent violence against women and children), (b) corporate funders (to be good citizens and to be seen as such), and (c) consumers (to maintain their family relationships). The three groups' interests were not identical. They rarely are. If you have a well-developed marketing imagination, you will not look for identical interests, but you will seek, and find, interests that complement each other.

Products

An organization's *products* are generally defined as tangible goods and services. In larger and more complex organizations, products are grouped into "product lines." For example, Black and Decker uses at least two lines—workshop and kitchen tools. A Black and Decker electric drill is a product, and all of B&D's low-cost power tools for the workshop make up a product line. A social agency might set up departments to conduct social, athletic, and cultural programs. It might also divide its service programs by age (from preschoolers to seniors) or geography. These groupings comprise an organization's service programs (product lines in marketing terms).

Products can also be defined more intangibly. If the toaster or coffee maker make up part of B&D's product line, why is it that the firm sold consumers on a reasonable way of getting more counter space? Is shelter and advocacy for victims what the Women's Crisis Center is all about? Are courses, workshops, and family holiday celebrations what the JEFF program is all about? Yes to all these. That hardly tells the whole story, however. Just as the promise of more counter space might sell a B&D coffee maker, the promise of quality family time might induce a family to participate in a communitywide Hanukkah family celebration. The promise of expanding its membership base might induce a congregation to make its facilities available at no charge. The promise of contributing to ethnic continuity is what might generate gifts from donors to underwrite the program. How programs are interpreted will depend on the publics being addressed and their interests.

Price

Price refers to the amount each of these publics is willing to pay. The price may be in dollars—paid by participants for services received (or on their behalf by third parties such as insurance companies), awarded in grants, allocated in yearly appropriations, raised in a bricks-and-mortar campaign, or donated in response to a telephone drive. Payment can be made in dollars or in noncash contributions such as the loan of facilities, donation of supplies, and allocation of volunteer time.

There are also social costs, psychological costs, and opportunity costs. Social costs refer to giving up one set of social relationships for another. When volunteers contribute two evenings a week to a hospice, they may be giving up customary bridge games, family time, or other opportunities to socialize. When a funding agency commits itself to sponsor your organization, it may be making a social commitment. When local leaders agree to serve on your organization's board or capital campaign cabinet, they are committing their prestige as well as their time.

Psychological costs refer to what one may have to give up in terms of personal image and sense of self or the stresses one must endure to gain other anticipated benefits. Working with dying patients is painful for both staff and volunteers. Making a commitment to a neighborhood association may require one to take emotional risks. Applying to a family agency for services may require admitting that one is not capable, at least for the moment, of dealing with one's problems without outside help and it may require at least a partial dependence on the helper or helping system. Working on a demonstration project may require agency staff to work long hours and to undergo stressful periods of uncertainty as a new program is put into practice.

Opportunity costs refer not to what is paid out but rather to what might have been gained from making similar commitments elsewhere. Thus, when the United Way allocates $250,000 to your organization, it has $250,000 less to allocate elsewhere. When a client enters a job-training program under Goodwill Industries' auspices, he or she may have to give up the opportunity of seeking training or employment from another provider.

The marketing challenge is to (a) reduce costs, defer them, or spread them among several suppliers; and (b) increase benefits to the point where the costs appear well worth the expenditure. Having committed themselves to support (or pay) your organization in one way, various publics may be more easily induced to support the organization in other ways as well. Thus, if the Area Agency on Aging planning staff have been involved in helping to design a particular service and are satisfied that your organization can and will perform it well, they may be more willing to allocate state funds to its operation.

Place

The term *place* most often refers to the geographic location of a service agency, the locations from which clients and other resources are drawn, or the locations where services are distributed. For example, a mental health center may be mandated to provide services to residents of a designated catchment area, but some may seek clients from other locales to maintain programs that could otherwise not be justified on the basis of local demand. This may also have implications for funding because local authorities may insist that costs be covered by the governments where clients are coming from. Some services are offered in a single facility, whereas others are decentralized or provided in the facilities of other organizations. In some cases, such as Meals-on-Wheels for the elderly and infirm, an agency's services are located in clients' homes. Each of these possibilities may have some impact on funding or the allocation of other needed resources.

Place also has other connotations for fund-raisers and grant seekers. It can be used to refer to the importance of a particular funder in an agency's support system or the place that the organization plays in the funder's output system. For example, if there are many group home facilities available, and a relatively modest supply of youngsters in need of protective care in a community setting, then the place of a particular group home in the array of potential contractors for the state welfare department may not be very secure. If there is a great need for group homes and no others are available in your locale, however, your group home may be in a very solid financial position.

It may even be able to place demands on the state agency for special consideration and for the resources needed to expand its facilities and services.

Promotions

A promotional activity can be aimed at selling a particular product, raising public consciousness, or properly positioning your organization for new relationships to targeted publics. Selling a product, in nonprofit terms, requires informing targeted publics that the product is available, where it is available, and at what cost. It also requires informing the public of the benefits of using a particular product. At first, this may seem overly commercial and not the kind of thing that a nonprofit service organization ought to do. Nonprofits do it all the time, however. For example, libraries advertise the availability of their bookmobiles or special reading services to the disabled, and museums inform the public of special shows or of the benefits of membership.

A charter school association may dispatch volunteers to speak to interested parents. Press releases or feature stories on special services or seasonal programs such as summer camps for the visually impaired are not uncommon. Some agencies even advertise clients, as in the case of those seeking adoptive families for hard-to-place children. Thus, selling is a fairly common activity in most nonprofits but, as the opening vignette suggests, it is not always effective. Before the corporate officers would consider allocating to the shelter program at the Women's Crisis Center, they had to become aware of their own need for a related service. In effect, their consciousness had to be raised.

Consciousness raising is of a slightly different order than selling. It is not aimed at increasing demand for a particular program or product but at increasing the likelihood that there will be support for the program or demand for it when such support or demand is needed. Most people do not become interested in hospice services or adoptions until they become aware of a personal need or until they become conscious of the needs of others with whom they share concerns. When agencies try to promote services for unwed mothers, teenage substance abusers, or the victims of domestic violence, they often find little public receptivity. Receptivity can be increased when offenders are redefined as victims or when the public becomes aware of the social costs associated with certain behaviors.

Promotional activities can take many forms and involve different collaborators. The local newspaper may carry features stories, news articles, or regular columns dealing with family violence. Similar content may be carried in agency newsletters, in corporate house organs, church or civic group newsletters, and so on. Television and radio might also be used for news releases and may carry free public service announcements. Public appearances and community education programs can also be used to promote programs and services and may be conducted under the sponsorship of local civic organizations. Which of these approaches does your organization use on a regular basis?

MARKET SEGMENTATION

Targeting Specific Stakeholder Publics

Market segmentation generally refers to a process of clustering consumer and supplier publics according to some criteria that are useful in determining levels of demand or increasing interest in your organization and its products. Agencies cluster their services and promote them to different publics whenever they design some programs for the aged and others for children or some for all the residents of the community and others for those who live in specific neighborhoods. They do not always engage in market segmentation as consciously, however, when designing a fund-raising strategy. Funders and other publics can be clustered around geographic, functional, demographic, and psychographic interests and characteristics.

Geographics

Geographic segmentation refers to the locale(s) in which service takes place. It can be created on the basis of size, density, or both. For example, some Area Agencies on Aging serve very sparse populations spread over multiple-county rural areas covering thousands of square miles. Others serve densely populated neighborhoods or clusters of neighborhoods in metropolitan areas. The term *catchment area*, familiar to those in the community mental health field, generally refers to geographic segmentation. Funders are also likely to be more interested in some geographic areas than others. For example, community foundations or the United Way will rarely support programs outside a designated geographic area. Foundations such as the Edna McConnel Clark Foundation, however, are more likely to seek programs of national significance to fund, regardless of where they are located.

Function

Functional segmentation refers to the way in which services are clustered around given problems: housing, job counseling, protective services, family treatment, and so on. For example, the Robert Woods Johnson Foundation (RWJ) is concerned primarily with funding health-related research or service programs. The definition of a functional area, however, is likely to change over time. When RWJ began its operations almost two decades ago, it was narrowly focused on medical research on cancer or heart disease. Today, it funds an extraordinarily wide array of research, service, and prevention activities at the local, national, and international levels. Knowing what a funder was interested in yesterday is likely to give you a good clue into what it is interested in today but may not tell you enough about what its interests will be tomorrow.

Demographics

Demographic characteristics include age, race or ethnic identity, religion, national origin, gender, income, education, position in the life cycle, type of employment, and so on. Some funders prioritize funding to specific groups—for example, the aged, children, Native Americans or other minorities, women, the disabled, or those whose income falls beneath a certain line. Individual donors may also have a commitment to certain populations. For example, philanthropists often target part of their giving to programs that serve populations that they have some connection to, such as coreligionists ("I want my children's children to have what my grandparents tried to leave me") or the less fortunate ("I know what it was to live without and I want to provide others with the same chance I got").

Psychographics

Psychographic characteristics are somewhat more subtle. They include such variables as personality, lifestyle, commitment to the organization, and even readiness to use a service. In the case of a charter school in a violence-prone neighborhood, separate programs may be set up for males and for females whose learning styles differ considerably because of community expectations. A decision may have been made to work with Latino youngsters first because there is a readiness among members of that community to take responsibility for both treatment and prevention (psychographic characteristic = readiness).

MANAGING DEMAND AND USING THE MARKETING IMAGINATION IN YOUR FUND-RAISING

Demand

Throughout this chapter, I use the term *interests* frequently. Consumer or funder interest, however, is not sufficient to generate demand. Interest must be backed up by a capacity to act on that interest to make a difference. For example, assume that clients of your agency are interested in a new family life education program. The costs, however, are such that few families can pay to attend. Even more important, neither transportation nor child care are available to those who are without their own resources. In these circumstances, the program may be available but inaccessible. Here, the agency's challenge may be to increase consumers' capacities to act on their interests by providing transportation and child care.

Demand is rarely static. To understand this, it might be helpful to use some "qualifiers." For example, we can speak of actual or potential demand or of full, faltering, excessive, or insufficient demand. Actual demand is reflected in the extent to which consumers, funders, auspices providers, and staff participate in or support a program. Potential demand reflects an assessment of what they would do if they were interested or had the capacity to do it. When there is capacity but no interest (e.g., on the part of potential concertgoers or funders), the marketing challenge is to increase interest in the agency's programs.

When there is interest, but relevant publics do not have the capacity to act on it in terms of time, money, or other resources, then the marketing challenge is to reduce the cost in time and dollars, to increase program benefits, or to redesign a program to make it more accessible. For example, if there is no way for clients to come to a program at the agency because of the unavailability of bus service, the marketing challenge might be met by offering private transportation, subsidizing cab fares, or relocating the program. Some funders are more likely to make "capacity"-oriented grants (e.g., funding child care) if they are convinced the public really wants to participate in a needed service. Others will be more interested in promoting interest (e.g., environmental education or alternatives to abortion).

SUMMARY

The recognition that many publics may have stakes in an agency's programs and services, and the development of programs that directly address those interests, is what distinguishes the social marketing approach to fund-raising and program development. The marketing imagination makes it possible to adjust products (programs and outcomes) to publics (those who have a potential interest in the product) and to address concerns regarding place, price, and promotions.

Opportunities for program development and expansion depend on relationships with various publics. Input publics provide the organization with the resources it needs to survive and to develop and deliver its products. An effective resource strategy requires development and orchestration of many resources from many suppliers. Output publics include the direct and indirect consumers of an organization's products. These may be individual clients, other organizations that receive intelligence or referrals from your organization, and others who transform your outputs into their inputs. Throughput publics include the staff, volunteers, and others who are involved in the transformation of resources into outputs through the agency's various services and programs.

Together, these publics make up the organization's markets. By segmenting various publics according to such characteristics as geographics, functions, demographics, and psychographics, it is possible to target fund-raising and promotional activities to specific populations and organizations.

SUGGESTIONS FOR FURTHER READING

Fine, S. H. (Ed.). (1990). *Social marketing: Promoting the causes of public and nonprofit agencies.* Boston: Allyn & Bacon.

Kotler, P., & Andreason, A. (1991). *Strategic marketing for non-profit organizations* (4th ed.). Englewood Cliffs, NJ: Prentice Hall.

Kotler, P., & Roberto, E. L. (1989). *Social marketing: Promoting the causes of public and nonprofit agencies.* New York: Free Press.

Lauffer, A. (1984). *Strategic marketing for not-for-profit organizations: Program and resource development.* New York: Free Press.

McGrath, A. J. (1988). *Market smarts.* New York: John Wiley.

II

Where the Resources Are and How to Get Them

3

The Bucks Start Here

Seeking Government Funds

Matchmaker, Matchmaker, Make Me a Match

As assistant director of planning for the Department of Mental Health, I try not to spend too much time in my office. My work consists mainly of providing consultation to local communities. I also serve as liaison to the Contracts Division.

I think of myself as a broker, a sort of matchmaker, if you will. It's no longer possible to think of discrete mental health services as the prerogatives of separate agencies. Too many problems are interrelated—homelessness, mental illness, substance abuse, family violence, poverty, etc. No single agency can do everything that's needed, and most service programs cross over many agency lines and professional disciplines. So I look for local organizations that might be brought together to work on common problems. I try to smooth relationships between them if there's a trust problem and try to help them identify common interests that also fit the state's agenda.

Grants were great tools, back in the 1970s, for promoting innovations. Local service providers liked grants because they could take the lead in defining how things were to be done. But today, the State funds local programs almost exclusively through purchase-of-service contracts that spell out what it wants done and how. Because the Planning Division works with mental health boards and planning councils throughout the state, the Contracts Division depends on us to tell them what the needs are, before designing RFPs (requests-for-proposals). And because we have close relationships with local providers, we are in a good position to interpret the state's interests to them.

For example, let's assume that one of our regional planning councils identifies a need for which the state should be issuing a service contract. Before the Contracts Division staff puts the specs into an RFP, I will meet with local people and others who might be interested in doing the work. It makes no sense for the contracts people to design an RFP that no one is going to be able to bid on or to do right. I generally share my impressions of need and capability with the contracts staff before they draft the request. And I give them the names of all the parties who should know about it and might bid on the contract. Those names are likely to include a substantial number of for-profit firms that are able to deliver services that are of high quality at low costs.

To make sure the process is as open as possible, we generally issue a "preliminary tender," spelling out what we want done and inviting feedback from all the potentially interested parties. These include relevant service providers and potential bidders, but they could just as well include local government officials, foundation heads, United Way staff, and so on. Their feedback is then incorporated into a final version of the RFP.

Mental health services, if they are to involve the communities in which they are located, must be truly community based. That's why we invest so heavily in community consultation. We're not only more effective this way, but we really save public dollars in the short-run by making fewer mistakes in the contracting process. By investing up front, we actually reduce the amount of staff time for contract negotiations, and we sure save money on poor funding decisions. What we strive for is a mutuality of perspective.

I spend a lot of my time looking for connections between the interests of, say, school authorities and mental health clinics, or community mental health centers and people running homeless shelters, home-care services to the homebound, or teen runaway programs. And if the resulting program ideas don't fit one of our current funding priorities, no problem. I've worked for many years with the heads of the major urban community foundations and United Ways in this state, and know most of the project officers that deal with mental health issues in several private foundations. If we can't fund it, chances are that there will be someone else interested.

This is not to imply that the state is always in the lead role. For example, women's groups were primarily responsible for creating shelter programs for battered women and their children. Once the shelters were established, they advocated effectively for a program of mental health services for victims and batterers alike. We, my staff and I, learned from them, and eventually—through some of our efforts— but mostly their own, new legislation was passed. This made it possible for us to work with shelter staff and others to find needed funds from both public and private sources to expand the shelter-based mental health programs.

GRANTS-IN-AID, PURCHASE-OF-SERVICE CONTRACTS, AND COPRODUCTION

Perspectives on governmental responsibility for the funding and delivery of social services are undergoing profound changes. These include the extensive substitution of contracts for grants mechanisms, the promotion of cooperative and collaborative arrangements between service providers at the more proximate level, and the sharing of responsibility for both funding and service delivery between the public, voluntary, and private sectors. Your success in locating and securing government funds depends on your understanding of those changes and how they are being worked out in your community. For example, although federal dollars continue to finance the major share of all public funding for the human services, state and local governments are the places where most decisions are made about who gets how much and for what purpose.

The 104th Congress created some major changes in the way in which many people think government should work. Congress completed parts of the Reagan Revolution in ways even he never anticipated. State and local initiatives are more important than ever, and the private and voluntary sectors are increasingly partners with government in funding and providing services. Although there is no question that government will remain in the business of funding services to the most needy, there is a loudly voiced opinion that government should not do it all and that the private and voluntary sectors should be encouraged to get more and more into the act—perhaps even writing the script.

Cost-containment considerations aside, however, without some government financing the most vulnerable citizens would suffer greatly. The role of government in the human services is to even the odds for the most needy. That role may undergo continual transformations, but it is not likely to disappear.

In this chapter, developments that have affected the way government has funded its domestic assistance programs during the past third of a century are examined. Particular attention is paid to grants, purchase-of-service contracts, and coproduction efforts that involve community groups in the provision of public social services. This chapter focuses on how governments engage in grant making and some suggestions for making your proposals most attractive are presented. You will learn how to find out about grant programs and what source materials are most helpful to you in seeking information on government grants. A more detailed discussion of purchase-of-service contracts (POSCs), the principle mechanisms for funding local programs and services, is deferred to the next chapter.

Pervasiveness of the Grant System

Government expenditures for foreign aid and domestic assistance are expressions of public policy. Grants-in-aid, contracts, loans, and certain kinds of cooperative agreements, such as coproduction, are the principal instruments used by the federal government to provide assistance to states, special districts, independent organizations, and individuals. Of these, grants continue to be the most widely used, even if some may not be directly available to service providers. There are several types of grants, each of which may have different levels of importance for you and your organizations. These include (a) project grants, (b) formula grants and entitlements, and (c) block grants.

The first two are sometimes referred to as categorical because they are targeted to certain publics or address specific functions. Block grants consolidate similar categories of funding and transfer both dollars and responsibility for their redistribution to state and local authorities. In turn, states and most local government units comingle their funds with federal dollars to purchase the services of nongovernmental organizations to carry out public functions such as road building and the provision of child welfare services. They tend to use four POSCs as their preferred redistribution tool. These terms are explained in the following sections.

Types of Grants

Categorical grants are used to fund specific, often narrowly defined activities. For example, they finance transportation and food services to the elderly, foster care and adoptions services for children, housing programs for the homeless, income and job training programs for the poor, and so on. Categorical grants can be distributed by formula or by competition. The competitive process leads to awarding grants to those who submit winning project proposals. Applicants must be able to demonstrate that they can do what the grant-making agency is interested in better than others or that their receipt of an award addresses an important need that is not being addressed elsewhere. These "project" grants are the kinds of awards that you and your organizations are likely to seek when submitting a grant application.

Although project grants are limited to particular categories of service, they tend to be more flexible in terms of purpose than other types of categoricals. Government administrators have considerable latitude in specifying what a project grant program is to accomplish, the duration of a project, the size of a grant, and its timing. For example, project awards may be several years in duration and need not be limited to fiscal year start-up times. Although some kind of local match or grantee contribution may be necessary, the proportion may be smaller than in formula-type categorical grants.

Awards may be made for a number of reasons, including (a) the transfer potential of a successful innovation from one setting or locale to another, (b) an interest in reaching an underserved population or geographic area, and (c) legal and other commitments to empowering specific groups. Depending on the grant program, beneficiaries may include both nonprofit or for-profit organizations in addition to lower-level units of government that compete for grant awards.

Formula grants are also categorical, but they are not competitive. The formulas that spell out how much is to go to a specific state, locale, or organization are established through enabling legislation. These are the laws that bring a program, such as transportation services for the elderly, into existence or the amendments that modify the law in subsequent years. Some formulas are altered by presidential order or made more specific via regulations set up by the relevant government bureaus in an effort to spell out the intent of Congress. Formulas specify the basis for distributing funds to the states and territories (e.g., on the basis of how many people are over 65 years old, fall beneath the poverty line, live in urban areas, are disabled, etc.). Formula grants almost always carry matching fund requirements. Thus, a state's Medicaid reimbursement might have depended, in part, on how much it was willing to contribute to the medical costs of qualifying citizens. This assured that both federal and state funds would be available. Such matching fund requirements are intended to do more than increase the funds available for operations. They are designed to promote a sense of ownership and commitment to federal programs and policies on the part of states, cities, or other cooperating governmental units by requiring them to contribute if they wish to receive federal dollars. The extent of local match requirements has changed over the years. For example, in the mid-1970s, nonfederal matches amounted to almost two thirds of all categorical grants but had decreased to 50% by the mid-1980s. They were virtually eliminated in some programs a decade later when Congress decided that states should determine how much they wanted to put into programs.

Some formula-based categoricals are used to fund services and others to fund individuals. Some do both. Examples are Aid for Dependent Children (AFDC) and Medicaid, which accounted for almost half of all federal grant dollars in 1996. These grants contributed to the administration of AFDC programs and their attendant services to clients. They also provided core funding for grants-in-aid to individuals, such as AFDC income maintenance payments, food stamps, and job training salaries. Formula-based grants to individuals are entitlements, which means that recipients are entitled to receive benefits on the basis of objective criteria such as income level or age. Such entitlements may be capped (to a number of years) or otherwise limited (as when they are accompanied by work or other behavioral requirements). Many have been eliminated by welfare reform.

Generally, the level of benefit will be arrived at through some agreement between the federal and state agencies responsible for a specific program. When a formula with a matching requirement is used, the higher the state contribution, the greater the federal share. States that are generous in their contributions receive more federal dollars, so their programs are likely to be more comprehensive and benefits to clients will be higher. They are allocated on the basis of need rather than government revenue. For decades, it was understood that if unemployment increases, the welfare rolls are likely to rise, and both the federal government and the states will pay out more dollars at a time when their tax revenues are reduced. This type of entitlement was under attack by the conservative wing of the Republican-led 104th Congress intent on deficit reduction and balancing the (federal) budget.

Because entitlements are not linked to government income, they have become frequent targets of cost-cutting efforts by those concerned with the size of government budget deficits. One way of reducing federal outlay is to consolidate discrete categorical grant programs into larger packages called block grants that cover broad functional areas (e.g., urban crime, education, services to the aging, or community development). Block grant recipients, generally the states, have considerably more discretion over the use of these funds than they have over more narrowly targeted and regulated categorical grants.

Block grants are sometimes confused with general revenue sharing, which does not require expenditures in designated categories. During the Nixon era, when revenue sharing received its greatest boost, between $5.5 and $6 billion per year went to nearly 40,000 general-purpose units of government. Approximately two thirds were local governments that suffered no restrictions on how the funds were to be used (save for the principles of honesty and good management). Whether funds are funneled to states and locales via block grants or revenue sharing, however, similar mechanisms are used by the more proximate unit of government to redistribute them locally. Contract mechanisms are the principal means for distributing funds intended for the provision of public services.

Contracting

Contracting for the conduct of publicly financed social services has substantially replaced other approaches to funding social service delivery. Although some purchase-of-service contracting was used to fund social programs in the 1960s during the Kennedy and Johnson years, it achieved initial prominence during Nixon's first term. The proliferation of categorical grants characteristic of the War on Poverty was reversed through the creation of block grants to states, municipalities, and specially set up local and regional instrumentalities (e.g., councils on governments). Nixon also tried to initiate a broadly based process of revenue sharing in which the governors and state legislatures would more evenly share power over the purse with the federal government. Nixon was only partially successful. Organized groups that had vested interests in each of the categorical programs made it politically risky. For example, Edward Newman, who was commissioner of rehabilitation at the time, recalls, "We had strong support among state commissioners and statewide developmental disabilities councils for the new program we were funding. They wanted more, not fewer dollars earmarked for the disabled. Any effort to take money away from the social and rehabilitation services and to put it into general revenue service met with outcries—even from governors who you might have expected would support revenue sharing."

The Reagan impact was even more profound, setting the stage for a major push by a conservative Congress in the mid-1990s to cut the federal budget while increasing the authority of the states. Nixon's approach to decentralization had been one of ambivalence regarding to whom local responsibility and authority should be shifted. For example, Title XX Block Grants covering child welfare and other social service programs went to the states. Community development grants went to cities, and manpower training program grants (the funding sources for the Comprehensive Employment and Training Act, a job training and employment program) were allocated to local governments, quasi-governmental units (e.g., community colleges and government-chartered agencies), and other community-based organizations.

In contrast to Nixon's relatively pragmatic and experimental orientation, Reagan's was more ideological and focused. Block grants were made almost exclusively to the states, giving them the preeminent role for carrying out federal policy and a large measure of both fiscal and programmatic control over the transferred funds. Under Nixon, however, states continued to be subject to certain regulatory requirements. Although they could define eligibility criteria for certain programs, they could not use funds allocated for one population —for example, a school lunch program for the differently abled—to provide services to another group—for example, Meals-on-Wheels for the elderly. Procedural regulations provided standards for state and stakeholder participation in planning for reallocation of federal dollars. Financial rules defined state obligations for participation in financing.

Reagan economists also used block grants as a broader strategy aimed at reducing public expenditures, at least at the federal level. In return for greater autonomy in how they could spend federal dollars, states were expected to pick up a larger share of program costs. To cope with this challenge, and with considerable encouragement from the federal government, states chose to purchase the services of private- and voluntary-sector providers. The Economic Recovery Program of 1984 clearly promoted an increase in the use of nonprofit and private agencies in provision of services to the needy. It included a Government Capacity Sharing Program that encouraged local governments to use contractors in the delivery of a broad range of municipal services.

This led to a rapid increase in the use of POSCs. Purchasing, rather than delivering services outright, also protected states from anticipated shrinkage in block grants. States reasoned that if the federal government cut the size of block grants, it would be easier to cut state spending by reducing outlay for contract services than by reducing the size of their own bureaucracies (in which civil service rules and union contracts shielded employees from the potential impact of downsizing). In most states, POSCs now account for well over 50% of all public expenditures for social services and by the end of the first decade of the twenty-first century are likely to represent virtually all state expenditures other than those retained for policy, planning, monitoring, and administration.

Coproduction

The term *coproduction* was used at the beginning of the chapter. Although coproduction sometimes includes purchase-of-service contracting, the two are both conceptually and operationally distinct. What they share in common is that both are conjoint arrangements in which government agencies are engaged in funding programs and services that may be delivered, all or in part, by voluntary organizations, private firms, quasi-government organizations, neighborhood and other civic association, self-help or advocacy groups, or private individuals. Coproduction is, perhaps, most clearly associated with President Johnson's War on Poverty of the mid- and late 1960s in which the national government attempted to empower disadvantaged citizen groups to manage their own social service programs, often bypassing stultifying and unresponsive state bureaucracies. The Community Action Program funded by the Office of Economic Opportunity and the Model Cities Program funded through the Department of Housing and Urban Development were the most prominent of all those programs promoting coproduction at the local level.

Coproduction involves two or more independent entities that agree to work together on the provision of a service or the delivery of a product—for example, a county government agency and an independent association of citizens or community activists who participate in service delivery. In contrast to the exchange of a service for a fee (contracting), Spiegel (1987) refers to coproduction as task-oriented reciprocity in which the collaborating partners retain their independence, each having the option to back out of the relationship and each with its own accountability structure. Sometimes it is easier to define a process by what it is not. For example, coproduction is distinguished from both cofinancing and coprovision, with which it is sometimes associated, and from both consumer participation and social action.

Cofinancing occurs when a community or citizen's group raises funds to support a service that is also funded substantially by a government unit. A contemporary example of cofinancing would be a communitywide association of African American groups, committed to improving education for black children, that fund-raises for a black male academy. The community group's funds were used to initiate planning for the school and to design or adapt curriculum materials that would focus on black pride and the contributions of African Americans to society. It was understood from the start, however, that the bulk of the new school's budget would be financed via state or local tax dollars filtered through an appropriate chartering agency (e.g., a school district or community college).

Coprovision does not require the financing of public or quasi-public programs, but it does involve community groups in deciding how public funds are to be allocated. For example, independently elected boards of public housing cooperatives might share responsibility with the city housing authority in determining how each coop's budget, which includes public funds, grants, and rent payments, will be spent (i.e., how much to pay off the mortgage, street or building improvements, recreation, etc.).

In consumer participation, recipients and potential recipients of services are involved by paid staff in providing some of the service to others. In effect, they are recruited and sometimes trained to volunteer. Volunteers in coproducing enterprises, however, do not participate as individuals or as consumers. Their involvement is as members of a distinct collectivity with a specific purpose (e.g., friends of the library, neighborhood council, housing coop board, parents for better education, AIDS care collective).

This distinguishes coproduction from other forms of citizen involvement that are often a top-down arrangement in which a bureaucracy involves citizens or consumers at its own discretion and in accordance with its own rules. It also differs from social action through which a group or coalition engages in an advocacy process aimed at getting some government body to change its behavior. Coproduction is a partnership arrangement in which the parties to an agreement share in the planning and implementation of a common program.

You may be thinking, "Very interesting. But why tell us all this in a book on grants, contracts, and fund-raising?" There are several reasons. Although currently there may be no massive federal programs aimed at promoting local initiatives or at building the capacity of community groups and others to engage in coproduction, the processes described are alive and well. By building on local initiatives and voluntarism, coproduction efforts are often supported by those on the political Right and the political Left. Bradley (1987) observes that coproduction provides a local perspective that professionals and others in government bureaucracies might otherwise miss and that it often reduces the overprofessionalization of services. This often leads to cost saving or cost reduction.

You might wonder, "Won't this affect our organization negatively?" Perhaps, but in an era of reduced public funding, coproduction is seen by some legislators and government officials as a way to cut costs without necessarily cutting services. The availability of government funding to citizen groups can be used to induce other funders and individual donors to make contributions that they perceive as leveraged—that is, are likely to generate even larger sums of money from government sources. For example, a familiar nonprofit family service agency was able to secure a foundation grant and a state agency contract in part because it had established a partnership with a local citizens group concerned with reduction of family violence.

Initially, their partnership was funded via a small demonstration grant from the United Way. Part of the demonstration included working with clients of the county welfare department. With backing from the county agency, they responded to a state RFP and received a contract. The state was particularly interested in the possibility that the program, which included coproduction, could be replicated elsewhere. State officials reasoned that it would generate considerable cost saving over more common contracting approaches. The foundation was interested in helping the partnership—which included the citizens' group, the family service agency, and the county—to promote similar collaborations elsewhere. Its grant was for conducting a conference and for the provision of technical assistance aimed at replication. Thus, coproduction led to a rather complex partnership in which one voluntary and two public agencies were engaged with a citizen's advocacy group in the production of a new service that received funding from multiple sources, including a foundation.

In Chapter 5, many more examples of multiple funding arrangements will be discussed, a number of which include both government and nonprofit project grants. In the remainder of this chapter, the focus is on how to find out about and get government project grants.

GETTING GOVERNMENT PROJECT GRANTS

Four Steps Toward Improving Your Competitive Edge

Step 1

Knowing who is funding what is the first step in improving your chances of getting a contract or grant. A description of the key documents you and others in your organization must learn how to use is provided under "Finding Out About Federal Project Grants and Grant Programs." Without them, you are not likely to know what is available. This is especially true in the case of project grants for which a government agency may not seek proposals as aggressively as they often seek bidders on contracts.

Once you have identified a government agency or program that you are interested in, take the time to talk with colleagues about their experiences with that program. Find out what worked for them and what kind of relationship they had with a grants officer or someone else from the agency with whom they interacted. Contact the grants officer. Like the state mental health planner quoted at the beginning of the chapter, he or she may be as interested in finding you as you are in finding the right state agency. Remember, you may be interested in getting your program funded, but the grants officer is on the lookout for organizations that can help the government agency achieve its goals—not yours.

Step 2

The second step is to put yourself and your organization in position to be in the know about new and emerging programs. That means being on the "distribution list." For example, if your organization fits certain criteria, it should be possible to arrange for the relevant federal agency to send you the copy of the *Federal Register* (see "Finding Out About Federal Project Grants and Grant Programs") that includes information about each year's "Combined Discretionary Grants Program." Contact with the right state agency should result in regular notification of contract and grant programs that fit your organization. Getting on a bidder's list (see Chapter 4) is another option. Relationships can be informal as well. Review the marketing concepts we discussed in Chapter 2, then consider the following two tactics described by experienced grants people.

Getting in Position

We weren't known for having any expertise in working with youth on drugs, but we had been working with teens on issues of self-esteem, school work, health needs, and so on. So when it became clear that the state was going to fund substance abuse programs and that low income teens were to be among the service targets, we wanted to be in position to be invited to submit a bid.

Our annual report was just about to go off to the printer. I made sure that in the section on priorities for next year, we included a bit about substance abuse prevention. When the report came out, I sent copies to the relevant state officials, and also a state congresswoman's staffer whom I knew, and circled the part about substance abuse. The congresswoman had been a central force in promoting the legislation that funded the program and I had known the staff person from work on other youth-oriented task forces in the past.

But that wasn't enough. We had to be doing something in the field, or appear to be. So we called a meeting of all the other relevant youth-serving and substance abuse agencies in the city, along with some politicians and community activists. The focus was on finding new ways of fighting substance abuse, and we made sure the media were present. Some good ideas were generated at the conference, and we were able to build on some of them in our proposal. But the best thing that came of it was that we were now seen as taking the initiative in dealing with a problem the state was interested in.

Don't Be Sexist; Send Reprints!

You have to know when a gift is not a bribe; it's a professional courtesy! I'm not talking about big gifts. It's the little things that can make or break a relationship. For example, I make it a rule never to take a potential funder out for lunch or a drink. Once I made the mistake of trying to pay for coffee when I was meeting in the cafeteria with a contracts officer from the department of education. She nearly snapped my head off! First of all, she pointed out, it was a sexist thing to do. Second, she wanted to make sure she would not be beholden to me for anything.

It was different when I sent her a copy of a report on something our community college was doing that I thought would interest her, or reprints from journals that I knew dealt with issues of professional concern to her and her department. Those weren't seen as personal favors. They were professional courtesies! And she returned the courtesy (it wasn't interpreted as a "favor") by making sure I got copies of proposed regs and other information she thought would be of interest to me.

Step 3

Before you actually write the proposal, make sure that you know what the funder wants. If concept papers and preliminary drafts are encouraged, do not miss the opportunity of getting free consultation from government officials.

Preliminary Drafts

If I can avoid it, I never submit a final proposal without first getting comments on one or more preliminary drafts. I keep those preliminary drafts short, concise, and to the point. I figure that if the feds want me to add more, they'll tell me. After all, if I fill a proposal full of garbage, they're not going to be willing to read it. So I let them tell me if they feel I've left things out.

And then I write that proposal the way the funder thinks it should be written. Usually I will ask how they want it. Sometimes a funder will say that I'm too academic in what I've written, that I should use simpler language and more illustrations. Sometimes they'll tell me that I'm too folksy, and I should make it more sophisticated in tone. Whatever they suggest, that's the way I write it.

Step 4

The fourth step is one you may not have to take. It is the use of other relationships to open doors and to keep them open. The grant seeker just quoted discusses the politics of grant getting in the following vignette.

Putting on the Pressure

Of course, things aren't always that easy. Sometimes you're going along really well when the funder hits you with a bombshell. Too many proposals are being submitted and you're competing with a lot of other people for a large share of a very small pot. Maybe there's been a cut in the appropriation and the program officer will ask you if you can do with $30,000 instead of the $80,000 you'd asked for. A time like that is when I have to make some hard decisions. Do I let it go at that and take my chances, or do I bring in the rest of the troops? Once when a funder called me to say there would be less money available for than she had anticipated, I pulled out a game plan that was a little bit risky.

First I was silent on the phone for about a minute and a half. This gave me a chance to collect my thoughts, and it worried the woman on the other end of the line. Then I told her I'd been silent because I knew how difficult it must have been for her to call me, and how aware I was of her own commitment to the program. I wanted her to know that I understood how she felt. Then I told her how I felt. I mentioned that, based on our previous contacts, I'd made certain promises to local people. Several agencies were ready to get involved in the cooperative venture. I spoke of how a lot of our local government leaders were going to feel about the project's being sliced down to under one third of our request. "What should I tell people?" I asked. I wanted her to know that I was going to be talking to our people, and that she might get some pressure from them. I didn't want it to come as a surprise.

"Tell them what you think you have to tell them," she told me, "and I'll see what I can do from here." I thanked her for calling. Immediately, I called the chairman of my board. We figured out which local people had the most influence with our congressman and with people in HHS

[Department of Health and Human Services]. We had these people place calls to Washington, telling them how disappointed people were at the cut in funds and how much local support there was for the project.

Two days later, I got a call from my friend in Washington. "You sure have a lot of people on your side," she said. "Submit a new budget. This time cut it by about 25 percent. We can give you that much." Well, that was better than cutting it by two thirds. I thanked her and said I was sorry if some of our local people had gotten too excited about the projected cuts and put the pressure on. "Well, there has been some pressure," she admitted. I made a note to do something for her later on. A couple of weeks later, I made sure that her superior got word from some of our local influentials about how helpful they thought she'd been. Six months later, knowing I'd have other dealings with her, I wrote a letter thanking her for having done something else for us and sent a copy to her supervisor. Those little gestures help.

Of course, you've got to be careful who you put the pressure on. It can backfire, especially when you use members of Congress or staff. The people in the bureaucracy don't like to be pressured by the people on Capitol Hill. And people on Capitol Hill don't like to be bothered with little projects. They don't want to use up their influence on every request that comes around. You've got to know when an issue is hot, how much resistance there'll be toward what you want, and how much of a stake the member of Congress or senator is going to have in that particular activity or in getting the funds for his or her locality. Sometimes it's better to use a staffer in a congressional committee than a congressman. Staffers have their own lines to the bureaucracy.

Still, you want to be careful. Line up too many guns on your side, let it seem as if you're politicking a grant through instead of having it reviewed on its own merits, and you're likely to be dropped like a hot potato.

Evening the Odds for the Most Needy:
Equity and Responsiveness in
Government Programs

With the entry of for-profit firms in the delivery of government-funded services, many traditional nonprofits express concerns about both their access to funding and the quality of services being provided to the most needy. Their concerns are not without foundation. Reality, however, is more complex than slogans and sound bites might suggest. Even in comparison with the apparent generosity of the 1960s, most government programs continue to be driven by norms of equity and fairness. Both lawmakers and the public officials entrusted with the application of policy must legitimize the use of limited public resources to help certain groups and not others.

Conversely, as analysis of block grants programs and other efforts at decentralization and deregulation show that the flow of federal dollars to the states and its redirection to localities is often as much or more the result of political influence than of need-based formula. For example, in a study of community development block grants, Dommel and Rich (1987) found that the "rich get (communities) richer" and those communities suffering from the highest incidence of urban hardship are not likely to get their fair share of federal dollars, if any at all.

To overcome such inequitable treatment requires spelling out governmental priorities as unambiguously as possible and defining eligibility standards for assistance. If this is not done at the federal level, it often is done at the state level. In much the same way as it defines eligibility for assistance and amounts of financial aid for individual recipients (by age, disability, or a poverty line), government also defines what organizations can receive assistance and for what purposes. You will need to understand government standards to increase your competitive edge.

In an insightful paper, Liptsky (1989/1990) points out that in the past 30 years or so, many nonprofit and for-profit organizations were created specifically to take advantage of the government's interest in contracting for the provision of specific services and/or services to specific populations. As the vignette at the beginning of this chapter indicated, however, government may also follow the lead of non-profit organizations and others in forcing social problems onto the policy agenda, especially when the extent of a problem and its location (e.g., AIDS) or ambiguities over eligibility (victims of family violence) make it difficult to establish entitlement programs.

Local agencies are not without influence. Hart (1988) found, in a study of state funding of children's services in Massachusetts, that service providers often functioned as a cartel, effectively lobbying for certain programs and restricting the state's ability to shape the policies and programs in new directions. Government can and does respond with new funding when emerging needs are documented or when there is community support for existing programs. Ensuring government support in an age of cost cutting, however, requires more than advocacy. It also requires a mix of funding sources that reduces sole dependence on the public purse.

This suggests that you and your organizations should consider two strategies when targeting the government for support: (a) responding to current priorities and eligibility criteria, and (b) working together with other advocates to change government priorities.

The latter strategy is part of a larger advocacy and longer-term development process that underlies much of what is suggested throughout this book. It includes elements of planned social change and social marketing. To maintain a focus on generating contracts and grants from government sources, however, we will now turn our attention to where you can find out what the government is funding and how to improve your competitive edge in applying for funds within the context of current priorities.

Finding Out About Federal Project Grants
and Grant Programs

There are several essential government documents that you should become familiar with. The following are foremost among them:

1. *Catalog of Federal Domestic Assistance*
2. *Federal Assistance Programs Retrieval System* (FAPRS)

The *Catalog* is the basic reference on federal programs, projects, services, and activities that provide assistance or benefits to the American public. It is published annually with quarterly updates in hard copy (printed pages). It is also available (at a lower price) on floppy discs (FAPRS) and on-line, where information is updated monthly. The *Catalog* includes all government programs, with information on the enabling legislation, types of grants or other assistance given, number and amount given last year or available for the current year, contact names and addresses, and how to apply (including application deadlines).

To get to the right agency on the hard-copy version, you may use any of a number of useful indexes such as subject, function, agency programs, agency names, and so on. For example, if you look up aging in the subject index, you might then find transportation, nutrition, or income-maintenance. Under nutrition, you might find Meals-on-Wheels, which is exactly what you were looking for. Also, you might have begun with the word *nutrition* and eventually found yourself directed to Meals-on-Wheels and aging. When you get to the right combination of words, the index will tell you what page to find the agency and program description within which Meals-on-Wheels projects for the aging are funded.

FAPRS supplies information on the basis of user input. Keywords are used to generate information that can be used to lead the searcher to program text that can be printed out. For example, typing in *aging* and *Meals-on-Wheels* can lead you to the appropriate program description that spells out the agency (the Administration on Aging) and its relevant support programs, grant or contract funding sources, how much money is available, procedures for getting more information or applications, application deadlines, and so on.

The *Catalog* is provided at no charge to governors and most state agencies, and to mayors, county chairmen, city planners, and chairmen of boards of commissioners at the local level. The easiest place for you to access a copy might be the public library and in local federal government buildings. You can purchase copies from any U.S. government bookstore or from the Superintendent of Documents, U.S. Government Printing Office, Mail Stop: SSOP, Washington, DC 20402-9328. For FAPRS diskettes and documentation on how to use them, or for on-line services, contact the Federal Domestic Assistance, Catalog Staff, General Services Administration, Reporters Building—Room 101, 300 7th Street SW, Washington, DC 20407; phone: (202) 708-5126 or (800) 669-8331. You can access FAPRS via two University of Michigan Web sites. See Chapter 15 and Appendix A for instructions.

3. *Government Assistance Almanac* (by J. Robert Dumouchel)

The *Almanac* presents the same information in a slightly different and, some people feel, more accessible format because it leaves out any information not essential to the grant or contract seeker. Entries include the following information: name of the program (e.g., emergency community services for the homeless); types of assistance (e.g., project or formula grant, direct assistance, or contract); purpose (e.g., demonstration or program operation); eligible applicants (e.g., states, nonprofit agencies, or individuals); eligible beneficiaries (e.g., low-income families and persons over age 65); range (or average grant size); HQ (agency name, address, and phone number for where to apply or to get information).

The *Almanac* is compiled annually from information in the Catalog of Federal Domestic Assistance. It is available from either (a) Omnigraphics, Inc., Penobscot Building, Detroit, MI 48226; or (b) Foggy Bottom Publications, P.O. Box 23462, L'Enfant Plaza, Washington, DC 20026.

4. *Federal Yellow Book*

Published quarterly, the *Yellow Book* lists the names, titles, addresses, and telephone numbers of all key federal officials by agency name. Therefore, if you know what agency you want, and need a name (generally a good idea when placing a phone call or writing a letter), this is your best bet (a similar document published by the federal government is available only to government officials).

This book is available from Monitory Publishing Co., 1301 Pennsylvania Ave. NW, Washington, DC 20004; phone: (202) 347-7757; or from its New York office: 104 Fifth Avenue, New York, NY 10011; phone: (212) 645-0931.

5. *Washington Information Directory* (Ann Advise, Ed.)

Published annually, the *Directory* includes information not only on federal programs but also on private-sector and voluntary organizations in the Washington area that deal with similar issues. A Ready Reference List near the end of the book also includes names, addresses, and phone numbers for state officials, members of Congress, mayors, federal government departments in Washington DC and elsewhere, and labor unions. The main section is divided into 18 chapters: 1, Communications and the Media; 2, Economics and Business; 3, Education and Culture; 4, Employment and Labor; 5, Energy; 6, Advocacy and Public Service; 7, Government and Personal Service; 8, Health; 9, Housing and Urban Affairs; 10, Social Services and Veterans' Programs; 11, International Affairs; 12, Law and Justice; 13,

National Security; 14, Agriculture; 15, Environment and Natural Resources; 16, Science and Space; 17, Transportation; and 18, Congress and Politics. Although these sections do not coincide with the names or functions of federal agencies, well-designed name and subject indexes are helpful in locating the appropriate program and contact persons and addresses.

This book is available from Congressional Quarterly, Inc., 1414 22nd Street NW, Washington, DC 20037.

6. *Public Welfare Directory* (Amy J. Weinstein, Ed.)

Not so much a description of programs, the *Directory* serves as a comprehensive list of U.S. federal and state as well as Canadian federal, provincial, and territorial agencies. At the state or provincial level, for example, it includes names and phone numbers for all major department heads within the public welfare system and offices, addresses, and department heads of related state agencies (e.g., education, Employment Security Commission, and mental health). The appendix describes interstate compacts (e.g., for placement of children with special needs), names of state directors of research, demonstration and evaluation units, key congressional human service committees, and so on.

This book is available from The American Public Welfare Association, Washington, DC; phone: (202) 682-0100.

7. *Federal Register*

The *Register* is a daily publication that provides information on regulations and legal notices issued by federal agencies, including presidential executive orders. It publishes changes in regulations, proposed legislation, and announcements of selected grant programs. For example, each year the Office of Human Development Services publishes a complete listing of its Combined Discretionary Grant Awards. Taking up a whole issue, it specifies each of the project grants available through several agencies (e.g., the Administration on Aging), complete instructions for how to prepare applications and by when they must be submitted, and relevant application forms (e.g., cover sheets, budget forms, etc.). The instructions are precise. For example, it instructs applicants to keep the total number of narrative pages to 10 or less (single-spaced and not photo reduced). Applications that do not conform to the format or that arrive late will not be considered.

Although many government agencies do not use the *Register* on a regular basis, others do. Among the users are various programs in the U.S. Department of Education and agencies associated with the Office of Human Development Services in the Department of Health and Human Services (e.g., the Administration on Aging or the Office of Children and Family Services). The *Federal Register* is available in many libraries and in all U.S. government offices.

Subscriptions can be ordered from the Superintendent of Documents, Federal Register New Orders Department, P.O. Box 371954, Pittsburgh, PA 15250-7954. Subscriptions can also be ordered by phone: paper or microfiche, (202) 783-3238; magnetic tapes, (202) 512-1530.

8. *Commerce Business Daily*

The *Daily* lists notices of proposed governmental procurements, contract awards, and sales. Although some may be relevant to your organization, chances are that state by state information, available elsewhere, may be more pertinent.

Subscriptions are available from the Superintendent of Documents, Government Printing Office, Washington, DC 20402-9371; phone: (202) 783-3238.

9. *Three Newsletters You Might Find Helpful*

In addition to previously mentioned standard, and often essential, reference sources, there are a number of newsletters that provide updated information on federal and other programs in specific fields.

ERC Newsbriefs is published by Ecumenical Resources Consultants and is a continuation of *LRC Newsbriefs*, which had been published by the Lutheran Resources Commission until the end of 1992. Published monthly, it provides information on late-breaking developments and often describes project grant opportunities still in the design stages. A typical issue will include information under the following categories: aging, arts and humanities, children, community development, drugs and alcohol, education, fund-raising, handicapped, health, homelessness, housing, management, minority affairs, parish life, rural, social services, tax matters, veterans, voluntarism, women, youth, grants and loans, and conferences.

You can subscribe via *ERC Newsbriefs*, P.O. Box 21385, Washington, DC 20009.

The Grant Advisor is published 11 times a year. It provides information on emerging grant opportunities from government, foundation, and corporate sources. Included is information on deadlines, eligibility, funding, and duration (and, of course, who to write to for information and application forms).

To order, write to *The Grant Advisor*, P.O. Box 520, Linden, VA 22642; phone: (703) 636-1529.

The *Federal Grants & Contracts Weekly* addresses project opportunities in education, human and other services, and in research. Issues include regular features such as (a) "Grants Alert," (b) "RFPs Available," and (c) "Grants Workshop." In a recent issue, the "Alert" column described the Jacob K. Javits Fellowships program that invites students to apply for $1.2 million in doctoral study grants in the arts, humanities, and social sciences.

Information About State and Local Government Grants

Information on state and local grant and contract opportunities is likely to be a bit less plentiful in some areas of the country. This is not because such information will be less useful—most contract dollars for the human services and many of the project grants available to your organization are likely to come from state and local sources—but because these systems may not be as fully developed.

A number of states publish a kind of "yellow book" directory that may include public agencies and their assistance programs and those of some major nongovernmental agencies. Some states have weekly and monthly newsletters that include some of the features of the *Federal Register* or *The Federal Contracts & Grants Weekly*. If not, they are likely to post notice of grant and contract opportunities in a newspaper published in the state capital. Almost all send periodic listings of RFP opportunities to all those who are registered with the state as potential contractors in the relevant areas. Other announcements may be found in the "legals" section of newspapers in those communities in which eligible applicants might be found.

If your organization provides social services or advocates for the most vulnerable populations, you may be able to get assistance in locating appropriate funding programs through your League for the Human Services, a nonprofit organization with operations in many state capitals. The league advocates for disadvantaged and needy populations and for social service providers. The league is often affiliated with a statewide United Way association or with a statewide consortium of private foundations or both. A list of these organizations is available through the Foundation Center in New York. The switchboard operator in the governor's or the attorney general's office will also know the league's address, as will a staffer in your local state representative's office. It may take a few hours to find out what there is and where, but it is not particularly difficult. Government agencies, after all, are not trying to hide what is available.

Information on your own local government programs is both more difficult and easier to obtain. It can be more difficult because counties, cities, and townships may not have as regularized procedures to inform the public or to engage relevant organizations in a bidding process as do federal and state government agencies. People tend to know each other at the local level, however, and the word often gets around early via committees and planning sessions as to where local government priorities are first likely to emerge. Although RFPs are also posted in the legals sections of local papers and elsewhere, they may appear too late for you to gear up or after someone else has already gotten into position.

Be on the alert for public hearings and read the minutes of public boards, councils, and commissions (which are often televised by local cable companies). A county commissioner in a mid-sized community stated,

> The one guy who knows what's coming down even before the decisions are made is Sheriff Merriweather. He's always at the table. And he's generous, sharing what he knows with other service providers. If there's a program for kids or for seniors, dealing with health problems or with sport, with safety or with culture, chances are the Sheriff's Department's got a piece of it.

TIPS ON GETTING INFORMATION
ON LOCAL GOVERNMENT FUNDING

Tip 1: A good source of up-to-date information on funding from local sources is the *Local Government Funding Report*, published weekly by Government Information Services in Washington, DC (but it may not have information on your own locale).

Tip 2: When all else fails, the state attorney general's office will be able to supply you with information about how to get information about state funding sources.

Responding to Government Priorities
and Funding Criteria

The government sets most of the priorities and the terms by which it dispenses assistance. These terms, however, like the times, are a-changing, as categoricals are folded into block grants, and these provide considerable discretionary authority to the states and other units of government. The closer the decision-making authority is to where services will be delivered, the more likely that service providers may have some influence on government programs and priorities and can help to shape the process even before grant and contract announcements are made. Also, as discussed in the next chapter, the larger and more comprehensive service providers can significantly influence both the purposes of the awards and the terms under which they are given.

SUMMARY

Grants-in-aid, contracts, loans, and certain kinds of cooperative agreements, such as coproduction, are the principal instruments used by the federal government to provide assistance to states, special districts, independent organizations, and individuals. There are several types of grants, including (a) project grants, (b) formula grants and entitlements, and (c) block grants. The first two are referred to as categorical because they target certain publics or address specific functions. Block grants consolidate similar categories and transfer both dollars and responsibility for their redistribution to state and local authorities. In turn, states and most local government units comingle their funds with federal dollars to purchase the services of nongovernmental organizations to carry out public functions. POSCs are their preferred redistribution tool.

REFERENCES

Bradley, J. L. (1987). Coproduction and privatization: Exploring the relationship and its implications. *Journal of Voluntary Action Research, 16*(3), 11-21.

Dommel, P. R., & Rich, M. J. (1987). The rich get richer—The attenuation of targeting effects of the community development block grant program. *Urban Affairs Quarterly, 22*(4), 206-211.

Hart, E. F. (1988). Contracting for child welfare services in Massachusetts: Emerging issues for policy and practice. *Social Work, 33*(6), 511-515.

Liptsky, M. (1989/1990). Nonprofit organizations, government, and the welfare state. *Political Science Quarterly, 104*(4), 625-648.

Spiegel, H. B. C. (1987). Coproduction in the context of neighborhood development. *Journal of Voluntary Action Research, 16*(3), 62-69.

SUGGESTIONS FOR FURTHER READING

Funding Research Institute (with Government Information Services and Education Funding Research Council). (1991). *Funding database handbook.* Arlington, VA: Author.

Gidron, B., Kramer, R. M., & Salamon, L. M. (Eds.). (1992). *Government and the third sector: Emerging relationships in welfare states.* San Francisco: Jossey-Bass.

Government Information Services. (1990). *How the government dispenses money, grants, and federal aid.* Washington, DC: Author.

Government Information Services. (1990). *An insider's guide to writing proposals for federal $$$$.* Washington, DC: Author.

Gutch, R. (1992). *Contracting lessons from the U.S.* London: National Council of Voluntary Organizations.

Kramer, R. M., & Grossman, B. (1987). Contracting for social services: Process management and resources dependencies. *Social Services Review, 62*(1), 32-55.

Maturi, R. (1991). States: A mother lode ripe for mining. *Industry Week, 240*(12), 79-83.

McVay, B. L. (1989). *Proposals that win federal contracts: How to plan, price, write, and negotiate to get your fair share of government.* Woodbridge, VA: Panoptic.

Peterson, G. E., & Howland, M. (1986). *The Reagan block grants: What have we learned?* Washington, DC: Urban Institute Press.

Saidel, J. R. (1991). Resource interdependence: The relationship between state agencies and nonprofit organizations. *Public Administration Review, 51*(6), 543-551.

Schiff, J. A. (1986). *Government social welfare spending and the private nonprofit sector: Crowding out and more.* Madison: University of Wisconsin, Institute for Research on Poverty.

Warren, R. (1987). Introduction to the special issue on coproduction, voluntarism, privatization, and the public interest. *Journal of Voluntary Action Research, 16*(3), 5-10.

Catalog of Federal Domestic Assistance

1200 Federal Assistance Programs at your Fingertips

Use a computerized system to search the Catalog for Federal assistance programs.

- Easy-to-Use
- On-Line
- Low cost
- Comprehensive, accurate

- Category searches
- Keyword searches
- Customize information formats
- Monthly *Federal Register* update

For information on how to access the *Federal Assistance Programs Retrieval System* (FAPRS), write:

Federal Domestic Assistance Catalog Staff
Reporters Building - Room 101
300 7th Street, SW.
Washington, DC 20407

U.S. General Services Administration
Information Resources Management Service

or call **(202) 708-5126**
or toll free **(800) 669-8331.**

**Catalog of Federal
Domestic Assistance**

Use your own
computer and
software to
search the
Catalog
programs.

**Now available
on floppy diskette**

- Set of nine 1.2 or 1.4
  MB floppy diskettes
- MS DOS/IBM PC DOS/
  Macintosh compatible
- ASCII characters
- 72 character fixed
  maximum record length
- Approximately 10 MB total
  data size, over 1200 files.

- Ideal for frequent
  users, libraries,
  publishers
- Complete with
  documentation
- Low cost, only $80
  per set or $140 for
  annual subscription
- Subscription includes
  complete June and
  December sets

To order the floppy
diskette version of the
Catalog, write:

Federal Domestic
  Assistance Catalog
  Staff
Reporters Building -
  Room 101
300 7th Street, SW
Washington, DC 20407

or call **(202) 708-5126**
or toll free **(800) 669-8331**

U.S. General Services
Administration

Information Resources
Management Service

HOW TO USE THE CATALOG

The following resource aids located in the front of the Catalog will help you to locate the assistance programs in which you are interested.

WHAT'S IN THE *HOW TO USE THE CATALOG* SECTION

- Information that will familiarize potential applicants with the contents of the Catalog, and pertinent criteria to consider before applying for Federal assistance

- Definitions for the 15 types of assistance, including both financial and non-financial types of assistance

- Explanation of the organizational layout of the Catalog, the program descriptions, indexes, and appendixes

- A sample program description illustrating the kind of information found in each section of program descriptions

FOUR WAYS TO IDENTIFY A PROGRAM FOR FEDERAL ASSISTANCE

AGENCY INDEX - PAGE AI-1

Identify assistance programs categorized by agency (subagency, or designated commission), listed by program number and title, or listed alphabetically at the end of the Agency Index. Review program(s).

FUNCTIONAL INDEX - PAGE FI-1

Identify assistance programs by cross-referencing programs within 20 broad functional categories and 176 subcategories. Refer to the preceding Functional Index Summary on Page FIS-1 for a complete listing. Review program(s).

SUBJECT INDEX - PAGE SI-1

Identify assistance programs by subject categories, popular names, or common keywords associated with the subject matter of the program objectives for the type of assistance you are seeking. Review program(s).

APPLICANT ELIGIBILITY INDEX - PAGE AE-1

Identify assistance programs according to the type of applicant who is eligible to apply for each program listed in the Catalog. Review program(s).

4

Putting Out a Contract

Government Purchase-of-Service Contracts and How They Work

Open Bidding

"Ron Moodey suggested I call you. Frankly, we didn't think someone with your background and reputation would be interested," Joan McClusky from the state's Department of Family Services told me when she called. "That's why we had not included your name on the initial distribution list. Would you still be interested in sending in a bid?"

"Hoping you would ask," I responded. "But before I put anything to paper, could we meet briefly to discuss what you have in mind?"

To be honest, I already knew what the state agency had in mind. Ron, with whom I had worked on federal job training programs in the 1970s and with whom I still kept in touch, had clued me in. "These folks are new at job training," Ron had told me, "That's probably why they didn't know enough to include you among the potential bidders for coordinating the state's efforts." That's the reason I wanted to meet with McClusky. Before writing anything, I wanted to let state officials know what I had in mind and to make sure that my ideas would be acceptable.

"I appreciate your extending the deadline," I began when we met in McClusky's office a few days later.

"No problem," she explained. "We can always reopen a bidding process when we are not satisfied with the quality of the bids that have come in." She was explaining the rules and protecting the agency from any charge of favoritism, but also letting me know that personal contacts were not going to substitute for quality.

"One of the things I am concerned about," I began, "is that some potential vendors might not hear about Family Service's job training initiative. All the established job training agencies are likely to, because they're already on your potential vendors list, and so will the big corporations that see this as potentially lucrative. But a great many potential trainers may not be on your list.

"If I were to coordinate the screening and selection process," I continued, "I would also want to work with you on creating an outreach strategy that would guarantee we get the best possible bids from the best possible vendors. Here's what I have in mind. . . ."

I explained how Texas and California had reached likely bidders, and engaged her in a discussion of how their approaches might be modified. By the time the meeting was over, we both knew exactly what I would be writing in my proposal. "Looking forward to seeing your application," McClusky said, "and thanks for sharing your ideas in advance."

BUYING AND SELLING SERVICES

Public Responsibility:
Private and Voluntary Production

Purchase-of-service contracts (POSCs) are the means by which government purchases the services provided by others and the means by which individuals, voluntary agencies, and private firms sell their services to the government. POSCs do not rid government of responsibility for the funding and delivery of prescribed goods and services. That is the goal of privatization. They do, however, create a system of sharing of responsibility in which government sets policies and covers all or part of the cost, and individuals or private, public, and voluntary organizations engage in service delivery. POSCs are not limited to the human services or to nonprofits. In fact, the human services and most nonprofit organizations are relative newcomers to service contracting. Federal, state, and county governments have long contracted with private-sector firms for conduct of public business, such as the building of roads and highways and the provision of public transportation.

Contracting out does not absolve government agencies from setting or carrying out policy. For example, although the federal government retains much of the responsibility for setting military policy, it contracts out for the research, for the recommendation of policy alternatives, and for the production of military equipment. It may even contract for the conduct of military actions via aid to other governments or through the support of covert operations by paramilitary organizations in foreign lands.

In this chapter, how government purchases of human services are conducted will be examined. The chapter begins with a review of recent developments and then describes the reasons why POSCs have become the principal mechanism for the allocation of public funds to the delivery of social services. The reader will discover that the contracting process can be informal at times (as the introductory vignette suggests), demonstrating flexibility on the state's part with regard to who it does business with and by what rules it plays. As the same vignette illustrates, however, the contracting agency can also set rigid standards and use rule-governed and competitive procedures in awarding contracts.

Beliefs about the extent to which POSC mechanisms contribute to cost saving and performance improvement will be analyzed. I will then suggest some ways for you to use these strongly held beliefs to your advantage in preparing a bid for funding. The steps in the bid-making and contract management processes will be described in some detail. The chapter will conclude with a description of a number of newer uses of POSCs by nongovernmental organizations.

Contracting for the Social and Human Services

Today, government agencies routinely purchase services that prior to the 1980s were almost always conducted by government agencies. For example, today, in addition to paying for the construction of prisons by private contractors, state and county governments may also purchase the services of other contractors for prison management or for the housing of local prisoners in jails managed by other jurisdictions. Some municipalities pay private firms to provide public safety protection, including public health, police, or fire fighting services. School districts contract with private firms to design curricula, train teachers, and even run schools. State departments of education charter schools and finance them directly or work through local government or quasi-governmental organizations empowered to provide the charter. State and county governments contract with for-profit and nonprofit organizations for the management of public parks and recreation services. In many states, mental health facilities and community alternatives are 100% in the hands of private and nonprofit providers funded in part via insurance (some of which is publicly funded) and grants, but increasingly through purchase-of-service contracts.

The expansion of POSCs for child welfare, mental health, and other human services has been extraordinarily rapid. In 1970, an insignificant amount ($27 million or approximately 1%) of all the funds expended for social services under the Social Security Act (including welfare) was allocated to the purchase of services from private contractors (Wedel, 1974). By the end of the decade, however, two and a half billion dollars in Title XX expenditures alone had been contracted out nationwide. Forty percent of these dollars (approximately $1 billion) had gone to for-profit providers, mostly to run group homes and day care centers. Soon, a wide variety of other programs aimed at "preventing, ameliorating, or resolving environmental, physical, or psychosocial problems" (Demone & Gibelman, 1989) were being purchased by the states. Many of these were new dollars, fueling the growth of service industries. The funding environment was becoming more competitive. The availability of service contracts and, especially, the entry of private-sector firms into what had been traditionally associated with the nonprofit world, were bound to make it so. Kettner and Martin (1987) report that by the mid-1980s, more than half the purchase-of-service funds expended on social services in western states were going to for-profit providers (in contrast with 17% for north central, 16% for northeast, and 9% for southern states). The percentages were tied to each region's historic experience. For example, Alaska's history of settlement was so recent that it never really had had a chance to build a well-developed voluntary sector with its own traditions and vested interests.

The passage of Proposition 13, occasioned by a statewide tax revolt in California, led to the slashing of property taxes in 1978. For 10 years, the impact was not felt. Surplus state funds and federal dollars were used to blunt the impact of lost revenue at the county and municipal levels. Services were not only maintained but some were even expanded. Major urban counties, such as Los Angeles and San Francisco, boasted some of the most advanced and varied social services available anywhere. Local governments and services received substantial funding via public transfers in the form of POSCs from the state. California, in turn, drew extensively on federal sources of funds.

By George Bush's first term, however, the tax revolt had spread to the federal level. Readers will recall Bush's famous "read my lips" pledge of "no new taxes." A tightening up of federal transfers occurred at the end of the Cold War, which in turn led to the shrinking of California's industrial base, heavily dependent on military contracts and bases. As jobs disappeared, state revenues from property, income, and sales taxes also receded. State officials discovered that one way to avoid making deep cuts was to reduce operating expenses, and this could be achieved by contracting out needed services to private-sector providers who promised to do the work at lower cost.

Massachusetts, Vermont, Michigan, Minnesota, Nebraska, Florida, and Texas caught up quickly, almost matching the western states' percentages of for-profit contractors. What Demone and Gibelman (1989) had referred to 10 years earlier as an "evolving contract state" was beginning to show some maturity. Some observers estimate that by 2010 more than 80% of all public funds expended for social services will be in the form of purchase-of-service contracts, with 80% of the contractors representing the private sector. Unfortunately, as Kramer and Grossman (1987) pointed out, despite some 20 years of extensive experience with social service contracting at that time, there appeared to be little research on its effects and insufficient recognition of how increased competition affects contractors. The literature on how POSCs work and their effectiveness was almost nonexistent. The situation is not much better today.

Just before going to press, I checked the Michigan State University Library, which possesses one of the country's major fund-raising collections. There were, at the time, 58 relatively recent "how-to" books with the words *grant* or *grantsmanship* in the title (e.g., "How to Get Government Grants for . . .") but only 3 with the words *POSC, contracts,* or *contracting*. Nevertheless, a good deal is known that can be translated into effective practice principles for both the funder and the service provider. For example, in a review of five studies of the POSC process in the human services between 1969 and 1981, Kettner and Martin (1987) abstracted 11 decision factors that affected state use of these mechanisms.

REASONS FOR SERVICE CONTRACTING
AND HOW PROVIDERS COPE WITH THEM

For purposes of this book, the focus is on those reasons most commonly used to promote or justify the use of POSCs. These generally fall into the following four categories:

1. Cost cutting and efficiency
2. Increasing fiscal control and accountability
3. Improving services and increasing their responsiveness, flexibility, and accessibility
4. Reducing the power of central government by transferring authority to more proximate units

Because these assumptions are sometimes accepted uncritically or voiced more as slogans than as the outcome of systematic observation, it may help to examine each more critically and to explore their implications for prospective contractors and other service providers.

Cost Cutting and Efficiency

Cost Cutting Leads to More Cost Cutting

The rapid growth of POSCs is closely tied to efforts to turn categorical grants into block grants to cut costs. Unlike categorical programs, which often have their own advocates within the bureaucracy and among the constituents who benefit from them (e.g., child advocates and advocates for the aging or disabled), block grants do not. Given the freedom to maneuver, by being relatively unfettered by federal mandates, it was argued that states could choose to be generous or stingy, increasing or reducing the size of programs or the benefits they provide. Reductions in federal allocations, however, put pressure on states to maintain existing programs by finding new sources of funds, cutting programs, or reducing costs in other ways.

How Costs Are Cut

POSCs can, and often do, cut costs, or at least shift them from one sector to another. Theoretically, there are at least three ways in which this can be accomplished:

1. Increasing competition
2. Limiting contracts to 12-month periods
3. Underfunding programs

How close is theory to reality? By opening bids up to a wider range of potential contractors, competition sometimes does result in cost-cutting innovations. One of the arguments often used to bolster this claim is that when private-sector firms, with their greater commitment to cost containment, are included in the bidding process, efficiencies are most likely. This is a nice theory, but to date there is no evidence to support it.

The second approach appears to be more successful. By limiting contracts to a year-by-year basis, states can eliminate programs that are considered inefficient or ineffective, that do not deal with emerging priorities, or that they can no longer afford because of budget shortfalls. Even here, however, there is some evidence that many programs cannot easily be cut because of constituent support for them at the local level. The third approach to cost cutting is likely to be more consistently successful—underfunding programs. In reality, this is often more of an exercise in cost shifting than in cost cutting. Contractors are sometimes required to generate matching funds or expected to bear the indirect costs associated with services purchased. Although some are able to find supplemental funds elsewhere, others compensate by reducing quality or by shifting the cost to others—for example, by contracting with temporary employees who work at lower wages and do not get fringe benefits.

How to Cope With Cost Cutting if You Are on the Receiving End

"Doesn't sound too promising," you might be thinking. "We have to cut our own infrastructures, hire staff whom we pay poorly (and who may be less qualified to provide the services we offer), and still have to raise more money to keep our operations going, the agency afloat, and to honor our commitments to employees. We wind up serving our clients poorly and have to subsidize the state for the right to do so!"

Could be, but it is not necessarily so, either in terms of the assumptions made or the helplessness expressed.

To begin with, many agencies and firms are now in the business of selling services that, in an earlier period, would have been provided primarily by public agencies. Clearly, there is enough business to go around or no one would be bidding on contracts, and organizations are able to do what they are in the business of doing or else they could not stay in business. In interviews with contractors and subcontractors, I have found the following strategies for dealing with sometimes threatening fiscal environments and coming out ahead to be increasingly common: (a) supplementing state contracts with other sources of supply, (b) expanding organizational size to create economies of scale, (c) diversifying in terms of markets and services, (d) subcontracting, (e) franchising, and (f) building consortia.

Providers are rarely required to limit themselves to the funds available through the contract. Nonprofit agencies have long been aware of the need to raise funds from multiple sources to supplement the services the state is willing to pay for. Among the sources of support are gifts from individual donors; federated agency allocations (e.g., those from United Way, Women's Funds, and sectarian federations); and other sources discussed in this book. For-profit organizations are beginning to look to similar sources but have been more apt to find new niche markets in which they do not compete with nonprofits that have access to supplemental funding or to cut costs though economies of scale.

Pursuing an economies of scale strategy can lead to greater efficiencies by reducing administrative and other overhead costs. For example, a group home for the elderly that serves 6 to 12 people is likely to be so underfunded that its proprietor will have to put in extra-long hours, underpay staff, and deprive some residents of needed service that the state will not fund. A larger agency, however, might include 10 or 12 group homes for the elderly, and a mega-agency serving 1,000 or more residents is likely to be in a much better position as long as there is a fairly stable supply of clients.

Larger organizations are often able to purchase supplies at advantageous prices and to hire specialists in recreation, rehabilitation, and counseling who can be assigned to several local units. They can also hire specialists who write proposals, negotiate and manage contracts with the state, and engage in other fund-raising efforts. Some social service providers have begun to take a page from medical care providers such as large hospital systems. Crossing state lines, they can contract with several state authorities, reducing their dependence on the political or economic factors that often influence services in a particular state. Others have protected their organizations by not putting all their eggs in one basket.

For example, a children's home under sectarian auspices in a midwestern state initially expanded its programs to include summer camps, neighborhood centers for delinquent youth, and tutorial services. It later added a health clinic for teen girls, a mental health program, and day care centers, and it went to an entirely different population to begin selling home-based services to the aging. Over time, its sources of contract funds expanded beyond the Child Welfare Division of the State Department of Social Serves to include seven other government contracting agencies. The director of a voluntary-sector family service agency explains, "And, of course, we're still getting money from affiliated churches and from the United Way, where we began. In fact, we're now also getting United Way dollars from suburban communities where we've opened up service centers."

Others have emulated the POSC process itself by purchasing the services of individual practitioners and smaller firms (in effect, subcontracting). For example, a large multiservice agency may contract out for counseling from private practitioners, accounting services from a firm with expertise in social services and state transfers of funds, or fund-raising. These contractors have learned from public agencies that subcontracting can save dollars and reduce long-term obligations. Some have also learned from the private sector that franchising can reduce risks by sharing the risk with local franchises.

This is a relatively new phenomenon in which a central organization negotiates contracts to provide services and then "sells the right" to do so under its own name to private entrepreneurs. This is what has begun to be referred to as the "McDonaldization of the social services" or the "Domino effect." Consider the following scenario. In a large metropolitan area, a number of relatively small children's service agencies began working together after the state department of public welfare, which contracted for specific services with many of them, added a provision to each of their contracts that they were to participate in design and management of a state-funded client information system. The information generated proved not only helpful in terms of better services to clients through improved referrals and case management but also led to eliminating some redundancies and overlaps. Now consider whether the following (imaginary) scenario might also be possible:

> Based on this success, and on their own initiative, several agencies collaborated on joint purchasing of supplies and equipment, even setting up a barter system between them. Eventually, they engaged in joint training efforts that led to lending each other staff with specific managerial and programmatic expertise. Over time, a consortium had been built that reduced costs to its members and increased their performance capacity but did not require that they give up their separate identities, boards, and other affiliations. In this case, efficiencies were not initiated by the POSC process, but they were promoted by the public agency that saw in the promotion of collaboration rather than competition opportunities to both improve services and reduce costs. Membership in the consortium was valued not only because of the direct benefits to its members but also because the state agency, understandably, was more favorably disposed to funding members of the consortium through purchase agreements.

Fiscal Control and Accountability

How the Contract Process Works
and How Costs Are Set

When compared with the grants process, POSCs certainly do have the potential for increased fiscal control. The contracting agency sets such terms as which services are to be performed, who is to be served, and in which locales. It can specify the types of facilities to be used and the qualifications of staff to be employed by the contractor, at what cost, and for how long. The arrangements by which government can contract with private and nonprofit vendors can be grouped into those that focus on either performance or costs.

When remuneration is based on performance, outcome is rewarded. Outcomes can be measured quantitatively or qualitatively. For example, a contractor might be paid x dollars for a unit of work (which might be defined as the successful placement of a disabled child in an adoptive home). The more efficient a contractor is (i.e., the more children it places or the more it places at less cost than allowed), the more likely it is to make a profit or to have funds available for other purposes (including improving service outcomes or effectiveness). The more effective a contractor is, the more likely that the contract will be renewed and that the contractor will be able to stay in business. A contractor that is not successful in placing "hard-to-place" children may not be reimbursed for some or all of the work done, or the contract may not be extended a second year.

In cost contracting, the public agency negotiates or sets a fixed fee for a number of units of service (e.g., placements made), clients served, or a specific set of activities. The fixed fee (price the public agency is willing to pay) might be set in advance and advertised via requests for proposals (RFPs) or other means. Alternatively, a price range might be announced, with the specific fee (fixed price) to be negotiated with each contractor in advance of its signing the purchase-of-service agreement with the state.

A fixed-price contract is sometimes not all that fixed. It might have an escalation clause allowing for unexpected changes in the cost of service or in economic conditions. Many contracts include payment incentives for rapid work or for improvements in quality. Others are set on a cost-plus basis, with the plus increasing if the cost decreases. Time and material contracts are also possible, but these tend to be limited to agreements with individual vendors who are paid by the hour, day, or session. Finally, the contract may include a clause that allows redetermination of appropriate fees or cost reimbursement at some point (e.g., 6 months) into the contract.

The financial or performance terms of the contract are also likely to define the terms of accountability—that is, the fiscal or performance measures that the contractor is expected to satisfy.

How You Can Cope With Fiscal and Performance Accountability Pressures

Although these terms may not initially appear to favor your agency or organization, you need not be victimized by them. There are two kinds of strategies a potential contractor can employ when the contracting agency's rules appear to be punitive or overly onerous, offensive, and defensive. These strategies are termed *assertive* and *compliant*, and both strategies are likely to net benefits for the organization.

Assertive strategies are aimed at influencing the terms of the contract. These include price factors (fixed costs, cost plus, incentive pay, etc.) as well as performance variables (how many, how much, where, and by when). For example, suppose the state agency insists on a change in your organization's client intake criteria requiring you to serve youth who are more severely damaged or present more behavioral challenges than your staff is prepared for. It may be possible for you to come to an agreement to gradually increase the numbers of youth with severe problems. That way, you have time to adjust your services and capacity to do the work. It may also be possible to get a state agreement to add a staff retraining line to the budget to allow you to build up the necessary capacity more rapidly.

Suppose the state advertises a fixed price for a given unit of service. If there are few takers, you may be in position to get the contract officials to reconsider the payment offered. Even when the state has lower cost contractors to choose from, government officials may see that there are benefits to contracting with some more high-priced vendors. An agency can negotiate to its own advantage if it has something of specific value to the state, such as experience, reputation, effective linkages with collateral providers, name, influential board members, relevant locale, and so on. A government agency may be willing to negotiate a supplementary amount to accommodate your organization's difference.

A defensive or compliant approach may have equal or even greater benefit to your agency by forcing staff to rethink the way in which they have been doing business and, perhaps, by changing itself. For example, it may require administrators to move from line-item to performance budgeting or for line staff to think of what they do in terms of outcomes rather than activities. This can lead to using new and different standards for assessing progress. Such changes can lead to goal modification or clarification and to new understandings of what is possible.

In practice, the impact of externally set performance measures is likely to be neither totally devastating nor totally welcome. Many providers find some requirements irksome and unwise, whereas other requirements may stimulate them to perform in new and improved ways that ultimately benefit the organization or its clients or both.

Improved, More Flexible, Responsive,
and Accessible Services

How Services Can Be Improved
Through Purchase-of-Service Contracting

If cost cutting was, in the mid-1990s, the most common rationale given for purchase-of-service contracting, service improvement was not far behind. Unfortunately, there is less empirical evidence than rhetoric to support the argument that POSCs are in the best interest of the client. I do not mean to suggest that services do not improve when funding patterns change. Research data, however, do not justify the strongly held beliefs that are often espoused to justify the use of contract mechanisms.

The following are some of the most commonly heard arguments made in favor of contracting:

1. Overregulation, characteristic of many government-run programs, tends to substitute for real quality. State and federal agencies suffer from all the rigidities that characterize most bureaucracies. It is unrealistic for the government to hire all the kinds of experts needed to perform the specialized services required in contemporary society. It is much more appropriate to hire individuals, agencies, and firms that are specialized to do the work required.
2. Voluntary-sector agencies tend to be more innovative, flexible, and responsive than government bureaus. Because of their extensive interactions with other community-based agencies and the commitment of both staff and involved community lay leaders, they are well suited to finding optimal solutions to clients' needs.
3. For-profit firms present similar advantages and, in addition, are cost conscious and able to apply business concepts to management decisions.
4. For some services—for example, legal aid or substance abuse counseling—and for some clients, going to a private or voluntary agency is likely to be more comfortable and safe than going to a public bureaucracy.
5. Some services are better rendered by contractors than by the state. For example, monitoring and evaluation are likely to be more objective if handled by an external contractor with no need to protect the status quo than by the same agency that conducts the services or purchases them from favored contractors.

How You Can Present Your Program as
Flexible, Responsive, Accessible, and Improved

Clearly, it is to your organization's advantage to stress the strengths of your program, especially if other contractors suffer by comparison with your organization. All too often, contractors have grown large and bureaucratic, suffering the same rigidities government agencies are accused of possessing. Small agencies are often bereft of imagination or of the other resources that can contribute to innovation and experimentation. Also, poorly trained staff, hired on the cheap, may lack expertise and commitment. Your competitive advantage is enhanced if these deficiencies do not apply, and if you can use at least a few of the arguments listed previously to justify why your organization should get the contract.

Interdependence and the Transfer of Authority

Sharing Authority and How It Works

As I have shown, proponents of both block grants and POSCs argue that by transferring authority from more central to more proximate levels of government, services are likely to be better attuned to local needs and more responsive. Also, by delegating responsibility for production and delivery of services to the private and voluntary sectors, responsibility is returned to local institutions more representative of the interests of their constituencies.

In some ways, the opposite seems to have occurred. Despite cutbacks in government spending, the economics of transfer masks a government penetration into sectors that had once been relatively independent. Service providers are often forced to decide between forgoing government funds or accepting government norms that dictate agency program priorities and operations. For example, government priorities determine which populations are to receive services (the mentally ill, the frail elderly, the homeless, or children at risk) and, within these groups, which persons are most worthy of services.

Contractors, however, may be in a position to influence public policies and priorities. Quality providers are often in short supply. Because the cost of locating new providers each fiscal year would be excessive, state agencies often develop cozy relationships with service agencies that have proven satisfactory in terms of cost and performance. These providers often help shape state priorities by demonstrating how one approach may be advantageous over another or by advocating for populations in need and documenting emerging needs. Thus, POSCs foster relationships that reflect various degrees of interdependence, sometimes blurring the boundaries between government and the private and nonprofit service sectors.

How You Can Take Advantage of This Interdependence

There are a number of strategies that service providers employ to make themselves more attractive, including the following:

1. Carving out a market niche in which there are few competitors and in which your organization is best positioned to provide a needed service

2. Demonstrating that your agency's programs are both productive and cost-effective

3. Building collaborative relationships with other providers (including service consolidation)

4. Working with others who will advocate for your organization (local politicians, influential lay leaders, directors of collaborating agencies that also receive state contract funding, etc.)

How to take advantage of interdependence may become clearer when the way in which the contract management process works is examined.

CONTRACT MANAGEMENT

The contract management process is conducted by or on behalf of the organization making contract awards. It includes the following five basic steps:

1. Recruiting potential bidders
2. Rating and selecting bids
3. Negotiating the contract
4. Monitoring and evaluating performance
5. Terminating or renewing the contract

It is important for potential bidders to understand how the contracting process works and how state and other organizations manage it. Although the process may appear to stack all the chips on the funder's side of the table, the potential contractor has considerable latitude in how to move at each step along the way.

Recruiting Bidders

Designing and Distributing RFPs

Once a decision to contract for a service is made, RFPs are used as a means to

- define the type of service the government wishes to purchase and the standards for practice;

- inform the public (or specific organizations and service sectors) that bids are being sought;
- instruct potential bidders on how to prepare quality proposals.

With regard to standards, the RFP may specify the characteristics of personnel, location of the program, cost or quality performance measures, affirmative action requirements, the nature of collaborations with other providers expected, or agency policy-making processes such as requiring consumer representation in planning or evaluation.

Although some RFPs may be sole-sourced or targeted to specific bidders, most are likely to be open to all prospective contractors. In addition to some of the notification mechanisms described previously, state agencies also send notices to trade associations, providers they know about, or to third parties that publicize the RFP to their constituents. Examples of third parties include metropolitan United Ways, county social service and mental health departments, and other contractors.

Once a contracting system is in place, the principal means of disseminating RFPs may be through bidder lists to select providers. These include individuals and organizations that request notification of any requests for proposals in areas where they have interest or expertise. Most of these lists are now computerized and include

- the name and auspices of the potential contractor;
- the kinds of work it can or does perform;
- populations served;
- geographic areas covered;
- names or qualifications of key staff;
- special characteristics (e.g., minority ownership);
- prior contract history with the state.

A keyword search may be all that is necessary to locate the most likely respondents to an RFP.

"Bidder's conferences" are held when the state agency wants to reach out to new contractors or when there are few experienced contractors available. These meetings can be open or closed, in one location or in many, or all on one day or spread out over many. Here, state officials explain what is expected, give instructions on how to complete the bid application, consult with potential contractors on specific issues that may be difficult to understand (e.g., pricing policy or quality standards), and so on. At some later point, consultation may be available in the form of review and feedback on preliminary proposals.

Government agencies, like most organizations, try to make life easier for themselves. For ongoing programs, they are likely to limit the bidding process to those individuals and organizations already on one of their computerized lists or to others that may be brought to their attention by consultants and other informants. Broader dissemination of RFPs may occur only when state officials wish to initiate new programs or expand to geographic areas where few potential bidders are available. Renewals of existing contracts are unlikely to be open to competition. The contracts officer of a state housing authority explains:

> When the contract period is up, we're likely to just renegotiate terms for continuation with the current contractor, even if we think performance was not fully up to our expectations. Setting up a new bidding process each year and negotiating a new contract would be terribly cumbersome and inefficient. Even more serious is that we could not get quality contractors to bid in the first place if they had to compete anew each year.
>
> To grow in capacity, service providers have to have some stability. We can generally assure compliance with our standards by working with the contractor over time. We might even add some funds to the contract to permit them to do better staff training, or help them link up with collateral providers with whom they should be working. I would say that once we make a contract commitment, we are more into capacity building and service improvement than into promoting competition.

When suitable contractors are not available, government agencies sometimes go beyond technical assistance to creating organizational infrastructures capable of bidding for and offering needed services or arranging interest-free loans for capital expenditures. When few suppliers are available, government may be very generous indeed.

When there is a surfeit of suppliers, funders use a number of mechanisms to limit the number of bids by using sole-source or limited-bidding contracts or otherwise narrowing the criteria for application to only a few qualified bidders. These are likely to be larger organizations with considerable experience and well-established contacts in government or with the ability to lobby effectively. For-profit agencies may have considerable resources available to invest up front—cornering the market, so to speak. This puts smaller, less experienced, or less endowed agencies at a considerable disadvantage.

Making Sure You Get an RFP

To make sure your organization gets the RFPs it is interested in, first contact the relevant state and local agencies to get on an appropriate bidder's list (there may be more than one, depending on the range of services you or your organization provide) and also subscribe to or otherwise get access to the journals, newspapers, and other organs in which competitive bids are likely to be announced.

Selecting Contractors

How Contractors Are Selected

When bidding is relatively open and competitive, or when government decisions are likely to be scrutinized, decisions will be made on the basis of some relatively objective criteria. These may be listed in the RFP itself or included in an application kit. When many applications are expected, a rating system may be set up in which review panelists score proposals on the basis of decided-on criteria. Panelists may include state officials, academics or others with relevant expert knowledge, representatives of professional associations or current providers, and so on. Rating scores are compared and proposals ranked. Even this process, however, is rarely fully objective.

Political criteria are likely to interact with "professional decisions." For example, it may be necessary to consider geographic location, professional affiliations of the contractors, the ethnic composition of the population to be served, the interests of an influential state legislator, and so on. The fewer the potential number of bidders, the more informal and political this process is likely to be.

*How to Increase the
Likelihood of Being Selected*

Find out what would give you or your organization a competitive edge. It always helps to prepare a good proposal—one that is honest, describes what you will do and your capacities, and keeps costs down. A well-written document, however, is not always sufficient. When competition is heavy, finding a way to distinguish your organization and its programs can make a big difference. Also, do not overlook the right connections. Here, I do not mean using pull or some unfair advantage but, rather, showing who you are connected to—for example,

- local officials who can vouch for you and your organization;
- collaborators who will work with you if you get the contract;
- consultants available to you on issues of importance to the funder and around which you may show some weakness (e.g., program evaluation);
- a larger organization of which you may be a part or that is likely to give you backup when needed.

Negotiating the Contract

What the Contract Contains

The contract is a legal document written in legal language. After a bid has been selected by the funding organization, the specifics are still to be negotiated. The following three issues may still need working through:

1. Price, timing, and payment procedures (e.g., fixed price, cost plus, and other payment approaches)
2. Operational requirements (e.g., client eligibility, staff qualifications, building location, or other specifications)
3. Monitoring criteria and procedures (e.g., how often, outcome measures, and compliance enforcement procedures)

Once tentative agreement has been reached, the contract is drafted and reviewed by both sides, but it must then go through a number of approvals. Kramer and Grossman (1987) describe a process whereby a San Francisco area Agency on Aging's contracts with providers had to be approved by its board of supervisors as well as by its finance committee, the mayor, the county attorney, the civil service commission, the purchaser, the controller, and the chief administrative officer. Each contractor may have had to go through a similar, if not as complex, series of approvals. A hitch at any point could have set the process back to square one. To avoid major delays, providers and funders would do well to know the rules and to follow them closely, checking with relevant parties even before the draft is put to paper.

WARNING: This process is not always smooth. Delays are common. Mixed interpretations lead to mixed messages and misunderstandings.

Negotiating to Your Advantage

From the bidder's perspective, the first three steps—finding out about the contract, writing the proposal, and then negotiating, drafting, and seeing the contract through the review process—are nonreimbursable costs. Organizations make these investments to be able to do the work for which they are in business. Winning a contract but negotiating poor terms is likely to put you out of business.

Well-established agencies with proven track records are likely to do better in the negotiations process than neophytes. They may already know how to negotiate, can point to earlier agreements that worked well, and because they may be able to engender trust they often obtain more flexible terms. Smaller bidders and those new to the process generally do better when represented by an attorney. You may know a great deal about what your organization does and about the populations it serves but much less about the legal and financial arrangements that may make it possible for you to do what you do.

Monitoring

What You May Be Required to
Tell the Funder if You Get Funded

Once the terms of the contract are agreed on, negotiations with the funder shift in focus from what is to be done to how it will be done and to acceptable levels of performance. Ongoing and periodic assessment of the work in progress is generally referred to as *monitoring*. Measuring outcomes and outputs is called *evaluation*. Although the monitoring process is reimbursed—that is, the cost of preparing reports and of evaluation can be built into the contract—funders rarely allow sufficient funds to complete the work required. Contractors often complain that (a) more information is required than can be of much use, (b) the frequency of reportage takes precious time away from service delivery, and (c) the criteria used to hold them accountable to the terms of the contract often have little to do with the real purpose of the program. For example, the numbers of contact hours may be measured, but little concern may be expressed about how these have led to improvement in client self-esteem or readiness to seek employment.

Protecting Yourself Against Unfair Requirements

There can be serious methodological difficulties in monitoring or evaluating services, especially those whose outputs are not easily quantifiable. Deciding at the start that monitoring and evaluation criteria are subject to review is often a good defensive strategy for both the funder and the contractor. Because the monitoring process can cause periodic strains in the relationship, it is often prudent to involve an evaluator in the development of relevant criteria, just as an attorney may be present in negotiating other aspects of the agreement.

Renewing or Terminating the Contract

When Contracts Are Renewed and When They Are Terminated

If performance is reasonably good, the contract is likely to be renewed at the end of the contract period. For efficiency reasons or because there are just too few qualified providers available, government agencies find it difficult to terminate contracts unless the contractor is clearly involved in illegal, unethical, or harmful practices. Revoking a contract can be as damaging to the funder as it can be to the contractor. Does this suggest the public agency has little power to enforce compliance? Not necessarily.

First, funders can reward effective work by increasing the size of the contract or the financial award and penalize poor performance by changing the terms of the contract. Second, it is possible to "invest" in an agency that has not been performing well by adding resources for a limited time in an effort to bring the program up to par. Third, it is possible to limit a provider's authority or autonomy to make independent decisions until it has proved its ability to comply with accountability requirements. When contracts do have to be terminated—because of malfeasance, incompetence, or a program has been phased out—helping the contractor phase down before phasing out may be necessary. When all is said and done, funders are the ones who made the contract and should assume some of the responsibility for a mistake or for a change in policy. It would not be fair for the clients of a discontinued program to suffer further.

Protecting Yourself Against
Sudden Termination

Clearly, the best protection is to do good work and to report it to the funder as required in the contract. As funds become tighter or as program priorities change, however, some contracts may be terminated or phased out. Your best strategies include (a) maintaining ongoing communication with funders and other relevant parties and (b) exploring other sources of support to expand or protect the program. A wide variety of potential sources are discussed in this book.

THE FUTURE FOR PURCHASES OF SERVICES

For the foreseeable future at least, public funds will continue to be allocated to the human services via purchase-of-service contracts. There is ideological support for the process from both the Right and the Left. Conservatives see POSCs as a way of reducing the size of big government, at all levels, and as an important means toward cost cutting. Liberals see contracting as a way of making social services more responsive and as a means toward improving service performance. Rapidly shifting priorities and the pressures to continually cut services or to privatize them, however, are likely to have significant consequences for local providers who wish to sell their services. The following are some predictions for the future, gleaned unscientifically from our interviews with both funders and contractors:

1. Larger, well-managed agencies, with greater capacity to absorb cuts in funds or to shift their services to new populations and needs, are likely to survive. Others, especially those that have not found a secure niche in safe markets or have not established effective cooperative relationships with other providers, will be increasingly vulnerable.

2. With less funds available for many programs, public agencies will place high priority on performance and budget accountability. Pressures from significant constituencies will have, as has been true in defense contracting and elsewhere, an impact on legislative bodies. The recent history of funding for victims of violence (no public support until advocacy groups raised the public consciousness), for family planning (negatively affected by the right-to-life movement), and for services to AIDS victims (denied or underfunded in many locales until legislators began to feel the pressure from constituencies or from personal experiences with family members and others who were victims) may point to lessons for the future. Providers will need backup from committed constituencies.

3. The most vulnerable, and hard to serve, populations are likely to be shunned by service providers because of the costs involved and the low rates of success unless public agencies clearly put an emphasis on equity considerations in funding purchase-of-service contracts and create more realistic output measures.

4. The most successful human service managers will be those with entrepreneurial skills, able to negotiate the contracting environment and to build effective resource sharing via collaborations with other providers in the communities where they do business.

5. Because there will be, for a time, increasing competition for fewer public funds, service providers will have to secure supplementary and alternative resources via other approaches to fund-raising, coproduction, and work with volunteers.

For many service providers, POSCs will be the major game, perhaps the only game, in town. Like other games, however, it is one that requires paying attention to the rules and to the strategies that lead to success.

SUMMARY

By the turn of the century, 80% of all government support to local service providers is likely to come in the form of purchase-of-service contracts. POSCs do not relieve government of responsibility for determining what services are to be funded or to fund services. They are, however, used to cut costs, increase fiscal control, and make services more responsive and accessible. They also increase the interdependence of the private and public sectors in the financing and delivery of services. The contract management process (government's responsibility) parallels the contract-seeking process (the bidder's concern). It includes (a) recruiting bidders (and getting known as a potential contractor), (b) selecting contractors (and writing proposals that are likely to increase your attractiveness), (c) negotiating the contract, (d) monitoring (and preparing progress reports), and (e) renewal or termination.

REFERENCES

Demone, H. W., Jr., & Gibelman, M. (Eds.). (1989). *Services for state: Purchasing health and human services.* New Brunswick, NJ: Rutgers University Press.
Kettner, P. M., & Martin, L. L. (1987). *Purchase of service contracting.* Newbury Park, CA: Sage.
Kramer, R. M., & Grossman, B. (1987). Contracting for social services: Process management and resources dependencies. *Social Services Review, 61*(1), 32-55.
Wedel, K. R. (1974). Contracting for public assistance social services. *Public Welfare, 32*(12), 57-62.

SUGGESTIONS FOR FURTHER READING

Bernstein, S. R. (1991). *Managing contracted services in the nonprofit agency: Administrative, ethical and political issues.* Philadelphia: Temple University Press.
Finley, L. K. (Ed.). (1989). *Public sector privatization: Alternative approaches to service delivery.* New York: Quorum.
Gurin, A. (1980). *Contracting for service as a mechanism for delivery of human services* (Grant No. 18-P-00170). Washington, DC: Department of Health and Human Services, Office of Human Development Services.
Gutch, R. (1992). *Contracting lessons from the U.S.* London: National Council of Voluntary Organizations.
Kamerman, S. B. (1984). The new mixed economy of welfare: Public and private. *Social Work, 28*(1), 5-10.
Karger, H., & Stoesz, D. (1991). The corporatization of the United States welfare state. *Journal of Social Policy, 20*(2) 157-171.
Kettner, P. M., & Martin, L. L. (1988). Purchase of service contracting with for-profit organizations. *Administration in Social Work, 12*(4), 47-60.
Maturi, R. (1991). States: A mother lode ripe for mining. *Industry Week, 240*(12), 79-83.
Prager, J. (1992, October). *Contracting out: Theory and policy* (Economic Research Report No. 92-50). New York: New York University, C. V. Starr Center for Applied Economics.
Saidel, J. R. (1991). Resource interdependence: The relationships between state agencies and nonprofit organizations. *Public Administration Review, 51*(6), 543-551.

5

Building on a Strong Foundation

Seeking Foundation Grants
and Foundation Partners

A Rejection Spurred Us On

Frank Santier of the foundation told me, "If it strengthens families, we're interested. Send me a concept paper." We did better than that, we sent in a full proposal and asked for comments. We got comments, alright . . . along with our turn-down letter.

I was stunned. I called Mr. Santier and asked the reason. "There are two," he explained. "One is substantive, the other is a matter of form." He explained that we had emphasized the needs of the women for safety, and that often meant getting away from an abusive relationship. "The foundation," he told me, "is interested in promoting family stability and development; not family dissolution. The abusive partner is the villain in your proposal. We see everyone in the household as victims."

That really got me thinking. I decided to visit the foundation office and explore our interests with them some more. Santier and Rosabeth Mitchel of the foundation staff gave us a full hour and a half. In that discussion we explored all kinds of possibilities. Problem was, the project was getting too big for us to handle. "We'll have to see what part of all this we can carve out for ourselves," I said. I concluded the meeting and thanked them both for their time. We did submit a new proposal. And we did get partial funding. The rest was raised through a capital drive and through an expanded allocation from the United Way.

Oh, yes. The matter of form. Our original proposal had been 38 pages long. It was loaded with details on the facility and how we would manage it, on the documentation of the problem, and so on. The second proposal was only 8 pages long. It had very few details, but it did spell out how we were going to contribute to family stability. The reviewers were satisfied; they didn't want to be bothered by details.

As Rosabeth Mitchel told me before we resubmitted, "Foundation staff may be interested in lots of details, and if you get funding we'll want regular reports. But our board people are the ones who make funding decisions, and we can't expect them to read a proposal it it's more than five to eight pages in length. They want to deal with policy issues. Don't overwhelm them with more than they need.

A bit timidly, I asked why we hadn't been told that instead of being rejected the first time around. Mitchel responded, "Because you didn't send us a concept paper. You sent us a fully developed proposal. If you really wanted feedback you would have called for an appointment earlier, or given us a draft Frank or I could have scribbled comments on or used as a basis for a start-up discussion."

Why Just a Postcard?

I've always been interested in neighborhoods and in empowerment. A few years ago a federal grant for neighborhood involvement might have been a real possibility. Today, it's out of the cards, especially for the kinds of purposes I was interested in. So I figured our best bet was to look for foundation support.

I went through a bunch of books at the library and located 67 likely prospects. I sent them each a two-page letter briefly describing what we intended to do and asking whether or not the foundation might be interested. The letter, I might add, was textbook perfect. It even included a Xerox copy of a photograph of one of our neighborhoods as an eye-catcher.

I got 65 responses, most of them on printed postcards; all of them polite turndowns. No explanation, no nothin'! Why just a postcard?

FOUNDATIONS: THEIR AGENDAS AND THEIR OPERATIONS

The central message in both these vignettes is clear: Because foundations have agendas, they are not likely to provide funding to groups, individuals, or organizations whose requests do not complement the foundation's purposes. Sending in a complete proposal without getting clarification about a foundation's interest generally will not work.

In the first third of the chapter, the overall impact that American foundations have had on the human services and other charities is reviewed. Current spending trends—what they spend money on and how much—will be described prior to examining "trendsetting" projects. These include foundation-initiated programs that generate substantial additional resources from the public and private sectors in the pursuit of comprehensive social change.

The operations and interests of independent, family, company-sponsored, community, and operating foundations will be compared, contrasting those that define themselves as having general in contrast to specific purposes. I will describe the more important information resources from which you can learn more about specific foundations and how best to approach them. The chapter concludes with suggestions on how to target those foundations whose agendas most clearly complement your own.

What Foundations Are and How They Differ

The term *foundation* tends to be used somewhat loosely. Because it connotes a certain amount of prestige, its use has been adopted by for-profit fund-raising companies, nonprofit research groups, voluntary service agencies, and not a few outright rackets. The Foundation Center's definition aims at more precision. In all its guides and information sources, it defines a foundation as a nongovernmental, nonprofit organization with its own funds (usually from a single source, either an individual, family, or corporation) and a program managed by its own trustees and directors, which was established to maintain or aid educational, social, charitable, or other activities that serve the common welfare, primarily by making grants to other nonprofit organizations.

This is a functional definition and not a legal one. Because any organization can call itself a foundation, the federal government has added the word *private* to its legal definition.

According to the 1969 Tax Reform Act, a private foundation must have charitable, religious, educational, scientific, or cultural purposes as described in Section 501c(3). Excluded are certain categories of organizations such as churches, schools, hospitals, governmental units, or publicly supported charities and their affiliates that are commonly referred to as "public charities" rather than foundations.

In 1997, there are more than 34,000 active grant-making private foundations in the United States. These include foundations defined as

- independent;
- family;
- company sponsored;
- community;
- operating.

Eight of 10 identify themselves as independent or family foundations. These account for three of every four foundation dollars expended. Company-sponsored foundations make up 8% of the total but account for $17 of every $100 awarded. The approximately 600 community foundations make up approximately 2.3% of the total but account for approximately 6% of the dollars spent. Operating foundations account for 3.4% of the total; their funds, however, are expended almost exclusively on their own operations. As will be seen in the next section, these distinctions may be blurring in much the same way that public- and private-sector distinctions have become fuzzy. For example, many community foundations could not achieve their goals without massive coinvestments by banks and corporations. Some independent foundations, such as the Carnegie Endowment, have operating programs of their own.

How Much Money They Have

In 1996, grant-making private foundations had combined assets of $200 billion and awarded grants totaling more than $10 billion. Foundations come in all sizes. About 500 (just over 1.3%) are big, with assets of $50 million and more. Four hundred (1.1%) are medium to large, with assets from $25 to $50 million. Medium-sized foundations come in two sizes: (a) $10 to $25 million (3% of the total or approximately 1,000 foundations) and (b) $5 to $10 million (3.7% of the total or approximately 1,300 foundations). Approximately 3,000 (approximately 8.5%) others have assets of $1 to $5 billion. That leaves 28,000 foundations, more than four out of five, with assets under $1 million.

This is a great deal of money, but from a macro perspective their grant programs are dwarfed by the size of public expenditures. They can often do what public agencies cannot, however, and often play a role in bringing government and industry together to work on communal problem solving. Although foundation giving represents only one of every five charitable dollars spent in the United States each year, their grants often have great impact. Because most individual donors do not usually pool their resources or plan their expenditure strategically, the relative influence of foundations can be significant.

Each year, new foundations, some with considerable endowments, are created. For example, in the 1994 Foundation Directory, 600 new foundations were listed, each with assets of $1 million or more. Thirteen had assets of more than $25 million, 4 had more than $50 million, and 3 reported assets of more than $100,000,000! These assets often grow over time. Most foundations invest their principal and base their spending on their earnings. Thus, when the stock and real estate markets are down, many have to cut back on the number and sizes of their grants. When the economy is in recession or certain sectors are in economic difficulty, corporate foundations may find themselves unable to meet their charitable goals. Because the U.S. economy, overall, appears robust, however, foundations are likely to grow over time in both size and capacity to give.

What Grant-Making Foundations Fund

There are a number of ways to describe funding patterns, including by type, purpose, or populations.

In 1996, the two most common types of awards were for program (43%) and capital (27%) expenditures, with the next largest category being research. Education was the most common purpose for which grants were made that year, with health a not so close second and human services taking third place.

Education received one of every four foundation grant dollars in 1996. Higher and professional education netted the largest share (65¢ of every education dollar). Elementary and secondary education received just more than 20¢ of every dollar of the funds expended, up from 16¢ in 1990, reflecting an increased concern with the quality of schooling. Community education, job training, preschool, and professional continuing education make up the remaining 15¢. The shift in funding toward elementary education may be a reflection of a few very large grants. In the mid-1990s, the Annenberg Foundation made grants of more than $50 million each to public schools in Chicago and New York City. Two years earlier, an Ohio foundation with a portfolio worth more than $200 million was established primarily to assist the state with its educational programs.

Although health ranks second in terms of dollars spent (approximately $17 of every $100), it is only in fifth place in terms of the number of grants made. This suggests that health-related grants are much larger in size than those made for other types of programs. There seems to be a trend to "hold the line" on health costs, however, not only by government and industry but also by foundations. The human services get more grants (21% of the total) but their awards tend to be smaller (totaling 14% of all foundation grant funds in 1995). The arts also get about 14% of all grant dollars, followed by science, the environment, international affairs, social science, and religion. Interest in overseas giving tends to remain relatively steady at 5%. With the end of the Cold War, however, grants to Eastern Europe have increased in number and importance, resulting in some loss to other sections of the globe.

Nearly half of all family foundations include some reference to religious purposes in their mission statements. No more than 5% of their gifts are for sectarian purposes, however, and of these, many are for nonreligious purposes, such as supporting social services under the auspices of the Jewish or Lutheran communities. On the surface, their funding behaviors belie what many foundations may claim about their religious purposes. It is likely, however, that many foundation trustees perceive all of their charitable giving as fulfilling religious ideals.

Although many foundations may not appear to target their giving to special populations, others do. For example, 12.5% of the funds allocated in 1995 went to programs that served children and youth (cutting across other categories such as education, health, and social services). Programs that serve minorities took almost 10% of the available dollars, women and girls approximately 5.5%, the differently abled 4%, and the elderly just more than 2%. In practice, the percentages may be even higher. The reason has to do with the different ways in which foundations list their funding patterns. For example, grants to local Y's and settlement houses may be listed under "general support" (for agency programs) but actually cover youth- serving programs that make up the bulk of services given.

A number of foundations with a traditional interest in children and youth have relabeled some of their grant giving as in support of the "family." This reflects a new emphasis on promoting profamily public policies, supporting demonstration projects, and expanding the availability of traditional family service programs. Some of these programs may not be much different from those defined as serving children and youth in other years. For example, the Anne E. Casey Foundation focuses on teen pregnancy and school dropouts through its New Futures programs in nine mid-sized cities—thus in effect focusing on problems of single-parent families. Under what category should these grants be listed: Youth or Family?

Funding for minorities has increased by approximately 25% since 1990 largely because of grants to educational and other organizations that serve African Americans. In 1992, two grants of more than $5 million were made to the United Negro College Fund for capital support, matched by a $7.5 million grant from the Kresge Foundation and a $5.2 million grant from the Annenberg Foundation. Other Annenberg grants to schools were aimed at improving the quality of education for students from low-income neighborhoods, which are predominantly minority in composition. In general, funding for the poor and less affluent has risen significantly as public programs continue to cut back. Student aid also appears to have picked up as some government-sponsored programs have been reduced and tuition costs have increased.

Tip: Funding categories are arbitrary. If you want to know what a foundation is really interested in, you have to dig beneath the surface.

Women and Minorities

A survey of approximately 800 of the largest foundations indicated that women made up 72.5% of all foundation staff in 1992, which is up from 66% 10 years earlier. The glass ceiling appears to be shattering, with 43% of these foundations hiring women as chief executive officers (CEOs), up from 26% 10 years earlier. Minorities have also made dramatic gains but have a long way to go. For example, the numbers of minority CEOs increased from 3 to 46, but that still accounts for less than 6%. Overall minority employment in foundations comprises 20.4%, up from 14%, but these are mostly in lower-level positions. They include few Hispanics, Asians, and Pacific Islanders and almost no Native Americans. Similar trends can be seen in the makeup of trustees but at a slower pace. Three of 10 board members are women, up from 23%, and minorities have reached nearly 9%—double the proportion of a decade earlier. Zehr (1993) refers to these as evolutionary, not revolutionary, changes.

Five Trends

If you receive or are seeking financial assistance from foundations, four emerging trends could be important to your organization. These trends include

1. A move toward continuing support in addition to time-limited project grants
2. Using resources to leverage donations and investments from other sources

3. Joining in funding partnerships with other funders

4. Supporting long-term processes aimed at community and capacity development

5. Investing in population groups with special needs or interests

From Seed Money to Organizational Support

Although many foundations still prefer project funding that does not tie them to specific organizations or commit them to the same program indefinitely, support for continuing programs seems to be holding steady at 30% of grant dollars allocated. This may not seem like a gain, except when one considers the number of demands on foundations to support programs that have suffered a loss of public funding. Continuation funding may simply mean allocating dollars for the second of a 3-year grant or a 1-year extension. It also, however, appears to reflect a response to the criticism many foundations receive for funding the start-up of projects but not paying attention to the infrastructure supports needed to assure that worthwhile programs will persist over time.

Susan Berresford, a vice president of the Ford Foundation, signals a change in perspective in some foundations (Leonard, 1989):

> If a project is a success . . . you want that [grant-receiving] organiza-tion to be stable. If it's scrambling around for every nickel and dime, with little degree of flexibility, that [stability] is very difficult to achieve. Providing general support does not mean transferring an organization from carefully monitored projects into some kind of relaxed state of not attending to getting its work done; it's the reverse: [general support] allows them to be thoughtful and reflective, to initiate new things and to do so in a business-like manner. (p. 42)

This trend does not contradict the message of the two vignettes that opened the chapter. Foundations do have agendas. Those agendas, however, often reflect a commitment to program and service longev-ity in addition to innovation.

Grants as Leverage

A number of the larger foundations, such as Ford, Kresge, the Pew Charitable Trust, and others, use their grants to attract new dollars.

By turning theirs into challenge grants, they put pressure on recipients to find additional sources such as government grants and contracts and United Way allocations. It is not just pressure, however, it is also an opportunity. The promise of a significant matching grant can be a powerful inducement to other donors. They, too, want to leverage their dollars. In previous chapters, I described a similar approach among government funders who often require local matches as evidence of community support or as ways of reducing costs to themselves. Foundations, however, may be less interested in saving money than in getting a bigger bang for their bucks and in reducing the risk of funding less than successful projects and organizations.

In New York, several foundations, alarmed at the tendency of arts organizations to have deficits every year, have begun experimenting with a "tough love" approach to helping recipients become more self-sufficient. For example, the Ford Foundation established the National Arts Stabilization (NAS) program with backing from the New York City Department of Cultural Affairs and the Lila Wallace-*Reader's Digest* Fund. Four-year "stabilization" grants are intended to help organizations such as the Alvin Ailey dance troupe, the Pan Asian Repertoire, and El Museo del Barrio. To qualify for a grant, organization must develop long-range plans and reduce their debt. Some have reported their first deficit-free seasons within 2 or 3 years after entering the NAS program. Similar programs are under way in major cities throughout the United States, with those foundations, such as the Pew Charitable Trust in Philadelphia, shifting their funding priorities from helping arts organizations survive to enabling them to help themselves to take charge of their financial needs and expenditures.

Funding Partnerships

Foundations increasingly seek funding partners among other foundations, with government agencies, and in the private sector. Joint funding reduces the risk to each partner and increases the range of programs or projects for which they can each claim some credit. For example, in the late seventies, encouraged by President Nixon's emphasis on privatization, the Edna McConnel Clark Foundation collaborated with the Federal Office of Human Development Services in support of innovative adoptions services. From the government's point of view, this was a way to promote "cost sharing." From the foundation's perspective, it was a successful effort at increasing the government's interest in and capacity to serve children with special needs.

Community Development

Some foundations have engaged in a systematic process of community development by taking a more comprehensive approach to planning and allocation. Eschewing small projects with uncertain futures, they focus on a specific issue and then use their considerable access to other funders to concert the efforts of many organizations on a common agenda. For example, the Marin (community) Foundation used the promise of allocating $1 million to a school district in the San Francisco Bay area as leverage to secure $6 million in state and local dollars for the same district. This was then invested in creating a new curriculum aimed at helping school authorities cope with the diverse needs of an impoverished community.

As work on the curriculum gained momentum, the foundation induced Lucas Films and Apple Computers to create a Center for Learning for Families in the schools. Next on the agenda was creation of a Cities in Schools program to attract public, nonprofit, and for-profit services, transforming school buildings into community learning and development centers. The Marin County model has generated considerable interest in the foundation world.

Targeting Special Populations

Women's Funds. During the past 20 years, a number of specialized funds have developed to address the needs of disenfranchised populations. For example, the Ms. Foundation, founded in 1977, was soon followed by the Astraea Foundation and other women's funds. The National Network of Women's Funds, which now has more than 100 funds, was established in 1985 at a conference in Washington, D.C. Women's funds now compete with the United Way of America for payroll deduction contributions in all federal government workplaces and in many state and local government offices (see Chapter 7).

"Women's" foundations view themselves as significantly different in terms of philosophy, funding priorities, and managerial styles. They tend to be less averse to risk in the types of grants they make, often more willing to take a gamble on sweat equity of volunteers than professional credentials of the staffs in the programs they fund. They may finance a group that has not yet achieved nonprofit status or that needs some start-up funds to get its act together before applying for a project grant. Their boards tend to reflect a much wider diversity than that found in traditional foundations. In addition to donors, community influentials, and others with expert knowledge, trustees are likely to include representatives of recipient agencies and the clients they serve, both lesbians and straight women, and people from a variety of social, economic, and cultural backgrounds.

Their giving focus tends to be directed to organizations that serve or advocate for (a) women denied access to opportunity, employment, or other community resources; (b) victims of violence; (c) low-income women and children; and (d) women and girls who face discrimination on the basis of race or national origin, sexual orientation, disability, and so on. Some are likely to make grants of as little as $500 or work hard at locating funding from larger and better endowed foundations.

Minority-Oriented Foundations. Minority philanthropists also tend to focus on "their own," and this is reflected in the agendas of a number of minority foundations. Ruffin (1990) observes that highly successful black entertainers and athletes are more likely than their white counterparts to start foundations. In an article in *Black Enterprise,* Curry (1990) reports on a Ford Foundation assessment that African Americans, as a group, are far more charitable than any other segment of the population. For example, Bill and Camille Cosby donated $20 million to Spelman College, Oprah Winfrey gave $1 million to Morehouse College, Isaiah Thomas pledged $300,000 per year to Detroit public schools, and so on.

In 1990, the Council on Foundations reported that its Pluralism in Philanthropy Project had helped promote approximately 200 minority foundations in the United States. At the local level, it is not unusual for a community or private foundation to allocate funds to a minority-oriented foundation or to help it manage its portfolio as it begins to take its first steps. Many minority foundations, however, have forged ahead independently with considerable success. Despite some assistance from general-purpose foundations, however, the growth in number and size of black-oriented foundations has not yet caught up to the largess of individual donors.

In general, African American foundations tend to help African Americans, Hispanic foundations help Hispanics, and an emerging group of Native American foundations (some using casino proceeds) assist those American Indians affiliated with a tribe or nation. Because for most minorities education has been a ticket to advancement, this is also where many minority-oriented foundations target their giving. For example, the Jackie Robinson Foundation provides approximately $500,000 in scholarships to more than 100 students. Some foundations target black colleges such as the Tuskegee Institute and Compton College.

The Seventh Generation Foundation, largest of the Native American funds, supports tribal council development and promotes economic self-sufficiency and other community development approaches. Its funds are available to applicants from any of North America's tribal communities, many of them with their own distinct cultural and linguistic traditions. Like other minority-oriented funds, it depends heavily on grants from larger foundations, such as Charles Stewart Mott or Ford. The Navajo and Cherokee nations run their own United Way operations. Both were established in the 1980s and raise and distribute funds on their own reservations. Like other United Ways, they are also exploring new methods of raising dollars that will facilitate the funding of innovative programs. In Detroit, for example, the black United Way operates much more like a foundation than a federation of member agencies.

Unlike the Seventh Generation Foundation, but similar to the two Indian United Ways, most minority foundations are geographically based. The Oakland-based Asian Foundation for Community Development focuses its giving in support of new immigrants from Laos, Cambodia, the Philippines, and so on. Its grants have been used for English-language training, acculturation, and job retraining and placement. The East Los Angeles Community Union owns several profit-making ventures but uses the proceeds for scholarships, social service and mental health programs, community cultural events, low-income housing for Hispanic residents of the community, and so on. A few direct their funds to programs in their homelands.

In many respects, these foundations and quasi-federated funding organizations, diverse as they may be, are following in the footsteps of earlier generations of Americans. The Jews, for example, perhaps the most impoverished and discriminated-against of the immigrant groups that arrived at Ellis Island at the turn of the 20th century, eventually created communitywide federated fund-raising and allocations programs that paralleled those of the United Way. Eighty years later, the Korean community of Los Angeles examined how the Jewish community's fund-raising and allocating processes might be adapted to their own conditions and traditions.

TYPES OF FOUNDATIONS AND HOW THEY DIFFER

General- and Special-Purpose Foundations

Some foundations, such as those designed to serve women or minorities (or cancer research or promote the field of dance) have special purposes, whereas others are defined as general-purpose foundations. A general-purpose foundation is likely to provide aid to a larger variety of social, educational, cultural, religious, scientific, or other activities. Sometimes, the differences are obvious, and at other times they are not. Sometimes, focus changes over time.

When the Robert Wood Johnson Foundation opened its doors with the mission of promoting health, its grants were limited to medical research. Funding went to established institutions working in recognized arenas such as cancer research. Gradually, its scope of funding expanded to include medical services. Its program now includes four priority areas: improving service delivery and organization to those who suffer from chronic health conditions, finding ways to curtail or better distribute rising health care costs, reducing the harm caused by substance abuse, and assuring that all Americans have access to basic health care. It provides funding for community education, consumer involvement, and other social programs. Thus, the foundation both expanded its funding range and focused on specific types of programs within several practice arenas.

Many of Robert Wood Johnson Foundation's health-oriented grants might fall under a social service or community development rubric in another foundation. Sometimes, the way in which a foundation reports its giving affects how it is viewed by others. For example, until 1992 both the Starr and Ford Foundations were listed among the top 10 funders of health programs. In 1993, however, both chose to report the amounts allocated to health under other headings—service, education, and so on. In effect, the stated focus might change, but the programs may remain substantially the same, at least for a while.

Independent and Family Foundations

The boundaries between independent and family foundations are sometimes indistinguishable. Their purposes may be relatively similar and both may be operated by professional staff with well-established procedures and funding guidelines. Both are likely to fund programs and projects from their endowments and these are generally derived from what the Foundation Center describes as a "single source"—an individual, family, or group. Often, they originate in fortunes made in business or industry.

For example, the Mott Foundation endowment was built up from an original gift of General Motors stock by one of the corporation's founders. The Edna McConnel Clark Foundation's portfolio began with a large bequest of funds from the founder of Avon Products. The Robert Wood Johnson Foundation began with a bequest of $300 million of corporate stock from its founder, the former chairman of the Johnson and Johnson Corporation. The Koret Foundation of San Francisco began with a gift of approximately $200 million by a wealthy merchandiser. The Weinstein Foundation of Baltimore began with almost a $1 billion gift from a produce importer. The Packard Foundation, recently established with a gift of nearly $2 billion, may dwarf them all.

Initially, and sometimes well into the life of a fund, donors and their families or trustees remain the dominant forces in the foundation's decision making. Although those large and medium endowments are likely to be run by professional managers, the boards will be handpicked to assure close adherence to the donor's wishes—for example, they may be family members, estate trustees, former business associates, or close friends of the donor. These are termed family foundations, which remain closely tied in purpose and governance to the original donor and his or her representatives.

Independent foundations, as the name implies, operate with greater autonomy. Although they may continue to represent the donor's wishes, most have developed totally independent programs and priorities. For example, the Ford Foundation, perhaps the archetype of independent foundations, has a much broader set of agendas than the founder might ever have envisioned. To a large extent, this independence is a factor of how the foundation's initial mission and its governance structure were created. Because of the enormous wealth and prestige behind them, Ford and other megafoundations are often able to work in partnership with government agencies at home and abroad in the selection of agendas and targets for funding.

Family foundations make up by far the largest numbers of private foundations in the United States. They vary greatly in size and areas of interest. With some notable exceptions, their endowments are generally under $5 million, and many may be only in the $10,000 to $200,000 range. Few have professional staffs; some family foundations are administered by a trustee who is probably a private attorney, a local banker, or a trust corporation with many other responsibilities. Many have religious purposes. Some are connected with social agencies, the primary supporter of an endowment program for specific projects in those organizations.

For example, the Roper Charitable Trust of Columbia, South Carolina, which was established in 1991, awards 100% of its funding to religious organizations such as the Washington Methodist College of Columbia. This was the will of the donor, Margaret Roper, and it is being "religiously" followed by the trustee, Goenn Wicker, a trust officer at the local branch of NationsBank of South Carolina. Approximately half of the Koret Foundation's annual giving is reserved for Jewish communal institutions. A significant proportion is directed to higher-education institutions in Israel. Other funds go to Jewish Federation annual campaigns or are allocated as projects to specific grant applicants in the Bay Area.

Seven of every $10 allocated by independent and family foundations go to programs in their locales. A general rule is that the smaller and the newer (in that order) the foundation, the more local the giving. The smallest among them do not have the sophistication or personnel to consider giving patterns that are more broadly geographically disbursed. For the same reason, many newer and smaller foundations are likely to welcome efforts of established foundations and federated funding agencies—such as the United Ways, Catholic Charities, Jewish Federations—to enlist them in collaborative efforts.

Community Foundations— Catalysts and Linking Agents

The *Foundation Center Yearbook* documents an approximately 10% increase in the number of community foundations during each of the past few years. Community foundations are set up exclusively to serve a specific geographic area, usually a city, and sometimes its adjacent townships. Cleveland established the first community foundation in the years immediately preceding World War II. Initially established to ensure proper stewardship of trusts and bequests, community foundations now actively seek funds from individual and corporate donors who prefer to have their philanthropic responsibilities administered by professional foundation managers. They are increasingly involved in human service and community development activities. These include downtown reconstruction, the building of pocket parks, and the support of social services for which other funds may not be readily available.

The trustees of a community foundation are likely to include a mix of prominent citizens and others who represent diverse populations. As with independent foundations, however, staff are often gatekeepers and the primary decision makers. Although many trustees and staff may be savvy about local needs, they may also need to be educated. Your success as a fund-raiser will be much improved if foundation staff are knowledgeable about your agency's services and the needs of the populations you are concerned about.

Approximately one third of the foundations spend no more than 1% of all community foundation dollars (or less than $100,000 per year). Another third allocate between $100,000 and $1 million. No more than 50 community foundations make grants totaling between $1 million and $5 million. A few, however, allocate five to eight times as much. The 10 largest community foundations had assets of between $150 million and $900 million in 1990, and some optimists are predicting that these assets will triple by the turn of the century. Endowment size, however, may have less to do with their influence than the innovative patterns by which they fund-raise and make grants. The brief vignettes in the following section may help illustrate this point.

Responding to Donor Interests

One of the best ways to learn about community foundations is to interview people who work for them or have had other dealings with them (after you have read the foundation's annual report). I will share some of my interview notes with you.

Duffy's Tavern Saves Kids!

The Detroit area was one of the last major metropolitan areas to establish a community foundation. It was badly needed; otherwise why would many of the area's largest private foundations take the lead in establishing it and providing some of the seed money for our initial endowment? Other dollars came from wealthy philanthropists like Henry Ford III and Max Fisher who had worked together on other joint efforts. Everyone understood, from the beginning, that big dollars from big donors would help legitimize our fund-raising effort, but that in the long run, our success could only be guaranteed if we built up small gifts from donors of more modest means. The message had to be that everyone can be a philanthropist, and we were there to make it possible. I remember one of our first gifts.

Several young attorneys had been going to ball games together since high school. As they got older, their favorite pregame hangout became a tavern near Tiger Stadium. Let's call it Duffy's. Well, the classmates grew up, got married, and had kids. Duffy took almost grandfatherly pride in the children, who often came in to visit when attending a game with their dads. When Duffy passed away, one of the tavern group called to set up an endowment in Duffy's name.

The proceeds were to be invested in children. I asked two questions. First, did they want to spend the money over a 1-, 2-, or 3-year period, or did they want to set up an endowment from which only the proceeds would be spent? They wanted an endowment. Then I asked if they wanted to be involved in decision making about each grant, or would they prefer leaving the actual grant-making decision to staff. They preferred the latter. We then drew up papers of agreement that included guidelines for how the money should be allocated. Now we provide them an annual report on how their gift is being used. You might think that putting together hundreds of little gifts like this is more trouble than it's worth. Not at all. We see this process, almost as much as the grant making itself, as contributing to our goal of community building. The community is made up of many individual, family, and small group efforts. We try to bring the philanthropic impulse into a coherent framework. Some of our own donors would not have been able to set up programs on their own, and many would have shied away from creating their own foundations. In fact, what our various funds are, are minifoundations that they have made possible.

Community Priority Funds

Approximately 20% of the assets held by community foundations, such as the Duffy Children's Fund, are earmarked for specific purposes or populations. Recognizing that potential donors often want a say in how their gifts will be used, community foundations have begun to market field-of-interest or community-priority funds. Such instruments serve to focus the foundation's giving to areas it wishes to give priority attention—the arts, minority empowerment, children at risk, and so on. By giving designated areas higher visibility, it also increases the foundation's marketing effort and gives donors a sense that they are participating in a special mission.

Explains a foundation executive, "This moves us beyond being an instrument for estate planners. We can now engage the giver, during his or her lifetime, in planning with us." She notes that a few foundations have begun to experiment with the creation of advisory groups for community-priority funds, thus involving donors and others in decision making.

Working With Estate and Investment Planners

Some foundations have also created new kinds of partnerships with estate planners. In Kalamazoo, Michigan, a number of brokerage firms and investment houses had created tax-exempt portfolios for their clients to use in making charitable gifts. When clients began asking them for advice on where and to whom to give, they needed help. The Kalamazoo Community Foundation obliged. A partnership is emerging in which investment firms perform the tasks they are most suited to, whereas foundation staff members play the roles for which they are best prepared.

Community Partnerships

Community foundations do much more than fund-raise and make grant awards. They provide technical assistance to organizations that may or may not ever receive foundation grants, bring foundation and government funders together to address common concerns (and engage in common funding), and initiate and respond to community growth, development, and empowerment. These are public functions, which is the reason why community foundations are often thought of as more public than private. The following two examples provide a vision of the possible.

The Community Relief Fund

The California Community Foundation, which serves Los Angeles and Southern California, reported grants of almost $10 million in 1992. Some were small, such as $12,500 to the Community Partnership for setting up an "incubator" for emerging charitable organizations, or $24,200 to the House of Ruth (a shelter for abused women and their children) to employ a part-time fund-raiser.

The 1992 LA riots, however, required a more focused comprehensive effort. In partnership with the ARC Corporation, it created a Community Relief Fund. The fund's first task was to engage local private- and public-sector grant makers in the development of coordinated strategies for addressing problems that both stemmed from and contributed to the riots.

The foundation was clearly using its prestige and leverage to engage others in coordinated philanthropy and community development. It had to. When facing issues such as hunger, homelessness, unemployment, and urban blight, community foundations cannot come close to picking up the slack caused by cutbacks in federal, state, county, and city funding.

The Cleveland Foundation's newsletter, "Keeping the Trust," describes how its long history of involvement in neighborhood development resulted in targeting federal assistance to four neighborhoods and an empowerment zone designation that has already generated millions of dollars in private-sector investments. The following is a brief synopsis.

Cleveland's Empowerment Zone

For some time, the foundation had, together with the Rockefeller Foundation, helped support research at Case Western Reserve University's Center for Urban Poverty and Social Change. The findings from a 1989 center report on conditions in Cleveland area neighborhoods provided an information base for the work of the foundation's Commission on Poverty and its successor organization, the Cleveland Community Building Initiative (CCBI).

Five years later, when the federal government announced its empowerment zone strategy, Cleveland had already done the primary and secondary research necessary to build an effective proposal. Volumes of data on neighborhoods were available, and thousands of volunteers and dozens of agencies were already involved in neighborhood empowerment strategies that linked service providers to community groups. A "village" concept was already in place, serving as the model for federal empowerment zones. A neighborhood by neighborhood jobs initiative that prepares inner-city residents for employment close to home had been operating for some time, setting the stage for a broader industrial retention and expansion effort. The Cleveland Advanced Manufacturing Program (CAMP) had already demonstrated a 10-year track record of promoting industrial innovation and training workers for high skill/high paying jobs.

The foundation and others had for many years supported neighborhood-based community development corporations along with a facilitating and coordinating body, Neighborhood Progress, Inc (NPI). The mayor's office had taken the initiative to orchestrate the work of Cleveland's financial institutions and Fannie Mae to help support NPI's housing efforts. A $2 million grant by the foundation to a

Neighborhood Economy Initiative created a community development bank and real estate development program to which the private sector contributed. With its $20 million in assets, the bank helped stabilize and raise property values. Taking heed of these efforts, many of Cleveland's major corporations created the $50 million development process, making sure that all the key players were "in" before submitting the federal grant application. It was a winning proposal. "It's as if Cleveland had been putting together a competitive game plan for the past ten years," said Jay Tabot, the foundation's senior program officer for civic affairs and economic development.

The empowerment zone strategy links jobs, job training, business needs, and access to resources. It has three thrusts: economic, labor, and community development. Clearly, the building blocks were all in place. The city's director of community development, Chris Warren, has been appointed by the mayor to head the Empowerment Zone program. The $90 million in new funds, available over 10 years, he predicts, should leverage an additional $2 billion or $3 billion in investments. He stated, "All of the [earlier] consensus building gives us a chance to hit the ground running."

The best of the community foundations are learning to work this way. They have long-term strategies that involve, as partners, local residents, social service agencies, educational institutions, the private sector, and government. When opportunities for new funding become available, they are ready to hit the ground running.

Company-Sponsored Foundations

Company-sponsored foundations are also becoming significant players in community development and social service delivery. Examples include the Alcoa Foundation, the Sears Roebuck Foundation, the Exxon Education Fund, and the Aetna Foundation. Although legally independent, these foundations have close links with the corporations they represent. For example, their boards tend to consist almost exclusively of company officers and their endowments tend to be modest because the corporate sponsors often use their foundation as the vehicle through which to allocate pretax charitable dollars each year.

In general, grants are made for the support of institutions or agencies that benefit the company's employees, its stockholders, or others with whom it has business relationships. Some corporations have used foundations to enhance their public images through the sponsorship of cultural and other programs. Most grants are made in communities in which the corporation has its headquarters, a plant, or a retail branch. The Ford Foundation's Local Initiative Service Corporation (LISC) has encouraged businesses in cities throughout the United States to increase their giving by offering matching funds that deal with economic participation of minorities. In San Francisco, several executives have organized a "2% Club" to encourage corporations to contribute more to the local community (2% or more of their pretax earnings).

Some company foundations make their grants at the headquarters level. For example, the American National Bank and Trust Company of Chicago Foundation makes awards for community improvement and development, arts and culture, human service programs, education, and medicine in Cook County, Illinois. Other corporations such as Dayton-Hudson, which has retail outlets throughout the country, are likely to have much more decentralized giving patterns, both geographically and in terms of decision-making authority. Managers of affiliated Target Stores, wherever they are located, are given considerable discretion in how to distribute grant funds and to whom. Some managers have taken the initiative to coordinate giving programs with other merchandisers in the malls in which Target may be the anchor store.

Growing More Foundation Dollars

There are several ways in which foundations can grow, including through

- investments;
- generating new gifts;
- comingling or leveraging their funds;
- start-up funding for new foundations.

The judicious management of investment portfolios is probably the most common way in which foundations grow. The current payout requirement for foundations (the percentage of total assets that must be expended each year to maintain 501c(3) tax-exempt status) is 5% of the foundation's income-producing assets, and the excise tax on foundation earnings is a mere 2%. Securing new gifts is not limited to community foundations. Other—already well-endowed—foundations do as well. For example, in the first 10 years of Franklin Thomas' tenure as president of the Ford Foundation, the organization more than doubled its endowment from $2.3 billion to $5.7 billion. Foundations can leverage their grant dollars by comingling them with government and private-sector funds and by coordinating grants with sister foundations. A final strategy is to fund the start-up of new, more specialized foundations, each with their own fund-raising and grant-making programs. This is what Doll (1992) describes as an emerging "civic symbiosis" in which a variety of organizations become partners in philanthropy.

For example, the Nord Family Foundation served as an incubator for the birth of the Community Foundation of Greater Lorrain County (Ohio). Nord contributed by providing start-up funds and staff assistance, promoting the new foundation's visibility, and expanding its funding base. In turn, the new Lorrain Foundation helped extend the family foundation's outreach, cofunded projects, and supported its initiatives. These and other emerging patterns are the hot topic at many of the sessions of the annual meeting of the Council of Foundations at which philanthropists share insights, learn from each other, and collaborate on shared policy agendas. As James A. Joseph, president of the Council on Foundations, points out, "Philanthropy is more than grantmaking. It requires a recognition of the connectedness between sectors and the interdependencies of people, communities, and institutions in society."

FINDING AND ACCESSING THE RIGHT FOUNDATION

Where to Get Information on Foundations:
The Foundation Center and Other Sources

Whether you are just beginning to educate yourself about foundations or looking for a specific foundation with an agenda that complements yours, a good place to start is with the Foundation Center, its publications, and its network of library resources. The center was established in 1956 in New York, where many of the largest foundations were located. Through its publications, libraries, and consultative services, the center helps grant seekers access information on nearly 34,000 active foundations as well as many private-sector and government funding programs.

The center publishes reference books and disseminates information through a nationwide public information and education program in the interest of matching foundation interests with nonprofit organization needs. It will not direct you to particular foundations, nor will it arrange introductions, but it will provide you free access to information at its New York office or at any one of its three branches (Cleveland, San Francisco, or Washington, D.C.) and through its more than 200 Cooperating (library) Collections. Reference librarians at Cooperating Collections can guide you to the appropriate information source in books, articles, and periodicals. Some can also walk you through computerized search services using both government and Foundation Center databases.

To find the nearest Cooperating Collection, call (800) 424-9836.

In its 1995 *Foundation Directory*, the center describes its publications as "the primary working tools of every serious grantseeker." The center's publications are divided into (a) directories; (b) grants indexes; and (c) guides, monographs, and bibliographies. Both the directories and indexes can be indispensable and, in fact, often provide the base data used by other profit and nonprofit publishers and search services.

In addition, the *Foundation Center News*, a bimonthly journal of general philanthropy, includes articles of interest to both foundation officers and board members and to grant seekers who want to understand the directions in which foundations are moving. A significant portion of each issue includes brief abstracts of grants of $10,000 or more made by the approximately 1,000 largest foundations. This is the source of information compiled for the *Foundation Grants Index*. The Foundation Center's directories and the *Foundation Grants Index* are available on-line. Searches can be conducted by accessing DIALOGUE, a company that has dozens of databases, at least two of which used Foundation Center materials. If you do not have a computer with a modem at home or in your office, check with your closest Cooperating Collection librarian.

There are, of course, other sources. Most states have affiliates of the Council of Foundations, and these state organizations may publish their own directories that have even more current information on small and local foundations that may be of specific interest to your organizations. If you cannot locate your state council, write to the Foundation Center in New York or check for a phone number for your state League for the Human Services. The league is an advocacy organization that works closely with United Ways and other voluntary sector agencies and that sometimes publishes a state guide to foundation and other funding.

In many states, there are also public, voluntary and nonprofit, and for-profit organizations that publish their own guides and directories and that can provide both search and consultation services to you. You can get information on these from the league, your United Way, the state Council of Foundations, and the library. There are also national organizations that package information differently than the Foundation Center and provide their own analysis that may be of interest to your organizations. The Taft Group (835 Penobscot Building, 645 Griswald St., Detroit, MI 48226-9833; phone: (800) 877-TAFT) is one such firm that publishes several newsletters of interest, including

Foundation Giving Watch, a 20-page monthly newsletter, includes lead articles on trendsetting patterns. For example, in February 1995, the Watch reported on the giving patterns of the 10 largest foundation funders of health care programs, a description of selected new foundations and their interests, updates on established foundations, and a FunderSearch service (in which Taft searches its database in response to a subscriber request, sends reports to subscribers, and may print part of a report to in this column).

Planned Gifts Counselor, an 8-page monthly, includes tax news updates, items of interests affecting planned gifts (e.g., recent studies or examples of litigation), and suggests seminars and workshops to attend. FRI Monthly Portfolio is another 8-page monthly that includes hands-on reports and suggestions on improving fundraising efforts. For example, it has a regular fund-raising "Letter Clinic" and "Tip of the Month" column.

CHARLES STEWART MOTT FOUNDATION
1995-1996 FUNDING PRIORITIES[1]

Mott Foundation grant making is organized into the following four programs:

Civil society

Environment

Flint (its home community)

Poverty

plus an Experimental and Special Projects Program.

Each reflects the foundation's commitments to individual and community capacity building, empowerment, human rights, diversity, and leadership and social responsibility. Approximately 20% of its grants are international.

Mott is particularly interested in fresh approaches to community problem solving and systems change that, if successful, can influence the policy level, generate long-term support from other sources, be replicated elsewhere, or all three.

Although Mott has no formal application form, it does encourage letters of inquiry that include a brief description of the project and the approximate funding needed. Formal proposals, if they are invited, should include the following:

1. A cover letter detailing the amount of funding requested and the time period, signed by the person ultimately responsible for grant contracts on behalf of the applicant organization
2. A project description that explains why it is needed, who it will serve, and what it is to accomplish
3. Information on the feasibility and sustainability of the proposed grant activity
4. Anticipated lasting benefits to the organization, program participants, and other relevant parties
5. An evaluation plan
6. A documented line-item budget
7. Relevant information about the organization seeking funding, including its staff capacity, board, legal classification, history, and accomplishments.

SELECTED PUBLICATIONS
OF THE FOUNDATION CENTER

Prices and details are available from the Foundation Center, 79 Fifth Avenue, New York, NY 10003-3076; phone: (800) 424-9836

Directories

Guide to U.S. Foundations, Their Trustees, Officers, and Donors

Two-volume set that describes more than 34,000 national and local foundations, with information on where you can find more information. Updated periodically.

Foundation Directory

Annual editions have three parts: the *Directory* (Part I) describes approximately 7,500 foundations with assets of more than $2 million or whose annual grants total $200,000 or more. Foundations are listed alphabetically by state. Entries include information on foundation priorities, application procedures, financial data, grant amounts, addresses, and contact people. Part II provides similar data on foundations whose grants total $50,000 to $200,000. The *Foundation Directory Supplement* is published 6 months after the directories are published, providing late-breaking information, address changes, and so on.

The Foundation 1000

As the title implies, this annual provides comprehensive reports on the 1,000 largest foundations in the country, including multipage foundation portraits, detailed breakdown of grants programs, and examples of recently awarded grants.

National Directory of Corporate Giving

Features detailed portraits of 2,300 corporate foundation and direct giving programs.

Corporate Foundation Profiles

More comprehensive information on more than 200 of the largest corporate foundations.

Specific subject directories indicate foundation and corporate sources of funding for such areas of interest as

AIDS
Aging
Arts and culture
Children, youth, and families
The economically disadvantaged
Elementary and secondary
  education
Environment and animal welfare

Health
Higher education
International and foreign
  programs
Libraries and information
  services
Religion
Women

Grants Guides and Directories

Grant Guides

Each guide (there were 30 of them, published annually in 1995) describe all grants of $10,000 or more made during the previous year. Indexes further help the grant seeker narrow the search on the basis of the funder's interests, geographic areas served, and types of organizations funded.

The Foundation Grants Index

Coves grant-making programs of 1,000 of the largest independent, company-sponsored, and community foundations, describing over 60,000 grants made in the previous year. *The Foundation Grants Index Quarterly* contains timely updates.

Who Gets Grants/Who Gives Grants

Information on who gets grants can help a grant seeker locate organizations that might provide insights into how a funder works and on what foundations are likely to be interested in an organization like the grant seeker's.

Foundation Grants to Individuals

As the name implies, information is provided on study grants, travel grants, and other supports to individuals rather than organizations.

Books and Guides

Foundation Fundamentals (Judith B. Margolin, Ed.)

The Foundation Center's User Friendly Guide

How to Locate the Right
Foundation and Approach It

Rick Herman, one of the contributors to Margolin's (1991) *Foundation Fundamentals*, suggests the following three-step search approach:

1. Develop a broad list of prospective foundations (I suggest no more than 30).
2. Refine the list by eliminating those foundations unlikely to fund your project because your subject field or geographic areas does not fit or because it had no history of funding your type of organization.
3. Investigate the remaining foundations, identify their special characteristics, and create short list of three to five in order of likelihood that they will be interested and able to help.

That is a fairly common listing and it is probably pretty good advice. I think, however, that it is overly mechanical. In Chapter 2, I described a social marketing perspective that addresses the interests and capacities of potential donors or funders. Unlike many of the books on grant seeking that talk about winning proposals, however, I prefer to think of winning relationships. You do not have to know someone at the foundation before you start a relationship. You will be much more successful, however, if you and your organization are known by someone that the foundation also knows and trusts. The point is that you have to know something about the foundations you are interested in, but you have to be known by them as well.

Some Tips for Initial
Communication With Foundations

Because many foundations have no paid staff, they may find it difficult to respond to unfocused questions. Even larger, well-staffed foundations may be so inundated with requests that they will respond only to certain types of inquiries.

TIPS FOR COMMUNICATING WITH FOUNDATIONS

Tip 1: Avoid approaching a foundation cold. Whether using the telephone or sending a letter of inquiry, demonstrate that you already know something about the foundation or someone connected to it (e.g., "Ron Edwards suggested I call because the foundation's concerns about the frail elderly complements ours"). In a phone contact, be ready with your questions and answers to questions a foundation official may ask you. Keep letters brief and avoid sending in completed proposals until you have cleared it with the appropriate person.

Tip 2: Most foundations do not publish annual reports, and the smaller foundations are not likely to have their grants described in readily accessible materials. All foundations, however, must file tax returns, and those returns list the grants they have made in the previous year and the size of each award. The Internal Revenue Service will send you those returns, but it may take time. If the foundation is in your state, chances are the Collaborating Collection will have a microfiche card for each foundation's federal tax return in your state. If you need a microfiche card from another state, your librarian can order one at no charge from the Foundation Center.

Tip 3: If at all possible, avoid going in without a referral. Smaller foundations, especially, like to deal with people or organizations they know or who have been introduced by someone they do.

There are many more detailed suggestions in Chapter 15.

REVIEW

Foundations come in all sizes: large, medium, and small. Although the boundaries between private foundations (independent, family, and company sponsored), community foundations, and operating foundations tend to blur in practice, they all have agendas that govern their grant-giving programs. Foundation agendas shape the extent to which they will be interested in funding certain types of programs, populations, and grant seekers. There are many sources of helpful information on what foundations are interested in and how they operate. Some are available through the Foundation Center and its affiliated libraries. These are helpful in the start-up process. In the long term, however, there is no substitute for building effective working relationships with foundations and with the others likely to advocate on your behalf.

NOTE

1. Adapted from the Mott Foundation "Philosophy, Programs & Principles" pamphlet published in Flint, Michigan, in November 1995.

REFERENCES

Curry, G. (1990, July). Building a better foundation. *Black Enterprise*, 55-58.
Doll, H. (1992, March/April). Civic symbiosis. *Foundation News*, 33(2), 41-43.
Leonard, J. (1989, September/October). Best supporting role. *Foundation News*, 30(5), 42-46.
Margolin, J. (Ed.). (1991). *Foundation fundamentals: A guide for grantseekers*. New York: Foundation Center.
Ruffin, D. (1990, May/June). Minority foundations: Not for survival alone. *Foundation News*, 31(3), 52-57.
Zehr, M. A. (1993, January/February). Evolution, not revolution. *Foundation News*, 34(1), 46-47.

SUGGESTIONS FOR FURTHER READING

Due, T. (1992, March/April). Tides of change: Miami foundations are helping the city become a laboratory for cross-cultural exchanges. *Foundation News*, 33(2), 18-23.
Joseph, J. A. (1989, April). Building a new era for organized philanthropy. *Fund Raising Management*, 42-48.
Hull, R. (1990, August). Community foundations, vehicles for giving. *Trusts and Estates*, 129(8), 14-18.
Leonard, J. (1992, January/February). Flowering fields of interest. *Foundation News*, 33(1), 48-51.
Massinga, R. W., & Carcal, J. (1991, May). Foundations and family-based services: Support, innovation, and leadership. *Journal of Contemporary Human Services*, 301-309.
Seltzer, M., & Cunningham, M. (1991, July/August). General support vs. project support: A 77-year-old debate. *Nonprofit World*, 9(4), 16-21.
Williams, R. (1992, July/August). From embers: Community-based organizations emerge as logical leaders in addressing post riot urban issues. *Foundation News*, 33(4), 14-15.

6

The Business of
Business Is Business

*Working on Common Concerns
With the Private Sector*

From Redlining to Redevelopment

They accused us of redlining. It wasn't true. It is true that some banks
were refusing to provide mortgage or improvement loans to people in
high-risk neighborhoods. But, we're an insurance company; not a
bank, and we did not make mortgage loans to anyone. And we were
selling insurance in every neighborhood, regardless of the risk. High-
risk policies cost more; but that's business. We've always had a commitment to the communities in which we have national or regional
headquarters. So we were willing to take the risks, even lose money
on some of the policies we sold.

Still, as the neighborhoods close to the inner city were deteriorating,
costs were getting higher. Boarded up storefronts were a common
sight. Thefts increased as some of the more stable residents moved
away and as some of the major institutions, the churches and banks
pulled out. A major fire or two seemed to break out every week. We

suspected arson in some business establishments and in some deteriorated apartment buildings. And as everyone knows, health problems are most severe in poverty areas. There is no question that neighborhood deterioration was costing us money.

Self-interest, for this corporation, is indistinguishable from its concerns for the community in which it does business. Read on.

Although we did have to close some of our offices or pull out some of our agents, we never refused a bona fide request for insurance. We weren't redlining, even if that's how CORP saw it. CORP is a network of neighborhood associations that calls itself the Community Organization and Rehabilitation People. They lumped us together with the banks, picketed our offices, issued damaging press releases. Frankly, it wasn't good for our public image.

And it didn't fit our view of ourselves as a community-spirited company. A number of the executive staff were pretty defensive, wanted to counterattack in the press. Interestingly, the board wasn't defensive at all. We had a number of church, business, and labor people on the board who felt strongly about the attacks on the company. They felt even more strongly about profits. And they believed just as strongly in our social commitments as a company and as an industry. The problem was that profits, image, and commitments seemed to be out of sync. "As you know, the archdiocese provides some support for CORP," one of our board members pointed out. "We know they (CORP leaders) tend to be seen as extremists, but we've always found them to have done their homework. If they are targeting this company, we should examine the charges seriously."

What characterizes corporate philanthropy in many settings is the range and extensiveness of new partnerships with community agencies and associations.

The board chairman agreed. He established a task force to recommend a course of action. One of its recommendations was to sit with representatives of CORP. I participated in the first meeting. I was empowered to offer CORP a grant for training local residents in community development techniques and for increasing CORP staff. At first they thought we were trying to buy them off.

"Look," I explained, "we are not about to abandon the city. Unstable neighborhoods cost us money, and we are fully aware that they create tragedies for the people in them. If you can help stabilize the neighborhoods, we all stand to gain." They agreed to think on it and we set up a series of planning meetings. At the second session, CORP came in with a number of demands. Money for organizers wasn't enough, they argued. They wanted us to invest in building rehabilitation projects: fixing up homes and redeveloping shopping centers. "Why not use your investment portfolios to reduce your insurance risks?" they asked. They offered to take us on tours of several neighborhoods to show us what was needed and to meet some of the people we would be investing in. We went.

After several more meetings, we agreed to put up $4 million for short-term rehabilitation and new construction loans if CORP, with our help, could induce banks to put up the money for long-term loans and if CORP could establish local neighborhood nonprofit corporations to manage each project. It took about six months to put the deal together. CORP insisted we also reopen neighborhood-based insurance offices. We did.

We're now three years into the experiment. None of our loans have defaulted. Once the banks were threatened with law suits for redlining and saw that we were willing to put our money on the line, several agreed to enter into cooperative agreements on long-term financing. From our perspective, the experiment has increased our profits and reestablished our image as a forward-looking, community-oriented company. It's good business.

Income from the sale of policies has grown; and payments on claims has decreased considerably. Most important, three of the seven neighborhoods we have stabilized, and three of the others seem to be turning around. We may be too late on the seventh, but we've got some new ideas there, too.

When this story first appeared in the 1984 edition of this book, it represented a radical departure from the traditional business philanthropy. Not so today.

CORPORATE GIVING: PHILANTHROPY
AS BUSINESS STRATEGY

Giving Is Not Better Than Getting, It Begets Getting!

Corporate philanthropy is often described as the exercise of social responsibility that is good for business. Philanthropy is more than good citizenship. By investing in their communities, business concerns have increased the size of their markets and the productivity of their employees. In the corporate world, giving is not just good for business: It is good business.

In this chapter, I describe a wide variety of business-sponsored philanthropic efforts. The beginning of the chapter examines a non-cash approach—one aimed at reducing costs and improving productivity by tapping corporate know-how. Then, a number of nonservice solutions to social problems (i.e., interventions that do not require expanding an agency's service programs) and more complex examples of collaborations between organizations in the public, private, and voluntary sectors are reviewed. The chapter also examines what can happen when local entrepreneurs invest as much energy in doing good as doing well. The second half of the chapter addresses the more traditional means—grants and gifts—through which many companies dispense their philanthropy. Finally, I suggest where you can learn more about specific corporate givers and how to build relationships with them.

Reducing the Need for Grant Funds
by Streamlining and Improving Services

Sandra Schnall begins her remarkable story of San Antonio's public-private partnership between the Texas Department of Human Services and 16 corporations, including IBM, Southwestern Bell, Datapoint Corporation, Levi Strauss, the Humana Women's Hospital, several banks, and a motel chain, by stating,

"[We found that] managers were looking for different ways to deal with the imbalance between needs and services. If we could streamline the business aspects of the Department—[in] areas such as telecommunications, building site planning, purchasing, and automation —we [would be able to] allocate more resources to client services. By giving corporate leaders a firsthand look at the day to day workings of a human service agency . . . we hoped to gain persuasive advocates for human service needs.

"While we were clearly seeking the help of the corporate sector . . . we have been able to help them," Schnall continues. "One executive who was concerned about his frail elderly mother did not know assistance might be available to her. . . . Corporate executives received valuable information for use in their companies and in . . . their own lives. Business leaders also came to realize that . . . clients who become self-sufficient would be potential consumers of the private sector's goods and services."

One result was that the department now had a group of high-powered advocates who interacted regularly with other business leaders and politicians. Clients, some of whom had never expected to meet an executive of IBM or Levi Strauss, were not only helped directly but experienced the uplift of being appreciated by persons they considered "important." Texas is not alone in promoting public-private collaboration aimed at improving management in state government. Nor was it the first state to do so. Ten years earlier, in 1983, New York State's Office of Management and Productivity was created by executive order of the governor. Its innovations included the Loaned Executive Program, government agency productivity awards (financed by the business community), and other efforts aimed at cost savings and improved services.

Reducing the Need for Grant Funds
by Shifting to Nonservice Strategies

Involving corporation execs as volunteers and advocates is one approach to reducing the need for funding. Another is to reduce the need for the services by involving business in "nonservice" activities. The following are some examples:

In Arlington, Virginia, a developer who sets aside a certain percentage of flats for low- and moderate-income families in a middle-income project receives special easement of zoning ordinances governing the height or density of apartment buildings within the development.

In Baltimore, Maryland, a citizen's movement sparked by the Roman Catholic archdiocese induced the Gas and Electric Company (G&E) to raise $200,000 from the private sector to be distributed to the city's poor who are unable to pay their utility bills. It saved the G&E money by eliminating the need to shut off utilities to those who could not pay their fuel bills. People would have suffered, and the unpaid bills would probably have totaled more than the money raised and distributed.

Shared housing arrangements, mediated by a family service agency, resulted in private and public grants for the rehabilitation of several privately owned buildings in a Northwest community. The landlords benefited by having needed repairs made to their buildings and by full occupancy, even though they charged reduced rents.

In St. Louis, Missouri, a group of business leaders raised several million dollars, which were then matched by the Ford Foundation, for the sponsorship of minority business enterprises. These businesses received technical assistance from both the private sector and from voluntary and public agencies. The sponsors benefited from a decrease in crime and unemployment that could have led to property tax increases.

These are examples of nonservice strategies, a term intended to imply that a social agency is not required to dispense a service to assist a client population. Thus, in Arlington, the county does not have to build or subsidize as much public housing as might otherwise be needed. In Baltimore, the public welfare department does not have to provide heating subsidies to those who cannot afford to pay their utility bills.

Responsibility Reaps Rewards

Jacqueline Davidson, associate editor of *Small Business Reports*, interviewed several entrepreneurs—owners of small businesses who were able to optimize on both profits and personal commitments to public service. She reports that Gary Hirshberg, cofounder of Stoneyfield Farm, wanted to launch a business he could feel good about. Yogurt Works was his way of helping area residents "stay on the farm" by buying their milk and turning it into moochandise that included milk products, mugs, T-shirts, cookbooks, and other items.

Vacationers are invited to visit the Londonderry, New Hampshire, plant. Half of the $1 per adult fee for tours goes to farmers or farm organizations. Employees report that they love having visitors and take pride in showing outsiders how they work. Work has become as much a community-building process as an income-producing activity. A biannual "Moos From the Farm" serves a dual purpose: promotion of the company's products and education about health, nutrition, and life on the farm. More than 1,000 customers participate in an Adopt-a-Cow program, which helps local farmers cover their costs. Adopting families receive frameable pictures of their very own cows!

In Corona, California, Nature's Recipe manufactures and sells premium-quality pet foods, packaged without use of carcinogenic chemical preservatives. That may not seem like much to non-pet owners, but it means a great deal to those who care for both their animals and the environment. Jeff Bennet, the company's founder, was even more interested in keeping kids from ingesting harmful substances, so he invested company profits in a Say No to Drugs campaign.

One tactic was to print up baseball-like trading cards with pictures of police officers on the front and anti-drug information on the back. When the firm's marketing manager expressed interest in Corona's annual Special Olympics event, Bennet encouraged his involvement and gave him time off to work on it. Soon, other employees began initiating their own good citizen projects. Becoming known as a company that puts something back into the community may not have affected sales directly, but it gave Nature's Recipe employees a sense of pride. Notes Bennet, "And that translates into higher productivity."

When Paul Saginaw and Ari Rosensweig established Zingerman's Deli, they wanted it to be the best restaurant possible. They also hoped to help revitalize a downtown business area called Kerrytown, which houses a farmer's market and dozens of one-of-a-kind restaurants and shops. By anyone's measure, they have succeeded. You will find Zingerman's listed among the finest eating places in the United States. Ask anyone who lives in Ann Arbor and you are likely to hear as much pride expressed in Zingerman's as in the University of Michigan's football or basketball teams. Even with a loyal customer base, however, some food goes to waste at the end of every day. Therefore, after one of their employees suggested packaging the surplus food for the homeless and the hungry, Foodgatherers was launched.

Zingerman's employees and other local volunteers pick up and package surplus foods from all the participating restaurants in town. They share responsibility for delivering meals to those in need, using one of the deli's office computers to keep track of requests, supplies, and deliveries. Chuck Kiefer, director of SOS, an antipoverty agency in nearby Ypsilanti, reports, "It beats having to depend exclusively on an annual can drive and recruiting our own volunteers. . . . And why shouldn't everyone have access to high-quality meals?"

Kevin McDermott (1991), in an issue of the *Dunn and Bradstreet Reports*, concluded that small-business owners "have strong motivations for civic involvement and that's a good thing for communities" (p. 18). Sometimes they need a little assistance. He describes how Gifts-in-Kind, an Arlington, Virginia, nonprofit helps for-profit businesses clear out their old inventories, thus taking a tax deduction by contributing surplus to social agencies in need of usable equipment and supplies.

Bigger national and multinational corporations also donate to charity, but some have a tendency to pull back when their gifts prove controversial. For example, a number of corporations cut back on their support of family planning clinics when faced with criticisms from abortion foes. They are less likely to be dissuaded from dealing with some of their own internal issues. Corporate efforts to promote and to celebrate multiculturalism are a case in point. Recognizing that by 2050 the average American will be African, Asian, Hispanic, or Native American, many large corporations have initiated ways of overcoming ethnic barriers within the workplace. Among them are Levi Strauss, Monsanto, Tandem, Sara Lee, Apple, and Wells Fargo. These companies have gone beyond in-plant celebrations of national and ethnic holidays.

One company representative stated,

> In our first efforts to celebrate the difference among our employees, we highlighting foods and customs in company cafeterias. Then we began mentoring new employees with varying ethnic backgrounds.

Both of these programs had been intended to make employees feel welcome and valued in the workplace. But people aren't just multicultural at work. It took a while, but we now encourage our employees to be themselves and share who they are with others at the plant and in the community.

Newer community-oriented approaches include giving employees time off to work on company-sponsored projects in ethnic neighborhoods and elsewhere. For example, Levi Strauss's Project Change creates community task forces to address cross-cultural understanding and to decrease local interracial tension in communities in which they are headquartered or have major plants.

Employees and other community residents participate on these task forces. The good work they perform, and often the setbacks, becomes the subject of conversation at the plant. The results are not always positive or comfortable, but they appear to be essential. Ann Kyle-Brown (1992), a San Francisco consultant on multicultural affairs, suggests that "One of the biggest challenges of achieving true multiculturalism is developing a clear, compelling vision of how Americans can live and work together" (p. 37).

CORPORATE RESPONSIBILITY:
PUBLIC GAINS AND PRIVATE GOODS

In my experience, human service personnel are often unaware of company efforts to do good in their communities. Evidence of the exercise of public responsibility by private firms, however, is all around us. Myopic vision can result in missing some important opportunities for collaborating with the private sector. To illustrate, some additional examples of corporate involvement in the community are described. In looking them over, you may wish to consider how one or more of these efforts might fit your agency's agenda.

Running and Race

Running shoe manufacturer Reebok awarded a $750 grant to Northeastern University's Center for Sport in Society to carry out Project Teamwork, which sends specially trained athletes into Boston's high schools and junior highs where racial tensions abound. Lotus Development funded an interactive art exhibit that deals with multiculturalism at the Boston Children's Museum and funded a mediation team when racial tensions flared up in a Boston high school.

Helping Schools

Schools receive considerable support from U.S. corporations. IBM and Exxon each have contributed more than $20 million to school improvement and reform. Many corporation executives have come to the conclusion that to make a difference in their lives, children must be reached early. Typical programs include funding child care and development centers, curriculum materials development, and other enrichment programs. Some facilitate employee volunteering in the schools. Others have created family libraries for use at home.

Chocolate Kisses

The Milton Hershey School Trust owns 42.2% of the Hershey Food Corporation's common stock and 100% of HERCO, the entertainment and resort company that operates Hersheypark. Income from the trust finances the Milton Hershey School, which serves more than 1,100 pupils from troubled backgrounds. Students attend on full scholarships. The trust provides college scholarships to its graduates.

Utilities and Learning

Illinois Bell's Project Homeroom linked 500 children and their families in Chicago schools, via computer, to national news services, encyclopedias, scientific data, and financial data. Arizona Public set up a Kids Voting program in which school children cast ballots for candidates and issues (but only if their parents were registered voters).

Aid for AIDS

Some corporations are not ready to engage in communitywide efforts until they have addressed issues internally. Multicultural programs are good examples as are AIDS education programs. It is not unusual for HIV-AIDS educational and prevention programs to begin with management education and then to extend to other employees. Like multiculuralism, however, the issue is rarely confined to the workplace. Companies often find that community involvement is essential for the provision of needed support to their employees. Collaborations with health and human service agencies that begin with an employee education focus often result in creating or expanding communitywide resources available to all.

Let's Go Krogering

When Kroger, a major midwestern supermarket chain, converted its check-out system to register tape, it gave away 8,000 no-longer-needed computers to area nonprofits. Charities regularly sponsor Kroger shopping days in which 5% of all sales go to the designated organization. Kroger employees have adopted almost 200 elementary schools, nationwide, where they work one-on-one with students.

From Super Bowl to Salad Bowl

In Atlanta, hotels, restaurants, and caterers donate to the poor and homeless through local food banks. This required some local legislative changes to deal with potential problems of liability, but with municipal and agency support and industry involvement it was not too difficult to change a local ordinance.

At the 1990 meeting of the Professional Convention Manager's Association (PCMA), a resolution was passed to encourage PCMA members to work with convention centers, hotels, and tour operators on similar programs. First success? The National Football League contributed that year's Super Bowl Party Leftovers to a food bank. Major manufacturers also contribute to food banks. Kraft donates $10 million in foodstuffs annually and its company foundation targets approximately $15 million annually to eradicate child hunger.

Creative Idea Banks

Food banks must be replenished daily. Creative idea banks create their own nourishment. In South Carolina, the Palmetto Project—sponsored by 20 blue-chip companies—collects creative ideas and programs that have succeeded in other states and matches these with concerned businesses and community leaders. Consultation is then given on how to work together with relevant service agencies.

Banking and Investing

Taking advantage of the Clinton administration's promotion of the Fannie Mae Neighbors Program, Avondate Federal Savings created a First-Time Homebuyer Program that provides money market–rate financing with only a 5% down payment. Similar efforts by other banks led to the creation of Neighborhood Housing Services of America, which aims to help at least 10,000 low-income families to buy homes with the help of local banks.

In downriver Michigan communities, employees of the Ford plant volunteer to reconstruct and refurbish homes of the indigent elderly every year. They screen applicants for need, organize volunteers, secure donated goods from local hardware stores and lumber companies, and arrange low-cost bank loans when necessary.

Share Our Strength

Since 1984, when Bill Shore created the antihunger organization, the SOS budget has grown from $30,000 a year to more than $16 million. His founding premise was that a charity should be run like a business, which not only "distributes the wealth" but also creates new wealth. For example, in an unusual arrangement between a charity and a for-profit corporation, SOS negotiated an agreement with American Express (AMEX) in which AMEX pays SOS 3% of the bill for all restaurant charges made during the last 2 months of the year. AMEX benefits by being identified with SOS's Charge Against Hunger campaign. Many restaurants that had refused to accept American Express cards because the charges are a bit higher than VISA or MasterCard now welcome the card. Some have even agreed to match AMEX's contribution. In turn, they have received their own SOS endorsement. In 1997, SOS expects to earn more than $7 million from this source.

Professional Associations Helping the Homeless

Banks are not the only ones helping Americans find homes. Members of professional societies and trade associations are also realizing that they can make a difference. Local affiliates of the American Bar Association have created volunteer and pro bono legal services for the homeless in places such as Kansas City, Missouri, Boston, and Washington, D.C. They also do more mundane things, however, such as letting the homeless use office phones to call prospective employers or taking phone messages for the homeless.

A county-sponsored Apartment Association in Texas provides 10 days of free temporary housing to families who lose their homes through natural disasters or fires and who have no place to go. The Red Cross helps locate and place families in need.

Working with volunteer architects, students, local housing officials, and teachers, local chapters of the American Institute of Architects have refurbished the dilapidated and boarded-up McAdoo Hotel in Shreveport, Louisiana, which now houses 45 homeless people; rebuilt an abandoned nursing home in Phoenix that now houses 31 homeless single women; and renovated homes in Minneapolis, Jackson, Mississippi, Brooklyn, and elsewhere. The National Association of Home Builders created the Home Builders Institute to engage in similar efforts and to secure necessary financing.

Corporate community service programs, such as those described previously, engage employees as volunteers and mentors in the schools and in informal education agencies (e.g., Boy Scouts, Big Brothers and Sisters). Some companies, such as Burger King, have created corporate academies through which workers and others in the community can gain management experience. Others, such as local hotel chain affiliates, provide internships for students in high schools and community colleges. Both students and teachers are recognized by "feel-good" incentives (recognition awards) and by scholarships for continuing their education.

Partners in Development

Collaborations between the private and the public sectors are increasingly common at the local level. Often, one success generates another. Residents of Putnam County, Missouri, became alarmed when the decline of the coal industry resulted in loss of population that threatened both the business and agricultural sectors. Business leaders, together with local government officials, school administrators, and others, created the Putnam County Foundation, to which businesses contributed funds. Once they saw what collaboration through joint funding could achieve, businesses and social agencies ventured into other bilateral and multilateral collaborations.

The Downside of Turning to the Private Sector to Solve Social Problems

There are, of course, downsides as well. The growth of "business improvement districts" across the country—nearly 1,000 of them have been created since the mid-1980s—is a case in point. Property owners in an area form a district by incorporating as a nonprofit, quasi-public institution and electing a board to govern it. As might be expected, the board is likely to be representative of the largest property owners. The district is empowered to "tax" local property owners (including themselves) to improve services in the area. Services might include creating shelters for the homeless, refurbishing dilapidated housing, fixing roads and streets, improving cleanup services, and contracting for additional policing. These become private solutions to public problems. For example, in New York's Upper East Side, the district, fed up with street crime, attempted to create a 500-person security force.

This sounds like a good idea, one might conclude. These programs appear to resolve problems and to cut the drain on public funds by financing their own services. In many cases, they even provide new sources of funding to nonprofits already well positioned to perform services needed by the district. So what is the catch? There are several. First, someone has to pay for these services. Because the boards of such districts tend to be composed of the largest property owners, others—owners of small apartments and private homes—often feel underrepresented. Moreover, what appears to be private funding by owners is often private funding by tenants who pay for the self-imposed tax through higher rents. By handling local problems on their own rather than seeking broader public solutions, richer neighborhoods and communities get better while less affluent communities continue to suffer. Bypassing rather than working with public service agencies often leaves those agencies weaker. This is especially true when districts attempt to create alternative institutions—such as their own garbage collection programs or police services. In the

long run, democracy may lose out as the more economically powerful forces in a community dominate its change agenda, with no way
for the ordinary citizen to "throw the rascals out" through the elec-
toral process.

Implications for the Nonprofit Sector

There are many ways in which nonprofits can and do influence
the private sector. First, most companies are not experts in assessing
community needs or the needs of vulnerable populations. Your
organization's experience in assessing needs may complement the
corporation's traditional approach to assessing market demand. Second, just as nonprofits can benefit from corporate managerial expertise, for-profit companies can learn from the nonprofit world. Assume, for a moment, that a manufacturer is designing a service for
its plant employees—for example, an early childhood or parent
education center. There is much that it could learn from nonprofits'
experiences with similar programs.

Third, corporations may also discover that their best bet is to
contract with social agencies and other service providers to provide
the needed services to their employees, perhaps even in the plant
itself. Examples might include management of a parent education
center, the development of HIV and AIDS education and prevention
programs, multiculturalism training, and so on. Fourth, agencies can
legitimize corporate involvement in the community by linking them
to established providers and supporters of nonprofit programs, including government and foundation funders. Finally, agencies can
provide an outlet for company surplus—equipment, supplies, and
the spirit of volunteering.

Remember, tapping into corporate philanthropy requires approaching a firm in terms of its self-interest and not your own.

Grants and Contracts

I have not included much information about grants in this chapter.
Despite the changes in the patterns of corporate philanthropy documented previously, however, companies dispense most of their charitable dollars through direct giving programs, and grants account for
the majority of funds given directly to nonprofit enterprises. In recent

years, the human services have increased their share of corporate gifts from approximately 25% to nearly 30% of the approximately $2 billion per year allocated to philanthropy. It is not very difficult to find out what companies are giving cash for and to whom. Much of the information on America's major corporations is documented in great detail in the directories described in the following section. Most are available in Foundation Center Collaborating Library Collections as well as in many other public and university libraries.

If you want more specific information on the local giving patterns of smaller companies in your own community, you may have to build your own database. Scanning the daily press or watching the evening news and getting on the mailing list for company newsletters are not bad starting points, but they do require being systematic and keeping good records if you want to maintain an up-to-date picture of what companies are doing. These sources may tell you whether they are interested in preventing AIDS, educating developmentally disabled children, promoting better understanding between the races, or dealing with the consequences of Alzheimer's disease. Approximately 20% of all corporate gifts tend to be nonmonetary (e.g., equipment, materials, and services). It is difficult to get standardized measures of the value of these in-kind contributions. Moreover, the motivation to give is sometimes geared more to getting rid of surplus than to contributing to a specific program or service. These factors make it difficult to obtain accurate data on giving patterns.

SELECTED DIRECTORIES

The Foundation Center (see Chapter 5) and other publishers produce materials that may become invaluable resources to you, like those that describe foundation giving (including company-sponsored foundations). The following are a few that I have found helpful.

The Corporate 500 Directory of Corporate Philanthropy

A "who's who" of corporate philanthropy is designed to make the search easier by listing all decision makers, regardless of position, in one index. "Grants-at-a-Glance" is a graphic summary (i.e., tables and maps) of important details about a corporation's giving programs. The Generosity Index measures giving against net earnings. Eligibility is discussed in greater detail than in many other publications and each profile includes a detailed analysis of giving patterns over time. Available from the Public Management Institute, 358 Brandon Street, San Francisco, CA 94107

The Directory of Corporate and Foundation Givers

A national listing of 8,000 major funding sources for nonprofits in two volumes; the directory lists funders alphabetically. Each listing provides concise summaries about who the corporation contributed to, for what purpose, the amounts of recent grants, and what kinds of noncash contributions it makes. Corporate and grants officers are listed, and application information (including restrictions) is described.

Indexed by state, operating location, grant type, recipient type, nonprofit categories, and major products or industry. Published annually by The Taft Group, 12300 Twinbrook Parkway, Rockville, MD 20852.

Matching Gift Details: A Guidebook to Corporate Matching Gift Programs

The Introduction describes why companies establish matching gifts and why nonprofits apply for them. Data list matching gift companies and indicate what they are likely to provide matches for and what they will not provide matches for. Gift-matching subsidiaries are cross-referenced with parent companies, and locations of matching gift administrators are provided. Published annually by the Council for Advancement and Support of Education National Clearinghouse for Corporate Matching Gift Information: CASE, 11 DuPont Circle, Washington, DC 20036-1261.

National Directory of Corporate Giving

Authoritative information on 1,700 corporate foundations and 600 direct-giving programs, most of them with lists of recent grants. Each listing specifies the kind of business the company is in, all plants and subsidiaries, and its charitable giving statement. Indexes help target corporations by geographic giving area, types of direct-giving grants, corporate officers, and so on. Annual publication of the Foundation Center, 79 Fifth Avenue, New York, NY 10003-3076.

Other Helpful Directories

International Corporate Giving in America and Abroad

The Taft Group (see above)

Global Contributions of U.S. Corporations

The Conference Board, 845 Third Avenue, New York, NY 10022-6601

Survey of Corporate Contributions

The Conference Board (see above)

Additional Sources of Information on Companies

Biographic directories: These include *Who's Who in Industry and Finance* and others.

Business directories: These include *Moody's, Dunn and Bradstreet*, and *Standard and Poor's.*

Corporate annual reports: These are generally available through a company's investment relations department; some companies may also list their charitable giving.

Corporate Giving Watch: A 24-page monthly publication from Taft: includes descriptive lead article, updates on major corporate gifts, descriptions of new giving programs, and a list of recent grants. The FunderSearch responds to reader inquiries and provides a search service to other readers.

Business magazines, newspapers, and trade or professional journals: *Barron's, Business Week, Forbes, Fortune, Money,* the *Wall Street Journal,* and many national and local newspapers describe innovative and trendsetting giving patterns; so do a number of the trade journals such as those listed under Suggestions for Further Reading.

DIRECT CONTACTS WITH
PRIVATE-SECTOR FUNDERS

Just as many companies want the public to know what they are up to, you may want particular companies to know what your organization does. That can be quite challenging. The object, after all, is not to find out what companies do but rather to get them interested in your organization and what you do. You can increase your visibility by (a) getting to know decision makers in local private-sector enterprises and (b) making your services available when you hear that the firm is in need.

Members of your board or staff may have connections to bankers, trust officers, heads of manufacturing plants, or branch directors of retail outlets. Why not appoint some of these people to committee or board membership or to be members of a fund-raising task force? Also, try the reverse. Get yourself appointed to task forces and commissions that are likely to include business executives. Yolanda Johnson, the director of a shelter for the homeless, explains, "I did not know anyone in the business community except a friend of mine who ran a pricey resale shop downtown. But Rona was active in a downtown revitalization commission and asked me if I wanted to attend a meeting. 'You serve a lot of street people and understand their problems differently than we merchants do.' So I came. I got active. And over time I joined several commissions dominated by business and government officials. Being at the table means that people know who you are and call you when they have a question or a problem. And it also means I can call them."

You can also find out about corporate concerns indirectly through contacts with providers already on the inside. For example, Employee Assistance Programs (EAPs) employ mental health professionals to help corporations manage troubled employees or provide aid to those with problems at home. EAP supervisory staff are also in contact with other mental health and social service providers. Because they are likely to know about company interests and agency needs and capacities, EAPs are often in a good position to share relevant information with other service providers and even to broker relationships between corporations and community-based nonprofits.

Larger companies often have a designated giving officer. Make a telephone inquiry or send a one-page letter of inquiry. The letter might be accompanied by a news story on one of your programs, a brochure, or some other attractive and interesting documentation. The phone conversation should be well scripted, demonstrating that you know something about the company's interests. Be ready with specific questions to ask. "Is the firm expanding its focus on education?" or "Do you fund sectarian program?" are appropriate. "What kinds of things is the company interested in?" is not appropriate.

Anticipate questions that you may be asked. For example, the person you are interviewing may interview you in return. Typical questions include

- "Who sponsors or funds you?"
- "What's your track record in this area?"
- "What populations do you currently serve?"
- "Who should we contact to get more information on your organization or its programs?"

If the person you are trying to reach is not in, leave your name and affiliation, with a brief "sound bite" statement of what you are interested in. Do not be vague with the receptionist. Executives do not like to feel that their time is being taken up by people on fishing expeditions. Sound familiar? It is the same advice as that presented in the chapters on government and foundation funding.

Some No-No's in Approaching Corporations

The following are a few red flags that could get you turned away:

- You are asking too much or too little, which shows that you are either dishonest or unrealistic.
- You seem to be more opportunistic than honestly interested in the project.
- Your track record is strewn with hurdles that have been knocked over.
- You are serving the wrong people or the wrong geographic area.
- There is not enough lead time to get the program off and running.
- You missed the boat. Nobody cares anymore. The project is not timely.
- The project is potentially controversial.
- You or your organization appear to be antibusiness.
- You have never heard of total quality management or quality performance measures.
- You, your organization, or your program are politically motivated.
- The project does not fit the company's image of itself or its current priorities.

Although these impressions may not necessarily be true, if these are the messages that get through in your communication, 5 minutes of attention may be all you get. What other issues are likely to raise red flags with the company you are pursuing?

Corporations as Competitors

We are accustomed to thinking of corporations as potential funders and collaborators. In Chapter 1, however, we also began to explore corporate involvement in the provision of social services. The passage of welfare reform legislation in the summer of 1996 is likely to generate a bonanza for big business and to challenge the very nature of the public-private-voluntary system as we have known it.

For example, Bernstein (1996) reports that corporate giants such as Ross Perot's Electronic Data Systems, Lockheed Information Systems (a subsidiary of Lockheed-Martin, the defense contractor), and dozens of smaller firms are competing to provide new state-run welfare eligibility, service, and training programs in Texas and elsewhere. She writes, "To state and county officials facing capped welfare budgets and financial penalties if they fail to move most recipients into jobs in two years, a fixed-price contract with a corporation has strong appeal" (p. 1).

The potential for abuse is enormous. For example, if determination of eligibility is tied to reduction in welfare rolls and to corporate profit, companies may find that denying eligibility increases shareholder profits. Corporate employers, however, are accustomed to rewarding employees for getting results, and if the goals of rehabilitation and employment are the criteria by which success is measured many current welfare clients may benefit from the changes in store. As these changes work their way through various state systems, however, they are likely to have a significant effect on corporate philanthropy when what had formerly been defined as a community service becomes a source of corporate profit.

SUMMARY AND CONCLUSIONS

The lines between strategic business decisions and philanthropy are blurring. In many cases, social giving is good business. This has led to more careful attention to what businesses fund and what they do not fund. Their choices are likely to put the corporation's agenda first, even if it is clothed in philanthropic garb. Others may continue to fund programs that reflect their chief executive's commitments. Many companies are likely to decentralize giving, providing more autonomy to local directors. In some circumstance, businesses may even take on quasi-governmental functions in their efforts to address local needs.

Businesses are interested in getting things done: solving a problem or improving a situation. This may also mean, however, that they will be less interested in small start-up efforts or demonstration projects. Most want to get the biggest bang for the buck, and that means leveraging their cash contributions in one of two ways: (a) reducing cash outlays by complementing them with volunteer service and other noncash contributions or (b) entering into collaborations with other corporations, community and private foundations, and government agencies.

REFERENCES

Bernstein, N. (1996, September 15). Giant corporations entering race to run state welfare programs. *New York Times*, p. 1.
Kyle-Brown, A. (1992, November/December). Creating something new. *Foundation News*, 34-38.
McDermott, K. (1991, September/October). The good neighbor thing. *Dunn and Bradstreet Reports*, 18-21.

SUGGESTIONS FOR FURTHER READING

Bartlett, N. (1990, Spring). The charity purge when corporations merge. *Business and Society Review, 73*, 29-31.
Braus, P. (1990, June). Sharing the harvest. *Successful Meetings, 39*(7), 87-90.
Colin, R. (1990, February). Getting corporations to give. *Association Management, 42*(2), 90-95.
Cordtz, D. (1990, May). Corporate citizenship: No more soft touches. *Financial World, 159*(11), 30-36.
Davidson, J. (1993, February). Responsibility reaps rewards. *Small Business Reports*, 56-63.
Dexheimer, L. (1988, December). Look who's helping the homeless. *Association Management, 40*(12), 28-35.
Embley, L. L. (1992). *Doing well while doing good: The marketing link between business & nonprofit causes.* Englewood Cliffs, NJ: Prentice Hall.
Fettig, L. (1991, Summer). Bootstrap rural development—How Putnam County took control of its own future. *Economic Development Review, 9*(3), 50-52.

Galaskiewicz, J. (1985). *Social organization of an urban grants economy: A study of business philanthropy and nonprofit organizations.* San Diego: Academic Press.

Hillman, H. (1980). *The art of winning corporate grants.* New York: Vanguard.

Hoeth, T. (1991, Winter). Public-private partnerships in state government. *Public Productivity and Management Review, 15*(2), 12-13.

Hutnyan, J. (1992, January/February). Accenting the "community" in the community bank. *Bottomline, 9*(1), 17-21.

Hyland, S., et al. (1990, Summer). Realigning corporate giving: Community development corporations. *Nonprofit and Voluntary Sector Quarterly, 19*(2), 111-119.

Katz, L. (1990, June). Corporate support and winning proposals. *Fundraising Management, 21*(4), 42-44.

Keehn, J. (1991). How business helps the schools. *Fortune, 124*(9), 161-180.

Klepper, A., & Mackler, S. (1986). *Screening requests for corporate contributions.* New York: Conference Board.

Logsdon, J. M., Reiner, M., & Burke, L. (1990, Summer). Corporate philanthropy: Strategic responses to the firm's stakeholders. *Nonprofit and Voluntary Sector Quarterly, 19*(2).

Mason, J. C. (1992, November). Corporate sponsorships help target the right audience. *Management Review, 81*(11), 58-61.

Noble, P. (1989, October/December). Entrepreneurs in community service. *Business and Economic Review, 36*(1), 6-8.

Piktialis, D. (1990, Winter). Employers and elder care: A model corporate program. *Pride Institute Journal of Long-Term Care, 9*(1), 26-31.

Rogers, L. (1991, August). What utilities are doing for kids. *Public Utilities Fortnightly, 128*(3), 16-19.

Sansolo, M. (1991, December). We can do something. *Progressive Grocer, 70*(12), 16-17.

Schnall, S. M. (1989, Summer). How big business can help the human services—and vice versa. *Public Welfare,* 6-17.

Shannon, J. P. (Ed.). (1991). *The corporate contributions handbook: Devoting private means to public needs.* San Francisco: Jossey-Bass.

Sklarz, D. R. (1991, April/June). Business-education partnerships. *Business and Economic Review, 37*(3), 15-18.

Stahl, D. (1993, February). Supporting affordable housing. *Savings and Community Banker, 2*(2), 16-21.

Therrien, L. (1992, November 2). Corporate generosity is greatly depreciated. *Business Week, 3291,* 118-120.

Victor, M. (1992). *Improving corporate donations: New strategies for grantmakers and grantseekers.* San Francisco: Jossey-Bass.

Zinkewicz, P. (1992, December). Life, health insurers target social issues. *Health and Life Insurance Sales, 135*(12), 14-16.

7

Donor's Choice and the United Way

*Seeking Support From United Ways,
Alternative Funds, and Sectarian
Federations*

Why Should Our Clients Suffer?
One Agency's Experience

"For the last few years, it's been downhill all the way," reports the director of a neighborhood center. "At a time when we're being flooded with new immigrants who need housing assistance, language training and acculturation, and job placement, the United Way has been steadily reducing its allocation. This year we were cut by nearly 17%. I know they've had problems with the annual campaign, but this 'donor designated' gifts approach they're using works against agencies like ours that deal with unpopular causes or populations. Our clients wind up being the ones who suffer when services are cut. We've explained our situation in our annual reports and budget requests, but it doesn't seem to help."

A Second Experience

"Until 3 years ago, there seemed to be no way we would ever get United Way funding," confides the director of an AIDS education project. "But then they instituted an open system in which any qualified provider can compete on a level field for United Way grants. On top of our being represented in the county's Combined Health Appeal, it makes our prospects look rosier and rosier."

UNITY IN DIVERSITY

Pressures on United Ways and other federated fund-raising organizations to allocate to worthy causes have increased dramatically during the 1990s, but for the most part their campaigns have not kept pace with demand. Unlike the first agency's experience in the opening vignette, however, clients do not always have to suffer. As the second illustration indicates, the ways in which money is raised and programs are funded are changing, and things can look a good deal brighter.

Donor-choice programs in which contributors designate how they want their money to be used are now an important part of the new United Way picture and are making headway with other types of federations. United Ways are also moving into new fund-raising and allocating approaches, including securing grants from foundations, collaborating with foundations on the giving of grants, and building their own endowment funds to make up for annual campaign shortfalls or enable them to take on new resource and community-building functions. Some function, at least in part, like community foundations, requiring petitioner agencies to compete for short-term grants rather than continuing to provide them with relatively secure annual allocations. The same is also true of sectarian and other federated fund-raising and allocating organizations (federated because member organizations have agreed to delegate some of their autonomy for fund-raising or planning or both to a central agency).

The experiences described in the preceding vignettes took place in two cities separated by hundreds of miles, but they could have occurred in the same locale. What distinguishes them is not geographic distance but rather a wide chasm in understanding about the ways of United Ways—how they do or could function. Whether you have found yourself on the defensive or on the offensive regarding your own local United Way organization, or if you need to check out the potential for support through other federated fund-raising organizations and payroll deduction campaigns, you may find the information in this chapter helpful.

United Ways and other federated fund-raising and allocating organizations are in a process of change that is no less dramatic than that which is taking place in government, business, and the foundation world. Fueling all this change is a desire on the part of prospective donors to determine what they give and to whom. In this chapter, how United Ways respond to donor-driven giving is examined. In particular, how this has affected traditional payroll deduction plans and led to creating new forms of designated giving that resemble patterns found in community foundations are examined. In some places, United Ways compete with or have launched their own alternative community foundations. In other locales, they find themselves squeezed out where they have traditionally had hegemony—the payroll deduction plan.

HOW UNITED WAYS OPERATE

The Ubiquity of United Way Organizations

There were approximately 1,900 independent, community-based United Way organizations in 1996. These provided support for some 48,000 local service agencies and chapters of national organizations. Of these local United Ways, 1,200 are affiliated with the United Way of America. Collectively, they employ approximately 6,000 professional staff people and perhaps 1 million volunteers who serve on boards, work on campaign drives, engage in decision making on community priorities and agency allocations, and perform a wide variety of other direct service and administrative tasks. In approximately one fourth of them, most in smaller cities, there are no paid professionals. Volunteers do everything from setting target goals for the campaign, creating and disseminating promotional materials, running the payroll deduction drive, to determining how much each recipient organization will receive.

Whatever the staffing mix, United Ways tend to be among the most efficient of all fund-raising organizations, devoting just under 15% of their income to campaign management and to community planning and priority setting. In 1990, they generated approximately $3 billion in charitable contributions via their annual campaigns—double the amount raised a decade earlier. Since then, however, payroll deduction campaigns, the bread and butter of United Way fund-raising, have been flat or diminishing. In 1992, 15 of the 25 largest United Ways raised less money than the year before, and 20 were unable to meet their own target goals. For them and their recipient agencies, some of which sustained 20% to 30% reductions in assistance, the news that year was definitely bad. Reductions in external support almost invariably lead to cuts in staff in members' agencies and in a cut in their services. The news was not all bad, however.

That same year, the San Francisco area United Way organization raised its campaign goal to $72 million, which was $14 million higher than the previous year's goal and a fourfold increase over the amount raised a decade earlier. The Boston United Way, although experiencing a $2 million campaign shortfall, was able to maintain its overall level of agency support via creative collaborations with foundations and by instituting new approaches to donor recruitment. These two organizations will be revisited later in this chapter.

Classic United Way Operations

Although smaller United Ways may be entirely operated by volunteers, the medium- or large-sized organizations are likely to have well-trained staff. These include social planners (often with social work backgrounds), fund-raisers, accountants, and specialists in particular practice sectors or arenas (e.g., health, the arts, community development, and so on). Some United Ways professionally managed volunteer bureaus.

Traditionally, those large enough to have paid staff tend to use relatively similar allocation procedures. Councils or divisions are set up to deal with specific areas of interest—for example, cultural and educational programs, social services, health programs, and so on. Each council is composed of volunteers who may have undergone some training before being appointed to the council or who may have worked on a variety of tasks and on subcommittees prior to their appointments. Each council received back-up help from one or more professional staffers.

The staff also works with "petitioner organizations"—those that will be requesting funds to be allocated by the council. This technical assistance is intended to assure that requests are in line with the "community's" overall funding priorities. These are set by the board, which relies on staff to provide it with information on community needs, particularly those unmet by other sources. Until recently, only member agencies could expect to receive an allocation, but once an organization became a member of the United Way it could expect a similar allocation on an annual basis. Member agencies expect regular appropriations, generally at the same level as the sums received for the previous year, adjusted for inflation. They are held accountable for the way in which those funds are spent; they must report on their programs and spell out the details if their current requests diverge in any way from those of the previous year. It is difficult for nonmember organizations to receive allocations.

United Ways perceive themselves as leaders in promoting sound accounting and financial reporting principles. *Accounting and Financial Reporting: A Guide for United Ways and Nonprofit Human Service Organizations* was first published in 1974. It is still one of the best guides available. It contains standards, models, and directions for use by United Ways in reporting expenditures and income and identifying expenditures and income of the agencies to which the monies are allocated. The financial records of almost all United Ways are audited annually by an independent public accountant whose examination conforms to generally accepted standards outlined in the accounting guide. All United Ways are encouraged to publish financial reports to the public that provide full disclosure of all revenues and expenditures.

A Bit of History—The United Way
and Other Federated Structures

The picture painted previously is vintage United Way. It was accurate for the mid-1980s when I interviewed a number of United Way lay leaders and executives. It is a picture that draws on a rich legacy that began with efforts by the Charity Organization Societies (COSs) more than 100 years ago and progressed through the development of Community Chests. The first COS was established in Denver, Colorado, in 1887 by a rabbi, a Catholic priest, and two Protestant ministers who conducted a single campaign to raise funds for 10 local agencies serving families and children. The COS movement grew rapidly, seeking new and better ways to "scientifically" manage the fund-raising and management processes.

The first truly comprehensive effort to raise funds from the general public and to reallocate them to local agencies, however, took place in Cleveland in 1913. Within a decade, Community Chests replaced virtually all Charity Aid Societies as central fund-raising and allocating organizations. By the late 1920s, more than 300 communities had established their own chests. These were to be true umbrella organizations able to address community needs more comprehensively. Because chests were founded, in part, by the service agencies that were to be the recipients of central fund-raising campaigns, they were especially sensitive to member needs. "In a voluntary community, we can't afford to drive anyone away," was a commonly expressed sentiment. Chests developed a consensus approach to decision making, thus almost guaranteeing that no member would feel outvoted or unvalued and increasing the likelihood that the original members would be committed to campaign efforts.

During this period, other federated funding efforts emerged, many of them under sectarian auspices. For example, the first Jewish federation was established in 1895 in Boston. Catholic, Lutheran, and other Protestant collaborative fund-raising efforts followed. As federated fund-raising and allocation grew, more money was raised, services were expanded, and many persons were helped. As perceptions of public responsibility changed, however, states and localities began assuming larger shares of the social service burden from the voluntary sector. With the advent of the Great Depression, even the best of the federated fund-raising and allocation efforts proved incapable, on their own, coping with large-scale dislocations, unemployment, and just plain misery.

In her insightful book, *The United Way: Dilemmas of Organized Charity*, Eleanor Brilliant (1990) addressed the propensity of United

Ways to allocate significant proportions of their funds to established organizations, many of whose local operations are affiliated national organizations (e.g., the Red Cross, the Y, and Girl Scouts) that provide traditional and well-legitimated services, or to local agencies with name recognition. In many communities, it is still not uncommon for United Ways to be criticized for operating like exclusive clubs, playing it safe by funding organizations that serve middle-class populations and that offend no one.

Newer agencies, created to address emerging needs or serving more controversial populations, were not likely to get United Way support until recently. Rarely were more than two or three new agencies per year likely to be admitted to full membership in a United Way, and new admits were likely to fit comfortably into "mainstream America." The less established agencies and those with less community support tended to be more extensively scrutinized for fiscal accountability and program acceptability before being admitted. This makes most local United Ways profoundly conservative organizations. The same was often even more true of other sectarian federations and of some alternative funds.

Today's picture, however, is much more complex. The poor performance by many established service agencies has eroded some of their legitimacy, especially given the growing demand from other organizations for federated funding. As demand for funding grows, many campaigns appear to be flat or shrinking. Donors have become more sophisticated in their review of agency practices. Many are demanding more personal choices regarding where their gift dollars are to go, challenging United Way boards that have traditionally held the view that it is their responsibility to determine allocations priorities.

CAMPAIGN SHORTFALLS AND HOW
SOME UNITED WAYS COPE WITH THEM

Why Some Campaigns Fall Short of Their Goals

There appear to be at least three reasons for campaign shortfalls, including

1. Structural changes in the U.S. economy
2. Increased competition from other fund-raising organizations
3. Government cutbacks, often leading to increased pressure on the voluntary sector

Changes in the Economic Structure

The United Way is facing a shrinking base for its workplace-oriented campaigns. This is especially true in regions of the country that have undergone major changes in employment. For example, when Defense Department budgets were severely cut following the end of the Cold War, states heavily dependent on military contracts faced significant economic disruptions. Layoffs of highly paid workers and managers resulted in a smaller industrial workforce and fewer contributors to payroll deduction plans. In turn, this put a financial squeeze on United Way recipient agencies at precisely the time that requests for service from families of the unemployed were increasing.

For example, in San Diego in the early 1990s, it was not unusual for agencies to receive 20% to 30% less in allocations than requested. The actual amounts received were likely to reflect significant reductions from the previous year. These changes paralleled earlier workforce reductions in other sectors occasioned by automation and competition from abroad. The shrinking of America's heavy industries was also accompanied by a reduction in the power of unions, which were traditionally major supporters of the United Way.

Many displaced workers and new entrants into the workforce are likely to find employment only in low-paying service jobs or through temporary employment firms. The latter tend not to generate the same kind of commitments as do more permanent settings. Not only are pay and benefits reduced (and intermittent) but so is the expectation that employees will contribute to their local communities through their employer. Employees of a Ford plant might compete with workers at a General Motors manufacturing facility to determine who contributes the most to the United Way. The same sense of collective effort is not likely to be found among employees of either Kelly or Manpower Services. Employees in other industries, such as fast-food and discount retail chains, are also likely to think of themselves as only temporarily employed in those settings. They are often younger workers who accept the low-paying, low-skilled jobs that are available to them, hoping to move on to better things.

The mid-1990s witnessed a new set of economic dynamics. A strong economy with its record-breaking rises in the stock market generated little, if any, increases in average worker take-home pay. More subtle changes also affected giving patterns. "I live in Vail," one economic analyst told me. "My corporate headquarters are in Baltimore. Sitting at my computer at home, I can do everything that I would do in Maryland. Save for monthly meetings, some of which are held in Chicago anyway, I would never get to Baltimore. Nor have I ever lived there. So why would I give to its United Way campaign?"

Competition From Alternative Funds

Although they continue to account for more than $9 of every $10 in employee contributions, United Ways are currently facing stiff competition from a number of "alternative federated funds," many of which have gained recent entree to corporate payroll deduction plans. These alternative federated funds include relatively traditional funds such as

1. International Service Agencies, which includes CARE, Oxfam, and Save the Children Fund and may include other designated charities that originate locally

2. Health-related organizations such as Combined Health Appeals and National Voluntary Health Agencies (NVHAs)—the latter includes national health organizations (e.g., the American Cancer Society or the Muscular Dystrophy Association) that are included in the Combined Federal Campaign (CFC) and the former may include the same national agencies plus a number of local affiliates or independent local health agencies and may be listed in state and local campaigns and in the private sector

3. United Arts Funds, which tend to be listed in state and local government or private-sector campaigns, because most of the recipient organizations are connected to municipalities or other public agencies— for example, local philharmonics and regional theater groups

4. Environmental Federation of America, which includes a score of national environmental groups and other environmental funds at the local and state levels

5. United Negro College Fund

6. United Service Agencies, which includes more than 60 member agencies whose services are national in scope (e.g., Traveler's Aid) covering health and social services dealing with the disabled, the poor, the homeless, legal advocacy for minorities and the indigent, and special services for women and children in need

The funds also include relatively new funds such as

1. Black United Funds (serving a dozen or more communities in the United States)

2. Women's Funds (many of them affiliated with the National Network of Women's Funds) that appeal primarily to female donors and that allocate dollars to programs that are designed to assist women and girls

3. Local and state Social Action Funds made up of coalitions of agencies that deal with issues, such as homelessness, AIDS education, family and community violence, that may not be adequately addressed by more traditional governmental and voluntary agencies

An Alliance for Choices in Giving was established in 1987 to promote similar choices in the private sector. It is composed of representatives of social action, environmental, and women's funds, as well as corporate representatives and others interested in increasing donor options.

The rapid growth of alternative funds was given a major boost by the creation of the CFC by President Reagan in 1987. For some time, the National Committee for Responsive Philanthropy (NCRP) and other advocates of "deregulating" voluntary giving had been promoting donor choice in payroll deduction campaigns. Reagan's executive order was followed by enabling legislation a year later. It provides for a single payroll deduction campaign that includes national agencies that are deemed eligible by the Federal Office of Personnel Management. There are now more than 100 alternative funds in the country, with many of them national in scope, some covering many communities in a single state, and others focused on specific locales.

CFCs operate in more than 500 locations in the United States where there are large concentrations of federal employees. Eligibility to participate in the Combined Campaign requires that the organization be recognized as having charitable, educational, or religious purposes, but that these are carried out by others on the organization's behalf. Thus, approval of the fund's 501(c)(3) tax-exempt status by the Internal Revenue Service is not enough. It must also demonstrate that it allocates its income through and for the benefit of the beneficiaries of other 501(c)(3) organizations. Eligibility rules for participation in CFCs are published annually in the *Federal Register*. In general, the national fund must have a local affiliate for it to be listed in a particular local campaign. Because local United Ways are so ubiquitous, the United Way of America (UWA) is invariably included. Money pledged to the UWA is reallocated by the national office to the affiliate in the locale from which the gift was made.

CFCs pioneered the way for other state, county, and local government agencies to open their payroll deduction campaigns to alternative funds and to other non-(United Way)-affiliated charities. The rapid headway made by alternative funds in public settings is, interestingly, beginning to take hold in voluntary settings (including in some agencies that have long been recipients of United Way funding) and in the private sector. CFCs, however, are not for every locale. Robert Bothwell, executive of the NCRP, estimates that a "minimum base of 25,000 (government) workers is essential for the success of a new alternative fund" before it can demonstrate the strength of its appeal to the business sector.

Alternative funds draw on two impetii. One is a growing awareness by specific groups that their interests are not being adequately addressed by United Way member agencies. This appears to be primarily true of women's, arts, social action, and minorities-oriented funds. These organizations also view the development of their alternative funds as a way of educating their constituents to become involved in philanthropic endeavors. The inclusion of alternative funds in payroll deduction campaigns is championed by advocacy and watchdog organizations such as the NCRP in Washington, D.C. The NCRP publishes information on many alternative funds as well as guidelines for how to apply to alternative funds for membership.

TIPS ON ALTERNATIVE FUNDS
AND COMBINED FEDERAL CAMPAIGNS

Tip: The best overall source of information on CFCs is *Catch the Spirit: Combined Federal Campaign,* which is compiled annually and is the official CFC brochure wherever local campaigns are conducted. The brochure, in the form of a booklet (which can be 80–100 pages long), includes brief descriptions of all participating federations: national, international, statewide (in the state in which the federal office is located), local foundations, and local service agencies and qualifying nonprofits. Brochures are available from the U.S. Office of Personnel Management or from the Local Federal Coordinating Committee. Check with your closest federal building for addresses.

Government Cutbacks

Government cutbacks have been discussed elsewhere. United Ways cannot make up for massive reductions in public expenditures. Cuts in Medicaid and federal nutrition programs and limits on welfare, however, all put pressure on the United Way and its recipient agencies.

Coping With and Overcoming Shortfalls. During the past two decades, many United Ways have used two methods to cope with campaign shortfalls, competition, and rising demand for service: donor choice and sunset allocations. The first is aimed at wooing donors and the second at controlling recipients. Donor choice has been adopted by many United Ways to "grow" the campaign and to counter competition from alternative funds. It is also a response to the growing sophistication of donor populations.

Donor Sophistication and Donor Choice. Donor choice also appears to be a partial antidote to donor apathy. Even where the United Way is the only designee of payroll deduction dollars, donors are likely to demand some involvement in deciding where their personal contributions will go. The San Francisco area United Way began offering choices to its donors as early as 1980. Many other United Ways followed suit. Although patterns may differ from community to community, the following is a description of how they generally work.

In their payroll deduction packet, donors receive a list of United Way "member organizations and agencies" (those that regularly receive allocations from the United Way) and a parallel list of other bona fide philanthropic organizations that are "managed responsibly." Donors are asked to specify whether

their entire gift is to go to United Way member organizations, with the United Way board making allocation decisions;

the gift is to go to the United Way but only to those agencies that serve a specific population (e.g., children, the aging, and those suffering from mental illness), geographic area (some United Ways serve adjacent communities), or service sector (e.g., social services, health, or the arts);

the gift is to go to the United Way but with a percentage of the donor's gift targeted to a specific United Way agency or agencies;

all or part of the money is to go to an alternative fund or to a United Way designated nonmember agency or agencies (with or without any of the restrictions or targeting discussed previously).

All this may seem cumbersome, and in practice many donors are likely to opt for the first option. People do like the idea of having a choice, however, even if the choice is to let the United Way board decide.

Initially, many United Way executives resisted donor choice fearing that uninformed contributors would make poor decisions, invalidating a more reasoned priority-setting process. That process includes professionally conducted community needs assessments, monitoring and evaluating recipient agency programs, and priority setting by an elected board. Member agencies feared that they would be losers in an environment that promotes trendy programs and that might degenerate into a popularity contest. Most of these fears have proven unfounded. Today, more than 90% of all United Ways offer some form of donor option. "In our first year with donor choice," reported a United Way campaign director, "donations grew by nearly 5% and they continue to grow as more organizations inform the public about their services. It also reduced the pressure on us to admit new agencies into full membership. Even without becoming member agencies, many now benefit from a united campaign effort."

Sunset Allocations. Because donors do not avail themselves of the full range of choices open to them, boards continue to play critical roles in determining community priorities. For this reason, a kind of "sunset clause" has been in place in many United Way communities. This term was current as far back as the Carter administration. Simply put, this is an effort to impose time limits on funding—for example, 3 to 5 years. After that time, all bets are off and even the most well-established agencies must justify annual requests in terms of emerging community priorities.

UNITED WAY OF AMERICA

Leadership and Coordination

Not much has been said about the United Way of America and the role it has played in both national and local developments. The UWA provides its members with technical assistance (including training in how to assist recipient agencies to use performance measures in their allocations requests), help with promotions and campaign literature, leadership development, and a unified voice in promoting a common agenda. Some observers perceive UWA as contributing to the system's conservative bent. I do not see it quite that way. National organizations with local affiliates are by nature going to be somewhat conservative, concerned as they are with systems maintenance. They can also be quite progressive, however, setting standards for member agencies, suggesting new directions for them to take, and providing them with the resources with which to respond to new challenges.

The United Way of America has done all those things, and it appears to have done them well. Otherwise, it would not have been able to maintain the allegiance of more than 1,200 local affiliate agencies when, in 1992, its president and chief executive officer, William

Aramony, was forced to resign under a cloud of fiscal impropriety. A year later, Elaine Chao, a former Peace Corps director and undersecretary of the Transportation Department, became chief executive officer. Chao instituted new approaches to fiscal oversight at the national level but otherwise continued and expanded programs set in motion by Aramony. These include professional and lay leader development programs, research and technical assistance, and the generation of how-to guides for strategic planning, budgeting, and fund-raising.

The UWA does not operate as a fund-raiser except when it is listed as a choice for contributors in the CFC. Funds raised in this way are redistributed by the national organization to local United Ways serving the donors' communities. UWA does, however, solicit foundation and corporate gifts to cover some of the costs of its national initiatives.

National Initiatives

The UWA's national initiatives (described in the following lists) and its legislative agenda may have some implications for your organization. Whether or not your organization is currently a United Way member or affiliate agency or benefits from its grant programs, it may be affected by one or more of the following programs.

Community Capacity-Building Initiatives

In an effort to help local United Ways remain current and targeted to emerging needs, the UWA has created a number of "initiatives" programs, including the following:

- The Housing Initiatives Program assists local United Ways to create public or private partnerships that support neighborhood-based, community development corporations and, in particular, those that address the goal of providing affordable housing to low- and moderate-income populations. The program began with a grant from the Ford Foundation in 1987 through which the UWA set up a competitive challenge grant program. Grants of $100,000 are awarded in support of local low-income housing efforts. In 1994, multiyear operating support and technical assistance were being provided to community development corporations in Chicago; Houston; Pontiac, Michigan; Rochester, New York; and York County, Pennsylvania.

- The Mobilization for America's Children (MAC) initiative is aimed at preparing children to enter schools ready to learn. MAC orchestrates a variety of educational and social service resources at the local level aimed at helping children succeed and remain in school through graduation. In the mid-1990s, 90 United Ways were involved in programs that linked UW agencies with schools and the private sector.

- Diversity initiatives such as Project Blueprint focus on "preparing people of color for volunteer leadership positions on the boards of United Ways and human service agencies." An initial 3-year grant from the Kellogg Foundation led to a pilot program in 22 cities. It was followed, in 1992, with a Ford Foundation grant to provide technical assistance to United Way organizations in approximately 30 communities.

- The National Youth Service initiative began with the assumption that young people are not a problem in their communities but rather can be important contributors to problem solution. Local efforts are likely to include Youth United Way campaigns, agency volunteer placement, and school-based educational and social action projects.

Government Relations and Legislative Action

The United Way of America also has a legislative agenda that includes support for

- early childhood development (e.g., Head Start and nutrition, child, and prenatal care);
- welfare reform;
- health care;
- education and literacy;
- emergency food and shelter programs for the homeless;
- collaborations between the public, private, and voluntary sectors on drug abuse prevention and treatment;
- promotion of voluntarism.

The UWA distributes materials to assist local United Way boards and their lay leaders who participate in related advocacy efforts at the local and state levels. In a number of cases—for example, the issue of literacy education—it has also facilitated the development of concerted efforts that link United Way member agencies to schools, libraries, and other relevant institutions.

TIPS FOR TAKING ADVANTAGE
OF WHAT YOU NOW KNOW

Tip 1: If your organization is not a United Way affiliate, find some other way to get into a payroll deduction program. This may require getting your United Way to institute a donor choice program, to join with other organizations to create an alternative fund, or both. Once you are "in," the income is likely to be steady, if variable. To increase your share, educate the public about your programs.

Tip 2: Whether or not your organization is currently a United Way affiliate, make yourself more attractive to your local organization. The following are some tactics employed successfully by others: (a) include key UW officials (e.g., lay and professional) on your board and program committees, and (b) redefine some of your programs in terms of UWA national initiatives (e.g., literacy training and minorities leadership) or in terms of its legislative agenda (e.g., welfare reform, low-income housing, and child advocacy). If your programs can help your local United Way to demonstrate the relevance of its programs, it may need you as much as you need it!

The same tips apply to building relationships with alternative funds. Find out what they are interested in and then get on the bus.

BEYOND PAYROLL DEDUCTION—NEW CHALLENGES
TO UNITED WAYS AND OTHER FEDERATIONS

For some federated fund-raising efforts, payroll deduction was never the name of the game. For example, sectarian federations such as Jewish federations and Catholic charities, which appeal primarily to coreligionists, are more likely to have narrowly targeted campaigns. Some work through congregations and diocese, whereas others raise funds via a structure that targets donors by community, organizational affiliation, occupation, or capacity to give (a euphemism for level of wealth).

The Eclipse of the Campaign and the Rise of Endowment Programs

Jewish federations, early pioneers in raising dollars through a single fund-raising campaign, have found that dependence on campaigns that have shrinking donor bases is not good business. In most large- and medium-sized Jewish federations, endowment programs have been developed that may eventually guarantee support for core services and populations in need. The campaign was never seen in purely fund-raising terms. It was perceived of as a community-building endeavor that promotes identity and affiliation with the Jewish community. In time, it may become more significant for community building than for fund-raising. By the year 2020, in many Jewish communities endowments are likely to begin eclipsing the annual campaign in terms of dollars expended and, by mid-century, are almost certain to dwarf the dollars raised.

"There are plenty of other places donors can invest their funds," reported a fund-raiser for Lutheran Charities. "Soliciting donors for the organization or even for a specific program is no longer cost-effective. You get as many or more turndowns as turn-ons. The name of the game is to find out what the donor cares about, not to convince him to care about our agenda. That does not mean ignoring what we know to be current or emerging community needs. I also see my job as helping donors target their gifts in such a way as to permit flexibility when those needs change."

This requires a highly skilled staff who can spend a good deal more time with individual donors than is necessary in a more traditional campaign.

What appears to be working well in sectarian communities also appears to be effective in some United Ways. Like other nonprofits, they too are finding that their donor base is changing. In some ways, it is beginning to resemble the donor base of community foundations. There are three times as many United Ways as community foundations in America, and many of them already have extensive relationships with wealthy donors, industrialists, and local businesses.

"We just could not compete," complained the president of a new community foundation. "The United Way was here first. Two years ago they decided to create a United Way Foundation. And they didn't limit themselves to traditional UW concerns. Fact is, they helped fund the library and the civic theater when county and state funds got scarce. So when we got a few business and professional leaders together to form a new community foundation, we found that the UW had preempted the field. Our challenge, now, is differentiate our purposes from theirs so as to be able to build a following and donor base of our own."

That may not be easy to do. In those communities that do not have community foundations, the UW effort may retard or dampen efforts to create an independent community foundation.

The following appear to be three options for how United Way "foundations" and community foundations can relate to each other:

1. Competition for donors and donor gifts
2. Cooperation in fund-raising or integration into a single entity
3. Agreements on turf boundaries

Competition is not necessarily bad. Like the competition for payroll deduction donors, competition for more substantial gifts may generate a good deal more money. Moreover, competition for donor gifts may translate into collaboration on programs and funding of joint projects. Cofunding is used to increase the amount of money available to projects that are deemed to have special merit or to need substantial sums of money to work effectively. Cofunding also reduces the risk for funders.

Beyond Donor Choice

Operating as a Foundation in Allocations
Rather Than Solicitation

Although donor choice has significantly influenced campaign strategies and placed increased importance on creation of more permanent endowments, an even more radical shift in orientation emerged in the early 1990s. The new approach forces agencies to engage in fierce competition with each other for United Way dollars, dissolving, perhaps forever, the consensus legacy of the old Community Chest. Under this arrangement, pioneered by Lansing, Michigan, and adopted by others such as the nearby Washtenaw County, Michigan, United Way and the national chapter (Washington, D.C.) of the United Way, (a) no agency or program will be guaranteed funding from year to year and (b) bona fide nonprofits that were previously ineligible will now be able to compete for funds.

Those organizations best able to present their cases in the language that will appeal to fund-raisers and donors are likely to get yearly support. Washtenaw United Way board chairman Benjamin Koerber predicts that "By throwing open the funding process to any agency that qualifies, [UWA] dollars will do an even better job." "Not necessarily," counter a number of recipient agencies.

"It's a terrible way to do business," complained the administrator of an antipoverty agency. "It is disconcerting for an organization not to know, from year to year, what it has to work with. Staff need job security and clients need to know whether they can depend on us. At a time when even some foundations and business enterprises are recognizing that they have to support the organization, not just the project, if they want long-term and consistent success, the United Way is telling us that we have to prove our right to exist each year."

The director of another long-term recipient agency stated "The problem is that our programs are multiyear, but the United Way's funding is tied to its annual campaign. If we could be assured funding for multiyear periods, with annual or semiannual reviews, we would have sufficient stability to maintain and improve programs."

"What worries me," added the director of a youth-serving agency, "is that there will be double and triple the number of agencies applying for the same amount of money, at a time when government funds are in danger of dramatic reductions. The competition will be fierce, and many important program are likely to be hurt."

"The anxiety is understandable," said a United Way spokesperson, "but the full change won't take effect all at once. We're phasing out automatic funding in which recipient organizations could expect to receive at least 90% of what they got the previous year. The phase-out will be in 25% increments beginning a year from now. At the end of four years, we'll have moved to a grant system from a common allocation pool. But not all the funds raised by the campaign or generated by the endowment fund will go into the pool. First, we will continue to respect donor designated giving. Secondly, the board has decided to fund a number of essential programs and to continue to support those organizations that will perform vital functions for the community. We'll also spell out our priorities, so that in time agencies can adjust their programs and application requests to areas the community thinks are most important."

Local agencies are not the only organizations that will be interested to see how these changes will play out. United Ways and other federations throughout the country are likely to closely examine the Washtenaw, Lansing, and Washington experiences for clues on how they too might redirect the way in which annual income is expended.

ORGANIZATIONS TO WRITE FOR ADDITIONAL INFORMATION ON FEDERATED FUND-RAISING

Council of Better Business Bureaus, Philanthropic Advisory Service, 4200 Eison Blvd., Arlington, VA 22203

Council of Jewish Federations, 730 Broadway, New York, NY 10003

National Committee for Responsive Philanthropy, 2001 S Street, Washington, DC 20009

United Way of America, United Way Plaza, 801 N. Fairfax Street, Alexandria, VA 22314

SUMMARY

Local United Ways are the prototypic federated fund-raising organizations similar, but not identical, to the many sectarian and sector-specific federations that contribute to the American voluntary system. The United Way pioneered and has long dominated work-place-related fund-raising via payroll deductions. Today, however, newer, alternative funds have begun to compete for donor dollars in many occupational settings as the idea of donor choice has gained popularity. Greater donor sophistication has led most local UW campaigns to also institute a form of internal donor choice in which contributors may specify the organizations, programs, or populations to which they want their contributions to go.

The United Way has engaged in some turf invasion of its own, expanding the designated giving options option to wealthy individuals and corporations in the form of endowment programs. This has generated the potential for competition with community foundations and other federations that also seek endowments and, in turn, this has led to an increase in collaborative fund-raising and allocations. Recently, some United Ways have begun to promote competition among potential recipient organizations. A traditional allocations approach, in which member agencies could expect continued funding from year to year, appears to be shifting to one in which programs and projects must be justified in terms of community priorities and agency commitment to quality performance.

WASHTENAW UNITED WAY ELIGIBILITY
REQUIREMENTS FOR FUNDING

Funded agencies must

Not "unnecessarily duplicate existing services" and "fill an identified gap in the human service delivery system or meet an emerging or unmet community need"

Establish objectives that are measurable, attainable, realistic, and relate to the problem area they are intended to address

Have an objective that is likely to result in "significant impact" on the community in need

Be legally incorporated as not-for-profit and have a letter of tax exemption from the Internal Revenue Service

Have a formal, volunteer governing body that will be responsible for the allocated funds

Not spend more than 20% of their total budgets on promotions or advocacy for the agency

Have a completed, certified audit for the most recent fiscal year and comply with governmental reporting requirements

Comply with nondiscrimination laws and operate with an Affirmative Action plan approved by the agency's board of directors

Agree not to conduct corporate or employee solicitations during the United Way campaign

---

SOURCE: Washtenaw United Way.

Table 7.1. United Way Priorities

Problem Area by Priority	Actual Allocation 1995-1996 ($)	Portion of Total Funding (%)
Youth at risk	941,319	30
Abuse/neglect	80,948	3
Basic/emergency needs	774,915	25
Alcohol/drug abuse	219,576	7
Mental/emotional health	378,145	12
Child care	183,359	6
Needs of elderly	241,502	8
Unemployment	50,540	2
Physical health	188,738	6
People with disabilities	41,095	1
Total	3,100,137	100

SOURCE: Washtenaw United Way.
NOTE: The amount of money allocated to a problem area is not reflective of the United Way priority placed on the problem area because not every problem area has a sufficient number of agencies to justify more extensive funding.

REFERENCE

Brilliant, E. L. (1990). *The United Way: Dilemmas of organized charity.* New York: Columbia University Press.

SUGGESTIONS FOR FURTHER READING

Allocating United Way money; A painstaking, often controversial process. (1993, January 12). *Chronicle of Philanthropy, 5*(6), 2.

Bothwell, R. O. (1989). Workplace giving: United Way or alternative ways? In J. R. Shallow & N. C. Stella (Eds.), *Grant seekers guide* (3rd ed.). Mt. Kisco, NY: Moyer Bell.

Committee, The. (1986). *Charity begins at work: Alternatives to United Way.* Washington, DC: Author.

Cook, R. V. (1986). *Study of United Way donor option programs.* Washington, DC: National Committee for Responsive Philanthropy.

Foote, J. (1991, January/February). The great divide: Donor designated giving. *Foundation News, 32*(1), 27-32.

Fund raising trends and ideas: Bracing for big cuts in the United Way. (1993, January 12). *Chronicle of Philanthropy, 5*(6), 26-31.

Hall, P. D. (1992). *Inventing the nonprofit sector and other essays on philanthropy, voluntarism, and nonprofit organizations.* Baltimore, MD: Johns Hopkins University Press.

Hodson, J. D. (1982). United Ways: Have you considered joining? *Grantsmanship Center News,* 42-45.

National Committee for Responsive Philanthropy. (1986). *Charity begins at work.* Washington, DC: Author.

National Committee for Responsive Philanthropy. (1987). *The workplace giving revolution.* Washington, DC: Author.

National Committee for Responsive Philanthropy. (1989). *The great charitable drive expansion.* Washington, DC: Author.

National Committee for Responsive Philanthropy. (1995). *Alternative fund statistics 1993.* Washington, DC: Author.

Perlmutter, F. D. (1988). Alternative federated funds: Resources for change. *Administration in Social Work, 12*(2), 95-107.

Porter, R. (Ed.). (1981). *United arts fund raising.* New York: American Council for the Arts.

Rose, M. S. (1994). Philanthropy in a different voice: The women's funds. *Nonprofit and Voluntary Sector Quarterly, 23*(3), 227-242.

Scala, R. (1992, May). UWA report uncovers widespread abuses. United Way/America feels the pinch. *Fund Raising Management, 23*(3), 9-10.

Stein, S. (1989, November/December). Sharing charitable turf. *Foundation News,* 53-55.

Wills, C. A. (1990, March/April). Uniting communities. *Foundation News,* 42-45.

8

In Association

*Securing Support From Religious,
Mutual Benefit, and Civic Organizations*

Association Through Associations

On returning from a visit to the New World, Alexis de Tocqueville
reported that

> Americans of all ages, all conditions, and all dispositions constantly
> form associations—religious, moral, serious, futile, general or restric-
> tive, enormous or diminutive. In this manner they found hospitals,
> prisons, and schools. If it is proposed to inculcate some truth or to
> foster some feeling by the encouragement of a great example, they
> form a society. (*Democracy in America*)

THE ASSOCIATION OF MEANING

Voluntary Associations

De Tocqueville's observations are as true today as they were in
1835, perhaps because a core American dynamic remains relatively

unchanged. Americans have always been on the move—from locale to locale, from identity to identity, and from one set of meanings to another. Moving also means being displaced, whether by choice or circumstance. It leads individuals and groups to seek their own place—one that helps them redefine identity and gives meaning to their lives. Relocating also provides people with the opportunity to define what is meaningful and to take on and shape their identities. They often do so in association with others who are seeking a common sense of place, identity, and meaning. When patterns of association are voluntary, the associations we belong to become, by definition, voluntary associations.

Americans band together in voluntary associations for mutual assistance, to solve common problems, to advance causes, to maintain a sense of continuity with a real or imagined past and a shared future, to express their spiritual yearnings, and to transcend their individual limitations. In this chapter, how the activities of religious, mutual benefit, and civic associations relate to the work of human service organizations is examined. I will tell you how you can find out more about relevant associations in your community and suggest some ways in which you can boost your fund-raising and resource development efforts through association with associations.

Religion and Mutual Aid as Motivators for Doing Good

Women and men have always banded together for purposes of mutual assistance and in search of meaning. According to David Macarov (1995), the roots of mutual aid lie in prehistory. Mutual aid was neither purposefully willed nor consciously undertaken. It was a survival mechanism. Families and tribes were among the earliest forms of association through which mutual aid was delivered. Smith suggests that prehistoric hunting bands may have been the earliest forms of cooperative association. As society became more complex, a wide variety of associations that extended beyond or cut across kinship groups were used to deliver specialized aid. Although government and other formal programs now assume many of the tasks associated with protection of individuals and groups, the impulse to engage in mutual assistance continues to motivate participation in voluntary associations.

From the earliest of times, humans also sought ways of understanding meaning and of transcending the limitations of both their understanding and corporeal reality. Religion and religious association were the principal means of doing both. Virtually all religions oblige their followers to engage in actions that promote justice and the welfare of others or to engage in acts of charity or both, thus bringing together the search for meaning and the impulse toward association. In America today, many religious congregations and the denominations with which they are affiliated coordinate and finance their own mutual aid and service programs. They also reach out to and provide assistance to others in need.

CONGREGATIONS AND COMMUNITY

Where in the World
Is Carmen Sandiego?

I first met Carmen when she was 12, a refugee—some would say an "illegal alien"—from a Latin American country, who with her mother and three sisters was given temporary shelter in our church. That was more than 14 years ago. And, believe it or not, I know where Carmen is now. Married and a mother of two herself, she's an active member of the Catholic Church in the old northside neighborhood. But she still volunteers a full day a week with us even though we're affiliated with a Protestant denomination. Although many churches tend to target their services to members of their own congregation or to coreligionists, that's never been our policy. That's why we took some initiative in bringing several other congregations from many denominations into an urban ministry.

Member organizations now shelter the homeless in church facilities on a rotating basis, staff a soup kitchen, and collect surplus food from participating restaurants through our Food Gatherers program. We're not housing refugees from abroad in the church right now, but we've got a new kind of refugee—the victims of domestic violence. There's a Safe House in town, the Urban Ministry along with some committed social workers made sure of that, but it's a small facility, often overcrowded. To make it possible for it to operate as a temporary shelter, we recruit families from this and the other churches who've agreed to participate to provide transition housing when the pressure is heavy on Safe House and when more permanent housing is not yet available. Living in a family context in a real neighborhood can do wonders for a woman and her children who've long lived in fear.

Our volunteering does as much for us as it appears to do for others; it gives us meaning in life, it permits us to act out our religious impulses. It gives us a sense of who we are and where we stand. Here we don't stand alone before our Maker. Here we work together to fulfill our purpose for being. Our work in association is redemptive in its impact.

Many of the social services in your community are likely to be the outgrowth of congregational efforts to respond to human misery and misfortune. Some programs are purely local. Others, like Habitat for Humanity, a church-sponsored program that draws community volunteers in the building or reconstruction of homes for the needy, are spun off from their original sponsors, developing institutional lives of their own. Another example is Mazon, which provides food for the hungry through the voluntary contributions of synagogue members throughout North America.

Such activities often reflect a religious impulse toward compassion that can also be translated into a desire to assume responsibility for the promotion of social justice. In many communities, congregations work together on issues of communitywide concern. The Church and Community Forum is a good example. Affiliated with Greensboro's Urban Ministry, the forum was established by six white churches to inform congregants of the consequences of government budget cuts on children of poor families. The first three educational meetings were targeted to their own members. A fourth session, however, was cosponsored with the Quality of Life and Budget Coalition, an umbrella organization of Greensboro's black congregations and civil rights organizations.

The joint session was followed by other contacts between the two groups, after which the forum urged the Urban Ministry to open a free medical clinic for the indigent. Volunteer nurses, doctors, pharmacists, and social workers from the six white congregations staffed the clinic. Encouraged by their success, congregants from the six mainline churches became active volunteers in several other local human service agencies. In North Carolina, as elsewhere, congregations are stepping into an emerging void occasioned by the shrinking of the welfare state. The religious impulse is clearly at work and is often reinforced by a savvy congregational leadership. The chairperson of an urban ministry in Texas suggests, "In an increasingly secular world, the religious community must find new ways to articulate religious values through civic commitments."

Facts About Congregations

In 1988, the Independent Sector, with grants from the Pew Charitable Trusts and the Lilly Endowment, commissioned a survey of religious congregations in the United States. Study findings were reported by Hodgkinson, Weitzman, and Kirsch (1988). There were an estimated 294,000 religious congregations in the United States, with revenues of approximately $50 billion. After covering their operating expenses, a total of $8.4 billion was left to cover charitable and other activities. Of this amount, $5.5 billion went to denominational charities (e.g., Catholic Charities or Lutheran Social Services), with most of it distributed at the local level; $1.9 million went to other charitable organizations; and $1 billion went directly to individuals in need.

Congregations also allocated 9% of their own operating funds to human services, 6% to health services, 3% to social justice and community development programs, 3% to the arts and culture, and 1.4% to environmental programs. Together (charity dollars and money used for church-conducted social services) this amounted to approximately $10 billion. Of this amount, at least $3 billion was not linked to denominational charities.

The following are a few generalizations you might find interesting:

- Larger congregations report providing more in-kind support to those in need in the form of food, clothing, and housing.
- The more conservative the congregation, the more volunteer involvement. Liberal congregations, however, are more apt to involve their volunteers in interdenominational service.

- Approximately 12% of volunteer hours are devoted to human services activities.

- Nine of 10 congregations make their facilities available to groups of congregants and 6 of 10 also make them available to outside groups.

If congregations contribute so much to human service and other community programs, and promote the habit of giving and volunteering among their congregants, why are relationships between congregations and social service organizations so limited? The problem of worldview aside, given the potential, it is curious that those engaged in the human social services are often less likely to devote time to learning about what congregations do than members of the religious community are to learning about social needs and social services. In Greensboro, the forum invited experts to make presentations on relevant social programs. Initially, there was no parallel effort on the part of the human service organizations to understand the concerns of the religious community. If it had not been for church initiatives, some opportunities to collaborate would have been missed.

Finding Out What Is
Happening in Your Community

Before deciding what kind of assistance or resources you would like to get from local congregations, it would be useful to know what their agendas are. There are many ways to find out, including the following:

- Keep a watchful eye on the press and clip out useful items.
- Get on mailing lists for internal bulletins or newsletters.
- Seek opportunities to work with key ministers and lay leaders via civic associations and problem-solving task groups.
- Ask staff and board members to share their understanding with you.

SAMPLING OF NATIONAL SECTARIAN AND CHURCH ORGANIZATIONS THAT SUPPORT OR COORDINATE LOCAL CONGREGATIONAL GIVING

American Baptist Churches in the USA
Valley Forge, PA

Presbyterian Church
Louisville, KY

Disciples of Christ
Indianapolis, IN

Religious Society of Friends
Richmond, IN

The Episcopal Church
New York, NY

U.S. Catholic Conference
Washington, D.C.

Evangelical Lutheran Church of America
Chicago, IL

United Church of Christ
New York, NY

United Jewish Appeal (UJA)[a]
New York, NY

United Methodist Church
New York, NY

NOTE: Prepared by Douglas Lawson.
a. UJA operates under secular auspices but is the major fund-raising organization of the American Jewish community.

ALL FOR ONE, ONE FOR ALL: MUTUAL BENEFIT AND CIVIC ASSOCIATIONS

All Fired Up

I really wasn't expecting it, but the Burn Prevention Project's first fund-raising effort took place at a fire fighters' annual picnic last May. Fire fighters and their families, other city officials, and interestingly, people who had been helped by the fire department at one time or another were all there. The chief got up and made a speech, then he introduced me. I spoke for about 5 minutes about how we all need to work together and I described some of the serious consequences of burns to individuals and their families. The chief came back to the mike and told everybody about the importance of the work of our project and asked everybody to dig in. I hate to get cute about it, but they were really "fired up." They collected over $500. The firefighters were ecstatic.

When I met with them a few weeks later, they felt proud of themselves, but as one of the guys put it, "We really can do better but we don't know much about fund-raising." That was my opportunity. Together we mapped out a campaign that included the involvement of parent-teacher organizations, the same PTOs with which the fire fighters worked when schools sent children to visit the fire stations in the community. And it included involving burn victims as well as people who had suffered property damage but not bodily harm through fires. It took only about 3 months of organizing to put everything in place. The annual picnic is now seen as a fund-raising event. They are about to start a semiannual letter-writing campaign. The fire fighters' auxiliary has opened up a thrift shop (and would you believe, it got its first major donation from what was left over in a clothing store after a fire).

It turns out that several of the fire fighters were active members of their local Knights of Columbus and Kiwanis chapters. They got their boards to agree to raise money for burn victims. Most of these dollars will probably stay in the community, but some may be directed to supporting some of the institute's activities, at least to purchasing some of our written materials.

This year we expect about $2,500 in gifts from that community, but that is not the entire point. By engaging people in fund-raising efforts, we have actually involved them in a process of consciousness-raising. I've spent about 20 working days in that community, and I suppose from a fund-raising effort that wouldn't be cost-effective. Not the first time around. But it will get more cost-effective as the community is able to take on more. Experienced with these approaches, we will be able to replicate them in communities throughout the country. We couldn't have found better partners than the fire fighters.

The Kiwanis and the Knights of Columbus are fraternal organizations that take on civic (community-oriented) and charitable tasks. Both are mutual benefit organizations (MBOs). Other examples of MBOs are police benevolent societies, coop groceries and other retail buying groups, friendly societies, self-help groups, unions, and professional associations.

A Bird's Eye View of Mutual Benefit Organizations

Michael O'Neil (1994), in a recent article on the philanthropic dimensions of mutual benefit organizations, notes that it is curious that the 400,000 MBOs in the United States "have been so neglected by the new field of nonprofit sector studies" (p. 71). It is even more curious that they have been virtually ignored in the more established field of fund-raising and in extensive literature on grant seeking. Many of these organizations do fund programs; they provide them with volunteer power, materials, and legitimacy.

Philanthropy, however, is not their primary motivation for existing. Their purposes are to benefit a particular group of people or organizations. Because most of them use other means than sale or trade to distribute goods and services, they are classified as nonprofit organizations. Because they are not primarily charitable organizations, however, they do not qualify for 501c(3) designation under the tax code and are not generally considered part of the independent sector. Nevertheless, in practice, many MBOs make significant charitable contributions to their communities, so much so that in some of their activities they look more like civic organizations (IRS Tax Code designation 501c[6]) than MBOs. For purposes of this book, I will focus primarily on fraternal beneficiary societies (IRS Tax Code designation 501c[8]and[10]) and voluntary employees' benefit societies (IRS Tax Code designation 501c[9]), which are the most likely to be of help to your organization.

As the previous vignette indicates, there are no hard and fast lines between helping members of one's own group and taking on philanthropic tasks that benefit other groups in society. The fire fighters do have a self-interest in getting people to be more safety conscious, but their involvement in fund-raising for the burn center also reflects an altruistic impulse. This broadening of focus is common in all mutual aid associations. It always has been. In America, in the mid-1880s, temperance societies helped their own members stay sober and cared for the spouses and children of alcoholics but also promoted temperance in society at large.

Immigrants in the 1890s formed *landsmanschaften*, a Yiddish term that refers to mutual aid groups of people from the same land or region. Many of these later became affiliated with B'nai B'rith (Sons of the Covenant), which began as a fraternal order but expanded to include educational and other functions. Other religious and ethnic groups formed parallel associations, such as the Scots and the Irish Charitable Societies, the Knights of Columbus (Catholic), Sons of Italy, the Ukrainian Workman's Circle, mutualistas (Mexican Americans), tongs (Chinese) and the many self-help groups of African Americans.

A mix of motivations sometimes infuses energy into these organizations. For example, Kauffman (1992) describes the three paramount values embraced by the Knights of Columbus when it was founded more than 100 years ago: diligence, devotion, and defense. Diligence referred to a commitment to hard work, in effect accepting elements of the Protestant ethic that characterized American society. Devotion represented a kind of practical Catholicism that placed emphasis on good deeds rather than faith or ritual. Defense reflected the need to be on guard against the anti-Catholicism that often characterized American nativism. With their parades and colorful sashes, the early Knights also reflected a cult of masculinity in their sense that they had entered a "brotherhood of man."

Men's groups, such as the Ancient Arabic Order of Nobles of the Mystic Shrine (Shriners), the Elks, Masons, Eagles, Moose, Oddfellows, Foresters, and so on, were eventually transformed from primarily fraternal to a mix of mutual benefit and public benefit (social cause or social service) orientations. Thus, the Kiwanis raise funds for a variety of causes and local social service agencies, the Shriners support their own regional and national hospitals, and so on. The term *fraternal* is used because that is exactly what they once were.

Only men could belong. Because the wives of the men involved also wanted meaningful tasks to perform, most fraternal organizations established women's auxiliaries, some of which moved off in their own directions. KI-Wives, sister groups to Kiwanis chapters, were founded in 1945 (approximately 30 years after Kiwanis International was founded). Thirty years later, many of its members were feeling like second-class citizens—unable to initiate projects and expected to follow the lead taken by the men's group. By the 1990s, the organization had taken on a major restructuring. Today, local chapters tend to operate on a coed basis, with little or no gender distinctions. A different dynamic is at play in B'nai B'rith: In the early 1990s, the women's organization disassociated itself from B'nai B'rith Men, forming their own association with an entirely separate name and identity.

Women have also initiated their own fraternal and civic associations that were never auxiliaries to any other organization. For example, in 1901, the Junior League was established to assist "young women of means in search of moral purpose." They began by raising money for the New York College Settlement, then moved on to take on broader programs of "neighborhood work." Today, Junior League chapters take on projects that deal with AIDS, the homeless, child abuse, mental illness, teen pregnancy, drug and alcohol dependence, and so on. League volunteers are often professional women with considerable education and skill. In other locales, league members raise funds through drives, thrift shops, and other means for a variety of social agencies and charitable organizations.

Members of minority groups and the less affluent did not feel welcome as members of early Junior League chapters, so they formed associations of their own. For example, a Colored Women's League actually preceded the Junior League by 5 years. It later evolved into the National Colored Women's League, which merged with the National Federation of African-American Women to form the National Association of Colored Women's Clubs. Local groups of African Americans provided an organizational base on which agencies and associations such as the Urban League and the National Association for the Advancement of Colored People were built.

The National Association of Negro Business and Professional Women's Clubs sponsors programs aimed at improving social conditions and encouraging self-reliance and self-respect, conducts consumer education and prison reform projects, disseminates information on pending legislation, and engages in advocacy activities. Jewish women's groups formed local councils to take on charitable projects in their communities or to raise funds for women's education and other causes. The National Council of Jewish Women currently has chapters throughout the United States and abroad that take on projects that serve both the Jewish and the general community. These are often aimed at providing openings in the opportunity structure for women of lesser means.

Some Comparable Information
on Civic Associations

Many of the associations that began as MBOs would more appropriately be designated as civic associations whose public rather than mutual assistance purposes are the central feature of their statements of mission. They are indistinguishable from other 501c(3) organizations. Many, such as the Junior League and Council of Jewish Women, were civic associations with bona fide public purposes from the start. The same is true of communitywide civic associations such as Lions and Rotary Clubs that involve professional and business women and men in promoting the public good.

Lions Clubs International perceives its purpose as creating and fostering a "spirit of understanding among peoples of the world." With contributions from hundreds of chapters around the world (including Leo Clubs for young adults), the Lions sponsor "SEE," a global vision program for the sightless. Through its SEE program, it sends specialists to developing countries to perform eye surgery. Its youth corps and youth exchange programs are involved in both learning and doing and in the provision of social, educational, and preventive services.

Many Rotary clubs have even broader missions, including the involvement of the local business sector in projects that promote public or community welfare. They support immunization programs in developing countries, offer scholarships through the Rotary Foundation, and organize exchange programs for volunteers from different countries. Ruritan International's purposes are to foster better understanding between urban and rural people, communities, and businesses. The Ruritan Foundation funds a variety of charitable and educational activities. Local chapters often set their own program goals.

Many of these associations have national bodies that define the mission and purposes of the organization. Policies are set at conventions. Formal structures may be designated to carry on the association's charitable and other programs. Local chapters, however, are often given considerable discretion over which local needs or causes to support—within the confines set by the national organization. Thus, members of a local Lions Club might engage in volunteer work with the homeless or raise funds to support a hospice for victims of AIDS in addition to their efforts to support international programs aimed at the seeing and hearing impaired.

The Best Sources of Names and Addresses of Associations and Their Periodicals

Volume 1 of the *Encyclopedia of Associations*, titled *National Organizations in the United States*, includes entries on more than 23,000 associations. These are grouped alphabetically by subject, and include addresses, key contact persons, brief descriptions of what they do, publications, computerized services, and convention dates and locations. Volume 1 has three parts. The first includes sections on (a) trade, business, and commerce; (b) environmental and agricultural organizations; (c) legal, governmental, public administration, and military; (d) engineering, technical, and natural and social sciences: (e) education; and (f) cultural organizations. Part II deals with (a) social welfare; (b) health and medical; (c) public affairs; (d) fraternal, foreign interest, nationality, and ethicity; (e) religion; (f) veterans, heredity, and patriotism; (g) hobby and avocation; (h) athletics and sports; (i) labor unions, associations, and federations; (j) chambers of commerce and trade and tourism; (k) Greek and non-Greek letter societies; and fan club organizations. Part III includes name and keyword indexes.

Volume 2 of the *Encyclopedia of Associations*, titled *Geographic and Executive Indexes*, provides other ways of accessing the same material. For example, the Geographic Index lists the names of all the associations described in Volume 1 by city and state. It includes addresses, telephone numbers, and surnames of the executives, plus entry numbers given in Volume 1. Volume 3 describes new associations and projects. Volume 4 deals with international organizations.

The *Encyclopedia of Organizations* series also has a seven-volume *Guide to Regional, State and Local Organizations* describing more than 50,000 nonprofit membership organizations such as those described in this chapter.

The *Encyclopedia of Associations* book titled *Association Periodicals* is a descriptive guide to journals, magazines, bulletins, papers, and reports issued serially by associations, societies, institutes, and other nonprofit organizations.

These volumes are available from Gale Research, Inc., Book Tower, Detroit, MI 48226. Gale also provides an updating service between editions.

Working With Associations—Some Instructive Examples

Considering how few human service agencies have ongoing relationships with MBOs and civic associations, and how important these relationships can be to an organization's fiscal and programmatic health, the lack of attention to these relationships is astounding. If your organization is only beginning to consider an "association strategy," consider some of the following ideas.

Get a Grant or Win a Scholarship

If national associations and their local affiliates give grants, find out whether their funding priorities fit your agency's program directions. Even if they do not, if they do fund college scholarship or other grants to individuals, get the information to your constituents or information on your constituents to the associations.

Alonzo Goes to College

Residents in a public housing cooperative in Indiana took a great deal of pride in Alonzo Reed, one of the young men who had grown up in the complex. Although a diligent student, his grades were not quite high enough to win a scholarship to one of the better universities. But he was a wonderful role model for other young boys and girls and the residents' council really wanted him to succeed.

The city's director of public housing knew that a new member of the housing commission had just completed a term as secretary of the local Rotary. After several meetings between the Rotary's scholarship committee and the coop's residents council, it was agreed that each of the community's public could recommend a promising young adult each year for a designated Rotary scholarship (i.e., a study grant).

All That's Fit to Print!

A complex tax initiative had reduced local property taxes but increased state sales taxes as a way of collecting and redistributing public income among poorer school districts. Opponents to the change had warned that state revenues would not be high enough to fund enrichment programs (e.g., music, art, and sports) at their former levels in wealthier communities. They proved correct. In fact, income shortfall led to reduction of educational programs for the developmentally disabled, unwed teen moms, and other special needs populations. It was clear to the Neighborhood Settlement that school-based programs for unwed mothers would be phased out within a year of the changes in the schools revenue structure.

The question was how to get the word out about the program's importance. Newspaper stories never seemed to do much more than make the agency staff feel good, and even a TV show that reported on the agency's effort to deal with neighborhood teen violence had little more effect than a twice-repeated sound bite. They found a partial answer in the *Encyclopedia of Associations: Association Periodicals*. A volunteer committee went through the Yellow Pages identifying all the mutual benefit and civic organizations in the community.

If the volunteers were unfamiliar with an association, they first looked the group up in the *Encyclopedia of Associations*. They made a list of those associations they thought might be supportive, then checked to see if they published newsletters on a regular basis. Calls to 46 associations that had newsletters yielded 40 that agreed to publish brief information pieces on teen moms—if the items were written with the association's interests in mind. Settlement house volunteers worked with members of each association on the wording of each story. Working on wording of each article with association members was, perhaps, as valuable as publishing the information. It created a cadre of people committed to doing something about the income shortage. Eventually, a community coalition was formed, composed of parents and members of civic associations, that advocated retention of special programs that were threatened by the budget shortfalls.

People Power

Most social agencies are chronically short of both cash and personnel. By working with local associations that have common concerns, they are often able to get much of the help they need.

Item: A Kiwanis chapter, working with a local residential center for retarded adults, not only dedicated half the income from their semi-annual recycled goods sale to the developmentally disabled but also involved teens and adults with disabilities in collecting used items, organizing them for the sale, and then staffing the sale itself.

Item: An emerging federation of children's agencies approached the Junior League for help with specific tasks, including fund-raising, proposal writing, preparing promotional materials, computerization, and legal advice. These are all skills league members possess. The problem was that there were too many requests and not enough league members with sufficient time. Solution: build a consortium with other women's civic associations, including some affiliated with religious and ethic groups. Result: a communitywide effort and an opportunity for women's groups to find common agendas.

Item: The Junior League was not in position to fund a playroom for the shelter, but it could organize its volunteers to make phone calls as part of the Whoa-Men's agency annual phoneathon. It did more. It culled more than 2,000 prospective donors from its own database, added them to the phoneathon list, and made sure they all were called.

Getting Association Support

The previous vignettes demonstrate what Michael Seltzer (1987) cites as the benefits of generating support from civic and other associations. They are a potential source of small amounts of money, available on short notice; volunteers, with special skills or who can be organized on your behalf by the organization or both; or useful contacts and referrals to other potential sources of support. They can also be partners in advocacy efforts, promoting needed social change or support for populations your agency may be concerned about. Financially, their involvement is legitimating—by providing evidence of community support that you may be able to use in a proposal for government or foundation funding.

The disadvantages include the extensive time that may be involved for little potential financial payoff, and the potential for disappointment when success involves the support of the many individuals who make up an association. Seltzer (1987) suggests a five-step approach to securing support from associations. Step 1 (discussed previously) is identifying potentially supportive MBOs and civic associations. Step 2, making an initial approach, can be crucial. It may include a phone call or casual (but planned) meeting with some of the association's members you may be familiar with (or that is arranged through a mutual acquaintance). If a more formal follow-up is warranted, move to Step 3—setting up a meeting at which the possibility of a common agenda linking the association's concerns and your organization's is fully explored. Consider having brochures or reports of your agency's programs available or conduct the meeting at one of your agency sites so that association members can see its work in action.

Step 4 includes one or more addresses to the association's membership in which the work of your organization and the way it addresses problems are vividly described. Consider the involvement of a well-known board member or a client representative (e.g., a teen mother who has already shown leadership in her high school group). Follow-up (Step 5) includes clarification of how a collaboration might work, proposing some possible next steps, and thanking the association for its interest.

SUMMARY

Often overlooked by resource-dependent human service organizations and other nonprofits is the support that is potentially available from voluntary associations. These include congregations and other religious organizations, civic associations, and mutual benefit organizations. These associations provide millions of Americans with opportunities to express their compassion for others and to demonstrate their commitments to community betterment and social justice. Collectively, they have the capacity to provide expert and other volunteer services and financial support for programs and causes in which they believe. Like other funders and donors, however, their interests must also be addressed. Associations have their own agendas, but their members may not be aware of how those agendas complement the interests and missions of your organization. The challenge is to build new partnerships in which all parties to the arrangement benefit.

REFERENCES

Hodgkinson, V. A., Weitzman, M. S., & Kirsch, A. D. (1988). *From belief to commitment: The activities and finances of religious congregations in the United States.* Washington, DC: Independent Sector.

Kauffman, C. J. (1992). *Faith and fraternalism, the history of the Knights of Columbus* (2nd ed.). New York: Simon & Schuster.
Macarov, D. (1995). *Social welfare: Structure and practice.* Thousand Oaks, CA: Sage.
O'Neil, M. (1994, Spring). Philanthropic dimension of mutual benefit organizations. *Nonprofit and Voluntary Sector Quarterly, 23*(1), 71-76.
Seltzer, M. (1987). *Securing your organization's future: A complete guide to fundraising strategies* (See Chapter 18). New York: Foundation Center.
Smith, D. H. (in press). *Grassroots associations.* Thousand Oaks, CA: Sage. **Au: update?**

SUGGESTIONS FOR FURTHER READING

Dawson, D. M. (1989). An overview of church resources for social and economic justice. In J. R. Shellow & N. C. Stella (Eds.), *Grant seekers guide* (3rd ed.). Mt. Kisco, NY: Moyer Bell.
Encyclopedia of associations (27th ed.). (1993). Detroit, MI: Dale Research.
Gitterman, A., & Shulman, L. (Eds.). (1994). *Mutual aid groups* (2nd ed.). New York: Columbia University Press.
Hall, P. D. (1990). The history of religious philanthropy in America. In R. Wuthnow, V. A. Hodgkinson, & Associates (Eds.), *Faith and philanthropy in America: Exploring the role of religion in America's voluntary sector.* San Francisco: Jossey-Bass.
Hall, P. D. (1992). *Inventing the nonprofit sector and other essays on philanthropy, voluntarism, and nonprofit organizations.* Baltimore, MD: Johns Hopkins University Press.
Joseph, J. A. (1993). *Black philanthropy: The potential and limits of private generosity in a civil society.* Washington, DC: Association of Black Foundation Executives.
Kordiylo, K. M. (1992). *The literature of the nonprofit sector: A bibliography with abstracts* (Vol. 4). New York: Foundation Center.
Kropotikin, P. (1925). *Mutual aid, a factor in evolution.* New York: Knopf.
Martin, P. (1991). *We serve: A history of the Lions Clubs.* Washington, DC: Regency Gateway.
Shelp, E. (1990. The infrastructure of religious communities; A neglected resource for care of people with AIDS. *American Journal of Public Health, 80*(8), 970-972.
Wineburg, R. J. (1994, Summer). A longitudinal case study of religious congregations in local human services. *Nonprofit and Voluntary Sector Quarterly, 23*(2), 159-169.
Wineburg, R. J., & Wineburg, C. R. (1986). Localization of human services: Using church volunteers to fight the feminization of poverty. *Journal of Volunteer Administration, 4*(3), 1-6.
Wuthnow, R., Hodgkinson, V. A., & Associates. (Eds.). (1990). *Faith and philanthropy in America: Exploring the role of religion in America's voluntary sector.* San Francisco: Jossey-Bass.

9

Noncash Support

Generating Gifts-in-Kind

The Art of Transforming
(Play)Dough Into Bread

I used to think I knew how to manipulate in-kind contributions. When a federal agency required a 25% match in a grant application, I always found some way to use in-kinds to generate the needed resources. For example, I would show the dollar value of volunteer time on the personnel lines. Once an auto dealership leased us a van for a dollar a year to transport kids with disabilities, and we simply calculated what it would have cost to rent a similar vehicle on the open market. I was also able to show what it might have cost to rent the conference facilities another agency was "lending" us. The $2,200 saved was reflected on the budget as an in-kind contribution. I saw all this as using a kind of play money—like Monopoly dollars—which did not really cost us anything. I guess you could say it was like turning play dough into real bread!

Self-congratulatory as it may have been, this administrator's inventiveness was limited. Contrast her experience with the following vignette.

Building Service Programs
on Noncash Contributions

When money really began drying up in the mid-1990s, we realized that dependence on grants and contracts from government agencies, foundation funds, and even cash donations from wealthy contributors was just insufficient. For years, we had been using noncash gifts as matching funds in grant applications or to supplement other funds. But today we find ourselves relying on noncash contributions—like legal services donated by board members and other supporters, promotional materials designed by members of a marketing firm, to do our everyday business. In-kinds have become primary rather than supplementary sources of income for us.

Look, we may have a bit more choice if someone gives us a grant of $10,000 to buy computers and other office equipment instead of donating the equipment. But last year we got a gift of 10 2-year-old 486 computers. Sure they were a bit slower than new Pentiums. But the firm that donated them to us threw in some printers, lots of software, and about $20,000 in consultation on how to set up our new client tracking system.

Both vignettes are from the same person, but they were made almost 20 years apart. The funding environment has changed greatly since the late 1970s; so have effective fund-raising strategies. Consider the following example.

A Music Camp in Israel

When Mary-Jane first contacted the Israel Association of Community Centers with an offer from a Chicago instrument manufacturer to send us 100 flutes, frankly we didn't know what to do. How would we distribute them around the country? Who would we use them for? I won't go through the whole process by which we discussed the options with center directors and a group of Chicago philanthropists. But what I can tell you is that the original offer led to creation of a national music camp that draws kids from rural communities and poor neighborhoods throughout the country. The program is now supported by donors from overseas as well as by the Ministry of Education and local municipalities. It collaborates with national music camps in other parts of the world. Among our graduates are a number of world-class musicians, and we've contributed to the culture of music in Israel.

In previous chapters, I alluded to the substitution of noncash gifts for monetary awards. In this chapter, I will go beyond the use of in-kinds as matching funds to explore a more comprehensive strategy that includes substitution of noncash for cash contributions or their transformation into cash or both. This chapter also examines the tax implications of noncash gifts for both the nonprofit organization and the donor.

NONCASH GIFTS: BETTER THAN CASH?

I will not go so far as to suggest that noncash gifts are better than cash, but in some circumstances they can actually be more productive. The Israeli music camp may be exceptional, but it is an exception that proves the rule. Noncash gifts can be divided into the following categories: (a) equipment, supplies, and facilities for current use or resale; (b) services and advice; and (c) those intended to generate new resources over time. Some are likely to be outright gifts, whereas others may be loans.

The Hard Core: Equipment and Supplies

Although nonprofits often accept donations of equipment and supplies by individuals on an ad hoc basis, such gifts are often more trouble than they are worth. For example, consider the gift of a pool table by a community member to a youth center. It may need to be transported to the center and its felt top repaired—two costs that the center may not be able to absorb. It may require staff monitoring during use and take up space needed for other activities. When given by an important supporter, such gifts can force the agency into a program or service it is not interested in.

Seasoned administrators know that out-of-the-ordinary events are often disruptive, in particular if there are no procedures for dealing with them. The Israeli Community Centers Association was able to respond positively because the organization had a history of dealing with cash shortages by turning commitment and interest into new programs. When the solicitation and use of noncash gifts becomes routinized, it also can become a major component of an organization's overall approach to generating support for its programs and operations.

The following are a few examples of donated items that can be used in lieu of cash by an agency that would have to purchase them:

Item(s)	*Benefit of Donation to the Donor*
Sports equipment donated by an athletic goods store at the end of the season	Saves trouble of recycling through a discount store, netting very little income
386 or 486 computers given by a firm upgrading its equipment	The used items were worth almost nothing on the resale market but a great deal in terms of tax write-offs
Office supplies by a local distributor	Good community relations
Lighting equipment by a manufacturing plant that had had an order canceled	Storing the equipment in anticipation of a new order would have been more costly than giving it away

A nonprofit might also accept gifts-in-kind for which it has no use other than for barter or resale. Examples include

- desserts donated by local restaurants for the annual "chocolate extravaganza" fund-raising event;
- used household items or clothing for the "friends of . . ." thrift shop;
- unneeded office equipment that the agency swaps with another agency for needed goods and services.

Some school districts have established warehouses for the storage and exchange of equipment between schools, creating a kind of scrip that establishes a value for deposits and withdrawals. Similar arrangements might also be possible for other nonprofit organizations.

Another option is to reduce costs to the organization by securing loans or low-cost leases of equipment and facilities. Examples include

- the lease of a van for $1 a year to transport senior citizens to heath care and other services;
- allowing the family service agency to use a neighborhood congregation's recreation facilities for a day care center;
- the "loan" of a brokerage firm's offices on a Sunday, when they are not normally in use, for an agency's phone-athon, its annual telephone solicitation campaign.

A current donation can also reduce the subsequent cost of purchasing supplies. For example, the purchasing officer of the corporation that donated $10,000 worth of used computers took an interest in the recipient's operations. Soon, he began to include the agency's needs when ordering new computer programs and office supplies. The agency had to pay for its purchases but was able to do so at reduced cost because of the corporation's saving through bulk buying. Similar savings are possible by piggybacking on a corporation's reduced travel costs, special hotel rates, and so on.

Organizations can also increase the value of their dollars by buying supplies together with other like agencies. For example, it is not unusual for churches affiliated with the same denomination to buy supplies together. This saves money and staff time and makes it easier for the distributor, from whom office supplies are purchased, to identify "good deals" or to anticipate seasonal needs. Increasingly, agencies serving similar populations, such as homes for the aged or mental health agencies, will do some joint purchasing. This may not be the same as soliciting in-kind contributions, but it is an example of the kinds of ideas that may be generated when you begin to think in noncash terms.

Services in Lieu of Dollars

Perhaps no area of giving has been as poorly documented as the donation of services. It is as if the value of consultation on office procedures or assistance with tax matters has less value than a donated computer. Some organizations, however, report that getting help in the form of volunteer service has almost unlimited potential. All too often, this is also an untapped potential. The following is a brief sampling of possibilities:

- consultation on job motivation and satisfaction and other personnel matters;
- managing an organization promotional campaign;
- layout, printing, and distribution of brochures and reports;
- accounting and other financial services and advice;
- legal or tax services and advice;
- management of annual campaigns or special fund-raising events;
- conference and meeting planning (which might complement donated facilities);
- recruitment and training of volunteers;
- Check writing, word processing, or other computerized services.

Somewhere in between equipment and supplies and services are

- piggyback advertising and no-cost advertising production;
- printing and duplication services;
- telecommunications services;
- providing contacts with or access to additional sources of supply.

Resource-Generating Resources

Some gifts can be used to generate current and future income through lease or sale. These could include

- artwork and collectibles intended for display (in museums, libraries, or in agency lobbies) or for sale;
- land and other real property, such as buildings and recreation sites, that may be used to house agency programs and to generate income from rentals;
- bonds, stocks, or other financial instruments that generate income or that can be sold to others;
- insurance on property (e.g., theft and fire), personnel (e.g., life and health), or performance (e.g., malpractice) that can reduce current agency cost or protect it against loss.

Better Than Cash?

Are any of these as good as or better than cash? Truth be told, cash is cleaner and neater. Some noncash contributions, however, such as the music camp, can lead to whole new programs. Others lead to major cost saving because they come with volunteer help. Noncash contributions often increase your range of contacts within the community and the likelihood that others—such as volunteers from the Urban Ministry or a consortium of corporations—will become committed to your organization or its cause. For example, several of the firms associated with San Francisco's 2% Club were challenged, a few years ago, by several big givers to increase their gifts to 5%. Most could not, but several were able to make noncash contributions.

"When execs from the banks, real estate firms, and building companies started volunteering their time with us," reported a settlement house worker involved in one of Cleveland's Empowerment Zone Villages, "we really began to feel that they meant it. Talk about empowerment! If the big guys cared about what we were doing, we felt that we must be doing something good. The effect on our morale was instantaneous, and spilled over to the residents of the community. Somebody cared, not just by throwing some dollars at us, but by putting in the time to help us figure out how we could do our work better and to think creatively about what we should be doing."

"We got more than we gave," the director of a Cleveland savings and loan institution reported. "Bankers tend to have very narrow vision. We're always thinking about risk in terms of collateral or growth potential. We too often miss the human factor in our dollars-and-cents equations. Empowered neighborhoods are safe neighborhoods, neighborhoods that people take pride in. That may sound like bull. It's not. But it wasn't until I left my desk on the 15th floor and began volunteering with the neighborhood finance committee that I really understood what this is all about. The satisfaction I experience from seeing this community begin to turn itself around and the appreciation I gained for the hard work done by the social workers who had been here before us—well, it's been an eye opener.

Like all other gifts, consider what the funder or donor is interested in—even if the donor is not yet certain of what that may be.

TAX AND LEGAL IMPLICATIONS OF
ACQUIRING OR DONATING GIFTS-IN-KIND

From the donor's perspective, there may be a number of advantages to donating gifts-in-kind instead of cash contributions. There may also be some special benefits to receiving them. Nevertheless, there are also some potential tax and legal pitfalls to both parties. Some of the tax issues are examined first, and then some legal concerns will be discussed. Finally, I will identify some typical questions of valuation (how to assess the gift's true value).

Tax Issues

Like cash contributions, gifts-in-kind may also serve as a deduction at both the federal and state levels and in some states may actually reduce tax liability directly through a tax credit. For example, in Michigan, a gift to a state institution (e.g., a university or one of its services such as a public radio station, service program for the elderly conducted by one of its units, or a charter school) can reduce tax liability by allowing the donor to take 50% of the gift's value as a tax credit up to a total of $400 in cash or in-kind (i.e., a $400 gift to a state institution reduces an individual's state tax by $200). Whether the gift becomes a deduction or a credit, the donor will have to clearly document the value of donated items.

The value of rent or service (potentially important to the recipient organization) may not be deducted. Donors, however, may deduct costs associated with providing a service (e.g., transportation or phone) and those expenses associated with managing property that is lent to an organization (e.g., cleaning and maintenance). Careful records must be kept, however, and such deductions are often subject to close scrutiny by the Internal Revenue Service (IRS). A donor might be do better, tax-wise, by renting the property and donating the proceeds or by donating the property itself.

To be deductible, property transfers must be, according to the IRS, "complete, voluntary and purposeful." A transfer that results from a misunderstanding or that is made under duress is not considered, for tax purposes, to be a gift. A partial or revocable gift, or one in which the donor retains some retainer rights, is not considered complete. To understand the reasons for this, consider a donor who wants to make a cash contribution to a charity. Suppose the donor fills out a pledge card, signifying his or her intent to donate a sum of money and dates it. You may feel that your organization can "bank on" the pledge because the donor has signed a kind of contractual obligation. The donor may, in fact, be legally responsible to make good on the pledge, but from the tax authority's perspective it is not a bona fide deduction because it is not clear that the charity can enforce payment. Just as a cash gift does not become a taxable deduction until it is actually transferred to the charity, a gift of property is not tax exempt until it is wholly transferred. For those items that must normally be registered or recorded with some official body—for example, a car or a house—no transfer will be considered to have occurred (for tax purposes) until the deed has been transferred.

Repeat: The property is not considered a gift, for tax purposes, if the donor indicates intent to transfer the property at some future time (e.g., paying a pledge over several years). The title, not just the vehicle or the keys to the house, must be handed over to the nonprofit. The transfer must be irrevocable and it may not have conditions imposed on it. For example, if a van, which was donated for purposes of transporting seniors to a day care center (the donor's intent), could be repossessed by the donor because he was unhappy that it was also used to transport children to day camp, the tax authorities would not consider this a complete and irrevocable transfer. Nor would the IRS consider the transfer complete if the former owner stipulated that she or he wanted it back when the agency has sufficient funds to buy another van or simply wanted to "borrow it back" during the summer months to use for the family's camping trips. There a few exceptions to this rule—for example, when

- the donor is a partial owner of the property (in which case, he or she must sign over all of his or her share);
- the gift is a home in which the donor continues to reside;
- the gift is for bona fide conservation purposes (in which case, those purposes may be stated in a set of rules governing the property's use);
- a trust is involved.

The value of the gift must be greater than that of any premium or inducement given by the charity in return for it. For example, a public TV station may use a T-shirt or coffee mug as a premium (inducement) to donors of given amounts, but the inducement must be valued at less than full consideration. The same is true of noncash gifts. Thus, if the public relations value of a gift to a charity is greater than the value of a business' gift on the open market, the gift may not be tax deductible.

Legal and Other Issues

There are also a number of legal and valuation concerns to consider when giving or accepting noncash gifts. For example, in community property states, it is presumed that any property bought during a marriage is owned equally by both spouses. Thus, for example, in California or Texas, a married person may only be able to donate one-half of the property owned in common.

Because some properties (e.g., homes or cars) are bought on credit, ownership may not rest 100% with the donor. Moreover, when a piece of property has a lien on it, or has appreciated over the years, the transfer may require some complex tax calculations. In the end, it may cost the potential donor and potential recipient too much to warrant the exchange. Consider the following example: A piece of lakefront property, appraised at $1 million, was to be donated by a married couple who were partners in a small manufacturing firm. Because they both really cared about inner-city kids, they wished to donate it to an agency whose primary program is the conduct of summer wilderness adventure trips for teens. Both spouses agreed to make the gift, so community property, a consideration in this state, is a nonissue.

Moreover, this is a gift that a member of the agency's board has been cultivating for some time but without a great deal of consultation with the agency's executive or discussion with other board members. The property is on the west side of the lake where state conservation authorities had declared the property to include protected wetlands, meaning that it would be OK for camping and hiking but not for extensive development. On his successful solicitation, the board member reported with pride, "This will always be a protected site."

To his personal embarrassment, the agency's board turned down the gift. There were two primary reasons. First, although the property was very attractive, no one on the staff or on the board was prepared to become involved in property management and development.

Second, accepting the gift for the purposes it was to be given would have had implications for the nature of the agency's camping programs (making them site based rather than travel based) that it was not ready to consider. Although some staff and board members saw in the gift an opportunity to increase its range of services, the overwhelming sentiment was that the gift would be diversionary. The agency's director explained later to the prospective donors, "We're a wilderness camp, and while we appreciate your generosity, much of the lake's shorefront is already too developed. With so many other people living along the shore, it is not a true wilderness area."

A year after the offer was made, the owners of the property discovered that a previous owner had permitted dumping of industrial wastes on the site. The dumping had occurred in an area not easily accessed. In fact, the only access was a road long unused and hidden by underbrush. When the waterfowl nesting in the area began to show signs of genetic poisoning, however, the Environmental Protection Agency investigated. The owners soon found themselves embroiled in a legal battle over responsibility for toxic waste cleanup. Had the charity accepted the gift when tendered, it might have been saddled with all or some of the financial responsibility for cleanup.

Nelson and Schneiter (1991) warn nonprofits that all that glitters is not gold. They offer several tips for separating the bad gifts from the good. They suggest asking tough questions of the prospective donors, such as the following:

- Have you ever tried to sell this property before?

- Who has clear title to the property?

- Would you consider selling it outright and making a cash contribution instead?

- Has the property been misused (e.g., land or water beneath it polluted or car been in an accident)?

- Does or can the property generate income that will support other agency programs (e.g., a bond portfolio or an apartment building with rental units)?

- Can the property be used in its current state or will it require substantial repair or development?

- Does the donor expect the gift to remain intact or can it be sold in its entirety or in part?

Perhaps even more important is being certain about what your organization can do with the gift, and whether it complements and supports its long-term mission and short-term goals.

CREATING THE CAPACITY FOR ACQUIRING, MANAGING, AND SELLING GIFTS-IN-KIND

Although you need to look out for potential pitfalls, the potential benefits of securing noncash contributions are considerable. In the current funding environment, some agencies would clearly have to close shop or curtail the nature of their business if they had no access to gifts-in-kind. If your organization is both new to this approach to fund-raising and serious about generating gifts-in-kind as a major component of its resource development strategy, however, it will have to engage in some thoughtful preparation and, perhaps, some restructuring. What follows are some tips I have garnered from experienced practitioners who make extensive use of noncash contributions. Look them over. If they do not seem too daunting, try them on for size, and do not worry if they do not quite fit yet. You will grow into them as your noncash strategies grow in size.

CAPACITY-BUILDING IDEAS FOR ACQUIRING GIFTS-IN-KIND

Organize for the Task

A good place to begin is the creation of a task group, composed of staff and board members, to examine the range of noncash gifts the organization has received in the past. Next, generate an inventory, a wish-list so to speak, of the kinds of gifts it might seek in the future. Some organizations may feel that they create such a capacity on their own. Consider the inclusion of representatives of other agencies that you normally do business with—other youth serving programs, group homes, services to the elderly, recreation agencies, cultural arts organizations, and so on.

TIPS FOR TASK GROUPS

Tip 1: Make certain the group has access to advisers who understand the legal and tax implications of noncash gifts, especially if real property is involved.

Tip 2: Get consultation from others who have had experience in generating the kinds of noncash gifts you are interested in.

Tip 3: Be sure to include volunteers who are committed to your organization and its mission and who also know something about the world in which they will be operating on your behalf: corporate officers, heads of other relevant nonprofits, attorneys, certified public accountants, real estate agents, and so on.

Once the task group has been formed,

- expand the original wish-list by also considering what is potentially available;
- determine the criteria you will use to decide which gifts to solicit or accept (e.g., equipment, supplies, property, volunteer time, items and assistance for use, barter, or resale, etc.);
- now set up committees or task groups to (a) solicit gifts and (b) determine whether unsolicited gifts should be accepted.

Gift Recruitment

The recruitment subgroup should gather intelligence on how other similar organizations generate gifts and then establish connections with potential individual and institutional donors. It may be possible to go right to individual meetings with prospects. It may be necessary, however, to take such intermediate steps as conducting parlor meeting with gatekeepers that might lead you to prospective donors. Such gatekeepers might include local real estate brokers or corporate executives who already meet in a "2% Club" or "5% club" to coordinate and stimulate corporate philanthropy.

Members of the group should share insights on how to spot opportunities in addition to recruiting them. For example, a loss incurred by a potential donor due to a canceled contract for delivery of certain goods or damage caused by a fire or natural disaster could be an opportunity for your organization. The potential donor may need an outlet for their damaged or surplus goods.

Screening, Review, and Acceptance

Screening unsolicited gifts is made a great deal easier (and less political) when there are clearly spelled out legal, tax, and fiscal criteria for their acceptance or rejection. It helps to be clear about a gift's relationship to organizational needs and the possibility that acceptance may lead toward goal displacement rather than achievement. The following is a list of questions that might be asked when a gift is offered.

SCREENING QUESTIONS FOR UNSOLICITED GIFTS

Does the gift substitute for a cash contribution (i.e., reduce need for cash outlay)?

Does the donated asset require expertise to use and do we have such expertise?

Does it require (property) management? Who will do it and at what cost?

Is the net income sufficient to warrant the expense?

What are the tax, legal, or dollar liabilities that we might have to assume? Is there any likelihood that the IRS or state authorities might challenge our interpretations?

Will acceptance of the gift require transportation, repair and maintenance, or storage expenses?

Can title be easily secured within a reasonable time?

May all or part of the gift be sold now or in the future?

Equally important is consideration of how the gift might contribute to achievement of short- and long-range goals and the extent to which it might lead to goal displacement. Sometimes the benefit to the recipient organization will be indirect rather than direct. For example, a grant from a prestigious foundation: It may confer prestige on the program and afford it considerable visibility.

Managing the Resource

The gift-in-kind may require specialized expertise for its management or its use. A van may require a licensed driver who the agency may have to hire if it does not choose to retrain one or more of its staff members. Those staff may not be comfortable in driving the van. It may also be necessary to periodically relicense the van, perform routine maintenance, or find a substitute vehicle when it is in service.

These are minor managerial and programmatic concerns that should be relatively easily accommodated. More complex are issues associated with accepting a gift of computers that may need extensive staff retraining and the availability of software consultants in addition to maintenance. Even more complex is the management of real estate, whether it be a rural, lakefront site with some developmental and toxic waste problems or an urban site with an apartment complex that both serves some of the agency's clients in subsidized housing and brings in revenue by leasing apartments on the open market.

Managing the resource may require expertise that is far removed from the traditional areas of expertise expected of the agency's staff (e.g., counseling, library science, camping, etc.). What may be involved is managing a business, and the business may or may not have anything to do with the agency's traditional business.

REVIEW

Until recently, many administrators and program coordinators assigned little weight to noncash contributions. Grant writers tended to list in-kinds in their budgets as ways to demonstrate cost sharing. They still do, but noncash gifts play a much more central position in nonprofit agencies' overall resource development programs. Some administrators seek donations of noncash contributions to round out or supplement dollar gifts or to make it possible to get more from a donor or donor organization than would be possible if only cash were being solicited. Noncash contributions, however, can be used for much more.

They can be used to generate income or turned into cash through sales and rentals, open up new program opportunities, and link organizations to each other through cooperative arrangements regarding the use or allocation of the resource. They can expand the range of organizations and community groups that support the charity. For these reasons, many nonprofits not only consider noncash gifts as seriously as cash contributions but also set up task groups to recruit, screen, and manage them.

REFERENCE

Nelson, D. T., & Schneiter, P. H. (1991). *Gifts-in-kind.* Rockville, MD: Fund Raising Institute.

SUGGESTIONS FOR FURTHER READING

Baetz, T. (1982, December). Tax planning for sophisticated charitable transfers: The divide between downright do-able and dangerous. *Taxes, 62*(12), 997-1009.
Herrington, B. (1992). In *Financial & Strategic Management for Nonprofit Organizations* (2nd ed.). Englewood Cliffs, NJ: Prentice Hall.
The Internal Revenue service also publishes a wide variety of documents dealing with cash-in-kind gifts, property valuation, revenue procedures, and so on.

10

Up From Apathy

*Generating and Increasing
Gifts From Individuals*

Indignity and Indignation

I had to undergo an abortion a few years ago. Let me put it another
way. I chose to have an abortion. My other children were grown. My
health is not the best. I did not want to take any chances for me or the
baby or put an added strain on our marriage. But the interrogation I
had to go through and the blatantly sexist comments of the attending
physician . . . it created even greater anguish than having made the
decision in the first place. I felt as if I had to defend myself and my
morality.

During the recovery period, I had a great space to think. I thought
about all those young kids who get pregnant without wanting to and
all the poor women who cannot afford to have children or who may
be too inarticulate to defend themselves against someone else's view
of morality. Since then I have contributed each year to Planned Parent-
hood and abortion rights organizations. I want everyone to have the
right to choose and to be protected from misinformation or misguided
advice and from external judgment. I'm not an activist and I don't get

involved in any other way. But I know that the money I am giving will protect someone else from indignity.

Once a Graduate, Always an Alum

For the first couple of years after I graduated, I gave at least $100 a year to my school's alumni association. That doesn't seem like a lot to me now, but it was a lot to me then. Although I was barely earning $100 a week before taxes, I couldn't do less. For four years I had received scholarship money without which I could not have graduated. I wanted other young people to have the same opportunity.

As the years progressed, I gave more; but I got more, too. The alumni association provides all kinds of membership services; a club with swimming and phys ed privileges, low-cost charter trips, and investment advice from those people who handle the university's investment portfolio. The more I got, the more I figured I owed. I began earmarking some of my savings for the university. I guess I got to be tagged a big giver, even though I wasn't as wealthy as others who were also giving a thousand or more. Being considered in the big leagues didn't hurt my law practice.

As an officer in the alumni association, I do more now than just give money. But I keep getting in return. There's a feeling of satisfaction in seeing the university grow, in maintaining my relationships to faculty I had admired and respected as a student, to making new contacts with people I have things in common with as a member of the community and as an attorney.

For Someone Else's Children

My parents didn't have much money, but they did have values. Those values still live through me. My present is really my past. I don't want to live forever. My children are alright financially. But you know, two of them intermarried. If I left them all my money and property, the government would get it anyway. That's why I am bequeathing money to the church. I may have failed in my lifetime, but others can take over after I die.

They are going to name the new overnight campsite for me. Maybe my great-grandchildren will go. They'll know who their great-granddad was and what he believed in. Maybe they will believe in the same things. At least someone else's children will. What's it all for unless you can give a little to future generations?

GIVING IT AWAY THE AMERICAN WAY

The foregoing sentiments are not unique. Voluntary support for causes and organizations has been the American way since immigrants first came to these shores. Cut off from the extended family support systems of their lands of origin, they established *landsmanschaften* and free-loan societies, took on collective responsibilities for widows and orphans, and established institutions to care for the poor, the sick, the disabled, and the otherwise disadvantaged. Often, those already well established in America created specialized services for new immigrants and others in need of assistance. Unlike societies with entrenched nobilities, American giving was quite democratic. Charitable activities permeated social sectors and strata. They still do. As your organization expands its efforts to solicit support directly from individuals, you may be surprised at the untapped reservoir of funds and goodwill that exists in your community.

As competition grows more fierce for public- and voluntary-sector funding, nonprofit organizations are increasingly reliant on gifts from individual donors. As the introductory vignettes show, however, the relationship between donor and recipient is a two-way street. Both have much to gain. In this chapter, I will distinguish between planned giving, annual giving, and a variety of special events and sales approaches to fund-raising. The motivations to give are likely to be somewhat different for each donor as are the rewards for both the donor and recipient organization. In Chapter 11, a number of campaign structures and programs through which money can be raised are discussed.

Why People Give Away Money

There are many reasons for giving. People have a need to do something worthwhile in their lives, to feel that they are contributing to the general welfare, and to see themselves as sharing with or taking responsibility for others. They also have a need to belong and to be associated with others they respect and by whom they wish to be respected. Almost everyone likes to be wanted, to be sought after, and to be a part of instead of apart from a group or association they feel is worthwhile. These motivations are supported by a sense of duty, a desire to pay back, and, not uncommonly, a sense of guilt.

There are also instrumental reasons for giving: advancement of one's career or occupational goals, tax benefits for oneself or one's heirs, and perhaps a desire to be remembered or "immortalized" by contributions to a cause. No gift can make one immortal, but it can extend one's contributions into the future.

Rounding Out Your Fund-Raising Strategy

For some readers, many of the approaches to raising money described in this chapter constitute their organization's primary income sources. That would be true of most community and family foundations, civic associations and mutual benefit organizations (MBOs), churches, and federation endowment funds. Even if most of your funds come through contracts and grants from foundations, united funds, MBOs, civic groups, or public sources, however, raising money from individuals can (and probably should) be an important component of your income strategy.

For some organizations, gifts from individuals make it possible to do things they could not have done otherwise—for example, purchase a new painting for the museum, create camperships for children from poor neighborhoods, or conduct a staff training institute.

For others, income generated from gifts, sales, and other means is used as the matching funds required by many grants or as evidence of community support needed for some contracts. It is quite likely, however, that gifts from individuals will, in the foreseeable future, replace some or all of an organization's income from grants and contracts. This is especially true for many cultural arts and human services agencies that have been accustomed to depending on public and voluntary funds that are increasingly hard to come by. Like other nonprofits severely squeezed by government cutbacks, yours, too, may need to develop strategies for bringing potential donors up from apathy.

New Development

In mid-chapter, we use the term *development* in a limited sense, referring to fund-raising aimed at program development. The term means much more, however, and some of the meanings associated with it may be new to you. Colleges, museums, and other nonprofits who depend heavily on individual donors for support refer to the entire enterprise as development and to the professionals involved in these activities as development officers.

According to Heetland (1992), development officers have two major goals: (a) creating an understanding of the mission, value, and accomplishments of your organization or its cause, and (b) turning that understanding into a commitment of support dollars. There are many ways to do this. Read on.

DEFERRED GIVING

Where There's a Will There's a Way

A tax attorney told me when I was researching this chapter, "There are three things you need to remember. First: 'Where there's a will, there's a way.' Second: 'Most bequeathers have gray hair.' And third: 'Deep down inside, all of us strive after immortality. All the rest is commentary.' " Here comes the commentary.

Perhaps some people do strive after immortality, but others know that their rewards will come from improving the lives of others. They may also be concerned with the future—with those who come after they have gone. They may have a concern with security, not necessarily for themselves but for those who will live in the future. Their concerns may be for the survival of an ethnic group or a cultural inheritance. They may be concerned about the security of others with whom they have identified in the past. Perhaps some are trying to work out a balance in their lives, overcoming a long-buried sense of loss through an act of expurgating guilt.

Not long ago, I asked an elderly woman what had compelled her to make a bequest to an organization with which I am affiliated. She replied,

When I was young, there wasn't a place like this for me, or if there was, I was too self-absorbed to recognize it. But if I were young now, this is the kind of place I would want to come to or have my children attend. And I would volunteer my time as a parent. Well, it's too late for that now, but it is not too late to make a modest gift that would give meaning to others and might even stimulate others to give.

Shades of Johnny Appleseed!

A Talmudic quotation comes to my mind. It comes from a small book observant Jews frequently read on Sabbath afternoons, the *Sayings of the Fathers* (1945, p. 45): "It's not your task to complete the job, nor are you free to desist from it."

People who make bequests often do so because they feel obliged to make a contribution, even if that contribution only begins the process that they will not live to see completed. It is that belief in the future and the desire to contribute to the future that characterizes financial bequests. Perhaps there is in their commitment a share in immortality.

Successful fund-raisers are masters at tapping such motivations. I say "tap" instead of "capitalize on" because I believe that is exactly what the process is all about. There is, in all of us, an untapped reservoir of unselfishness and a desire to do good. Many of us, however, do not know how or where to make our contributions, so we go with the institutions that have proven themselves—those with successful track records.

That is why most bequests tend to go to the more successful institutions. They go to Harvard more rapidly than they go to a smaller, lesser known, and much more needy school in a midwestern state. The mission or purpose of that small college, however, may be much more in keeping with the interests of a prospective bequeather—if he or she only knew of it. It is not necessary for the donor to pass on before the agency benefits from a bequest. A bequest can be made as a life insurance policy, an annuity, or another income-generating investment from which the agency draws now and from which it will receive a larger indemnity or death benefit in the future. A life-income annuity plan can be written for the donor, with the large sum going to your organization at a later time.

These deferred gifts provide tax benefits that may accrue to the donor's estate. The tax laws on estates tend to change frequently. If you plan to embark on a bequest program, consult a tax attorney or an estate planner, perhaps one connected with a bank or trustee organization. Becoming familiar with such people is not a bad idea for other reasons as well. As you get to know them, they will get to know you—and they will be able to advise their clients about the tax and other advantages of bequeathing money to your organization.

The better professional trustees know your organization, its programs, and its missions, the more likely that they will suggest just such a bequest when the time is appropriate. Involve these people as partners in the development of a bequest program.

They may be as anxious to find you, so as to serve their clients better, as you are to find them and their clients. Making a bequest puts one among the community's elite. Facilitating one may be next best. Remember, however, that under current tax laws it is possible to pass or transfer an aggregate of up to $600,000 without having to pay a gift or estate tax. That means you may be focusing on big gifts when it comes to deferred giving.

Planned Giving in
Contrast to Annual Giving

In contrast to annual or one-time gifts that can and often are used for current programs and operations, bequests and other forms of planned giving are deferred to some other time. The gift may be made now, but the transfer of assets or its availability for use is generally put off to the future. For organizations in need of funds today, delaying may not seem like a good idea, but for those that plan to be around tomorrow, deferral may be essential. Some of the reasons for this are discussed in the following paragraphs.

Planned giving is not for everyone. It tends to make sense for only a small number of people—those who

- want to protect their estates and their heirs from excessive taxation;
- are (potentially) committed to your organization, service population, or cause;
- know about deferred giving.

Because planned gifts tend to involve large sums of money or assets worth a great deal, they are not made impulsively.

Planned gifts tend to draw on long-held assets. It may be more difficult to part with something held on to for a long time (e.g., a house or a bank account) than the current income on which annual gifts are generally based. According to Paul Kling (1993), director of planned giving at the University of Richmond, "Planned gifts often involve intensely personal issues such as family inheritance, children and, ultimately, death" (p. 53). That is why they can take a good deal longer to generate than a single meeting or phone call. Development officers describe a long process of setting the stage that can involve establishing rapport with the prospective donor, the prospect's children and other relatives, attorneys and accountants, and other parties. There can also be a prolonged incubation period from the first inquiry to the signing of the papers.

The process is not always predictable. There are many "sure catches" that get away. Sometimes the potential donor wants out because the wrong instrument is being proposed. Kim Klein (1991) describes the following kinds of planned giving instruments:

Bequest: Generally a straight donation from the donor's estate to be paid when the estate is settled.

Charitable gift annuity: A contract between the donor and recipient organization in which the organization agrees to pay a fixed amount to the donor for the rest of his or her life in exchange for the donated property. In a deferred gift annuity, the annuity payments do not begin until the donor reaches a certain age.

Trusts: These tend to fall into four categories.

Pooled income funds operate like mutual funds. One or more donors may decide to pool resources into a fund that is managed by a trustee (which could be one or more of the donors or their agents). During the donors' lifetimes, they receive the income from the fund and pay taxes on it. At the point of death, however, the annual income is transferred to the nonprofit. This tends to work best for relatively small gifts.

Charitable remainder trusts operate like other annuities, except that if the trust does not generate sufficient income to pay the annuity it is not obligated to do more than it can produce in income.

Charitable remainder unitrusts are similar except that the payments to the donor are limited to a percentage of the income generated.

Lead trusts differ from the others in that what is given to the charity is the interest or earnings from a corpus rather than the corpus itself. Klein (1991) describes this as giving the fruit instead of the tree, in contrast with other trusts in which the tree is given and the fruit goes to the donor for life.

One way of moving annual givers up to planned giving is to mention planned giving approaches in all relevant organizational materials and meetings (e.g., annual reports, campaign literature, and board and fund-raising campaign meetings). Every time a planned gift is made, it might be mentioned or listed somewhere so that even those who give only modest gifts, in response to telephone or letter campaigns, become aware of this option.

ANNUAL AND ONE-TIME GIFTS

One-Time Memorial and Special-Occasion Giving

Most deferred gifts generate income after the donor has passed away. The death of a donor can also occasion memorial gifts from friends and family in memory of a deceased loved one. Typically, this occurs through churches and other religious or ethnic associations, but such gifts can be solicited by any organization, including museums, libraries, Y's, and child guidance clinics. Memorial gifts are generally made by members on behalf of members. The members in your organization may include paid staff, volunteers, participants on committees, advisory groups, and boards.

Memorials, however, are only one form of special-occasion giving. Also consider the following:

- weddings and anniversaries;
- christenings, bar mitzvahs, and confirmations;
- hospitalizations or returns from the hospital;
- graduations and promotions;
- special honors;
- arrivals and departures.

While you are considering these excuses to give (or solicit), also consider making it easier for people to honor friends and relatives. Print up cards (e.g., get well, condolences, and congratulations) that members can purchase or pick up from your organization. Include a message inside that indicates that a gift has been made in the recipient's honor to your organization or to a special program the organization sponsors. Indicate something about the organization and what it does. One gift may generate other gifts in the future.

Edifice Complexes

A more focused and well-orchestrated fund-raising effort may be required when the organization needs a new facility or to expand and modify an existing one—for example, offices, a campsite, a chapel, a meeting hall, or an athletic facility. Building fund and other capital improvement campaigns have characteristics of their own. First, they require carefully built plans and timetables. Second, they require considerable consensus on the part of a leadership group that is itself committed to making significant contributions.

There must be consensus regarding what is to be done, how the new structure or facility is to look, and the purposes it is to fulfill. Unlike some other campaigns and gift programs in which individuals can determine the purposes of their contributions or in which the organization makes the determination in relation to evolving needs and opportunities, what is often called a bricks-and-mortar drive requires that the major givers be committed in advance to the characteristics of the final product.

Almost everyone has an idea of what makes a building beautiful or functional. Some members of churches and synagogues and boosters of public buildings such as museums and community centers have been accused of having an edifice complex—that is, of being more interested in the pretentiousness of a new building than in its uses. If a more modest building would not be sufficient motivation to generate community giving, however, there may be something to be said for pretentiousness.

When working on the basic structure of the building—or some program site such as a recreation facility—the bricks-and-mortar campaign committee should also consider landscaping, equipment, and upkeep. It may not be sufficient to raise just enough money to burn the mortgage; it may also be necessary to raise enough to establish a special fund to pay the additional expenditures that the new or modified structure may require. A mortgage may be helpful to start the construction process early, but nonprofit organizations gain no tax advantage from mortgages. The faster the mortgage can be paid off, the less drain there will be on the organization's ongoing operations.

Build upkeep and fuel costs into the building fund-raising target. When fuel prices skyrocketed a few years back, I saw several organizations close at least some of their doors. A new recreation facility, office, or meeting place may not achieve its full potential unless it is well equipped. Consider the purchase of electronic data processing system, items for a physical education plant, art facilities, or other items necessary for the programmatic or administrative functioning of the organization. Many of these items may be donated by individuals or companies that prefer such in-kind donations to cash contributions. The tax advantages are the same, and it may permit givers to upgrade their own equipment. Your organization gets what it needs, even if the items are not new or the most advanced available.

With the exception of upkeep, capital campaigns must be clearly separated from concerns regarding operating budgets or ongoing programs. Unlike the others, capital campaigns are time limited, generally 2 weeks to 4 years in duration. That does not mean that they should be unrelated to programmatic concerns. It does mean that the fund-raising effort should be conducted separately and perhaps aimed at persons who do not currently contribute to other fund-raising efforts. Some people like to have their names or those of family members recognized on the new building or facility. Some will contribute to the Morris Jenkins Wing because they may wish to honor Mr. Jenkins, without any thought of having their own names associated with the facility.

One university, which solicits both big and small givers for its capital campaigns, honors all givers by selling bricks for $100 each and actually lists the contributors of each brick on a plaque located near each building entrance. I heard a student remark, "Hey, did you know your dad's laid a dozen bricks in this building?"

Building Also Means "Developing"

As the nomenclature suggests, development funds and activity support campaigns are aimed at the expansion or development in some depth of an existing program or the establishment of a new program or service. Funds are not raised for ongoing operations but rather for purposes of generating a new approach or reaching a new population. Development funds are generally long term in their orientation. They may be given special names that are easily identifiable and that attract contributions, for example

- The Minority Opportunities Fund;
- The Community Arts Program;
- The Holocaust Memorial Program.

Like capital drives, development funds also require a careful cultivation of various publics long before they are asked to contribute. In addition to individual donors, contributions to development may include business corporations and philanthropic foundations. The appeal to different publics may have to focus on special concerns: school lunches, increasing environmental esthetics, the putting in of playground equipment or park benches, or providing supports to the disabled or the aging.

Unlike bricks-and-mortar campaigns, development campaigns are not one-shot affairs. They are ongoing. When special funds have been raised for one program, new development campaigns may be established. Former donors may be tapped again and new prospects identified. Like other agency programs, development campaigns can be collaboratively sponsored by several nonprofit organizations or by several industrial and civic organizations working in concert on behalf of a single agency.

We Need Your Help Now

Some activities require immediate or emergency support. There may be no need for ongoing development or expansion. Such needs generally are based on organizational responses to predicaments or opportunities presented by the environment. Opportunities can become predicaments. For example, a museum may be offered a once-in-a-lifetime opportunity to purchase a rare work of art, a social agency may find itself the recipient of a professional-quality photo offset system that it has no room to accommodate, or another may be given the opportunity of purchasing the building it has been leasing at terms it can ill afford to pass up.

In the first example, the museum may have to seek special gifts to be able to pay for the work and at the same time not dismantle its budgeted long-range purchasing program. In the second case, the agency may need additional funds to redo part of its facility to accommodate the equipment. In the third example, the agency needs money to make at least a down payment on the facility.

More frequent, in recent years, have been the strains imposed on agency budgets and services by new and, in some cases, temporary consumer demands. In many areas of the country, social agencies, churches, and civic associations have worked independently or collectively on the distribution of food and emergency relief to needy families and individuals. Food banks and shelters were set up to respond to desperate circumstances. These were not perceived to be regular or ongoing services of the sponsoring or coordinating organization; therefore, development funds were not needed. An immediate, and perhaps one time only, infusion of funds in substantial amounts was needed, however.

These funds can be raised from regular givers—persons who may already have been tapped for development, bricks-and-mortar, or ongoing support programs. They may also come from new sources who are turned on by the opportunity or the predicament presented.

Endowments

Before moving on to an examination of sales and special events, I briefly explain endowments. These are funds or income-producing property (real property, stocks and bonds, and so on) contributed for the purpose of supporting a program or service indirectly. Endowment funds are invested. The income from these investments is then allocated to the support of the designated program or service. For example, the endowment of an academic chair may cost the donor $1 million. The income from the investment of those dollars—for example, $100,000 per year—will be used for the faculty person's salary plus supportive services.

Endowments can also be used for summer camp scholarships, special annual events for staff or volunteers, affirmative action programs, promotional campaigns, the purchase of equipment, the support of cultural events, or ongoing agency operations.

SPECIAL, ONGOING, AND ANNUAL EVENTS

This chapter has examined some fund-raising approaches that require a certain level of professionalism and technical sophistication. There are many other approaches to fund-raising that require the investment of creativity, imagination, and sweat equity. These are sometimes called "fund-raisers" or grassroots fund-raising activities. Many organizations employ a wide variety of fund-raising approaches in which support for the organization may be of little concern to the donor. The donor's gift may be more in the way of a purchase than a charitable contribution. The following sections present a few examples, many of which you are probably familiar with.

Treasures From Trash

In addition to soliciting cash, equipment, or supplies for direct use by the organization, your agency may find it profitable to collect or even purchase materials and services for resale. For example, treasure from trash-type sales begin with contributions of used household furniture and family clothing. These are then resold through bazaars, garage sales, white elephant sales, rummage sales, auctions, and organization-run gift shops. Making useful items available at low cost to low-income populations, as do many church or service club thrift shops, is in itself an important service.

Generally, little cash is required to be invested from the sponsor. Considerable investment in time and energy on the part of staff or volunteers is required. Sales events can be destructive to normal agency operations if paid staff are too heavily involved. Volunteers, however, may find bazaars or thrift shops and even yard sales to be rewarding in terms of the social relationships established, the recognition received, and the sense of achievement and accomplishment gained from having completed the work on behalf of others in need. They may benefit as much from these social exchanges as do the consumers of other agency services.

Recognizing this, some agencies purposefully involve clients in such activities. One executive reported, "If the teens wanted to keep using the facilities, we reasoned, they would have to raise some of the funds for rent and renovations. Within six months, they raised half the money needed for a lounge. Senior citizens raised the rest. Would you believe they share its use on different nights? Both groups are now fully committed to the purposes of the agency, and they've gained a new respect for each other."

An agency's primary service may be organized around production and sales. The work of Goodwill Industries and that of other sheltered workshop or home industries programs are good examples.

What Am I Bid?

Items or services donated by corporations, such as a lease or a discount on an automobile, office equipment, or free concert or theater tickets, may be resold by the agency directly or at an auction. Individuals can also donate services to be auctioned off, such as catering a dinner, entertaining at a party, doing someone's income taxes, or typing up to 100 pages without charge.

Art and antique auctions have become increasingly popular over the years. They can be organized around items donated, for which the giver receives a tax benefit, or may include merchandise purchased on consignment. An organization with which I have been associated contracts with a commercial auction gallery each year. It is the organization's responsibility to advertise and attract people to the auction. It is the gallery's responsibility to bring the artwork and to conduct the auction, for which the agency receives 20% of the proceeds.

Purchasers also receive a tax benefit for their purchases and frequently are able to buy items considerably below regular gallery prices. Art auction galleries frequently make their own purchases in large quantities, sometimes early in an artist's career. They also keep overhead low. For this reason, they make money while passing on considerable savings to the consumer. Works of art, antiques, and other collectibles can be certified as genuine by the gallery, thus further inducing the purchase as a sound investment.

Sales Enrich in Other Ways

Works of art, oriental rugs, or valuable handicrafts need not be sold only through auctions. A Boston gallery with which I have worked over the years provides local sponsors with an attractive package that includes artwork selected to reflect the consumer's interest and pocketbook. The sponsor receives a complete kit of instructions for the opening night. It includes a slide show about the exhibit, instructions for conducting a wine and cheese party, and flyers and announcements for distribution prior to the opening describing in pictures and words many of the items to be offered for sale. Sample press releases are also included.

The sale items arrive with instructions for display and for repackaging and shipping to the next destination. Costs can be covered in advance through the sale of an ad book or recruitment of sponsors who, through gifts of $25 to $50, are listed on the program or invitation to the sale. This initial gift can be applied toward the purchase of any item in the exhibit. Thus, the donor has the satisfaction of sponsoring the exhibit, receives recognition for his or her contribution, is assured a discount at the sale, and, of course, acquires a tax benefit. The sponsoring agency sees this not only as a fund-raising event but also as a cultural and educational service to the community.

Get It at a Discount

Discount days can be arranged through local merchants with very little time and effort on the part of the recipient organization. It is not uncommon for large food chains to provide charitable organizations with opportunities to make charitable contributions. The organization's members, on presenting the cashier with a coupon, can have 5% of their total purchase allocated to the organization. Information on the organization, along with discount coupons, may be made available at the door. Clothing, hardware, book, and record stores may also be induced to allocate 5% or 10% of sales in any given day, week, or month to a charitable organization or cause.

What kinds of arrangements are possible in your community? Should such arrangements be negotiated on a store-by-store basis or might it make more sense to involve members of the downtown merchants' association or shopping mall associates in planning such an event?

Discount books that provide the purchaser with reduced prices for dinners, movies, or merchandise are popular with merchants and individual purchasers, both of whom expect financial benefit and possibly a tax benefit. Ad books, which may include coupons, provide similar benefits to the donors. They can be given away at a special event or sold like discount books.

Reaching the Stay-at-Home

Why not try aiming sales at people who remain at home? For example, Hadassah, a Jewish women's organization, sponsors a lox box as an annual event in many American communities. People who purchase the box in advance are assured delivery on a given Sunday morning of a breakfast box that includes lox, cream cheese, bagels, and coffee cake. The activity not only energizers the organization's members and other volunteers but also makes all the participants feel that they are engaged in the communitywide event without ever having to leave their homes. Besides, it tastes good! Jewish organizations and other religious groups have frequently used a *pushke*, or home contribution box, in which family members deposit loose change. The box is collected at specific dates and the family involved is often provided with a certificate or a gift of some modest value in return for its contributions.

Getting Them Out Again

Overcoming Shame

The walkathon for Tay-Sachs disease netted about $9,000 last year. That may not be a tremendous amount, but the money was not the only thing we were after. The money was to set up a 1-week Tay-Sachs screening clinic. But there is not much sense in providing a clinic if no one is going to come, and this could be the case if people are unaware that they might be carriers. That is what the walkathon was mostly for. It educated the public, heightened awareness, and reduced whatever shame might be associated with coming to the clinic to be tested. It did just the opposite. It made people ashamed if they didn't come.

Most of us have participated in, paid for, or witnessed other marathons: walkathons, bikeathons, jogathons, even crawlathons. We have participated in other fund-raising events in which we received an immediate benefit for our contributions. Examples include the following:

- campaign dinners;
- barn dances and balls;
- hay rides;
- mystery bus rides;
- theater or concert parties;
- carnivals;
- fun nights.

We have also paid out some money in hopes of getting some back on bingo nights or Las Vegas weekends (in our hometowns). Some of these special events may occur on a one-time-only basis. Others will be held as annual events.

These special events do not just run themselves. They require carefully thought-out objectives and highly motivated participants who are ready to raise a targeted amount of money because of a shared sense of commitment. The activity may be seen as primarily fund-raising in its orientation, but it may have other, even more significant objectives. The walkathon for Tay-Sachs disease and the involvement of the fire fighters discussed in Chapter 8 were both aimed at raising the public's critical consciousness and altering behavior patterns.

Teaching Children to Be Philanthropists—
The Common Cents Way

Common Cents, a program in which children collect pennies—millions and millions of them—was born in a synagogue program and was adopted in 1992 by the New York Public Schools in response to Hurricane Andrew's devastating effect on the eastern seaboard. In 1996, 2 years after Chancellor Ramon Cortes invited Common Cents to expand further, 600,000 children in 540 New York public and 20 private schools were reclaiming more than a quarter of a million dollars in pennies. Penny harvesters, as they call themselves, leave cans at grocery checkouts and small bags at neighbors' apartment doors asking them to collect pennies and bring them to the harvester whenever it is full. In each class, or in schoolwide committees, harvesters sort and rebag the pennies. Thirty-pound sacks are worth $50.

Harvesters do more than collect and count. In their classrooms, children discuss the needs to which their dollars and cents will be allocated. Schoolwide Common Cents Roundtables in elementary and middle schools have budgets of at least $1,000 through which they can finance projects in their own schools or in neighborhood agencies that service children. Gary Pretzfielder, a 5th-grade teacher at the Rodolph Shalom School, reported, "We have conversations about what causes homelessness, about prejudice, and how money and commitment can make a difference. At the same time, we're dealing with some pretty basic math questions too . . . and we're working on communication skills as kids make arguments for particular projects and try to agree on priorities."

A citywide teen roundtable manages the Student Community Action Fund (SCAF). SCAF meets weekly, allocating grants of up to $19,000 for specific programs to local agencies. An adult community roundtable, made up of adults from all sections of the city and all walks of life, oversees the program and sets policy directions for it. For more information, write to Common Cents New York, 104 W. 88th Street, New York, NY 10024.

SUMMARY

There are a number of reasons why people contribute to organizations and charitable causes. These include a desire to belong and to be recognized and to be needed; commitment to an idea, a cause, or a group in need; the tax or other economic benefits that may accompany a contribution; the services received or goods purchased through a contribution; and a desire for personal immortality or for the continuance of a group, an idea, or a cause.

REFERENCES

Heetland, D. (1992, September). How to build a major gifts program. *Fund Raising Management, 21*(7), 54-57.

Klein, K. (1991, October). Beyond the bequest: Other kinds of planned giving. *Grassroots Fundraising Journal,* 3-8.

Kling, P. F. (1993). Planned giving and annual giving can cooperate. *Fund Raising Management, 22*(12), 53-54.

Sayings of the fathers. (1945). J. H. Hertz (Trans.). New York: Behrman House.

SUGGESTIONS FOR FURTHER READING

Resource centers from which you can get suggestions for further reading are provided in Chapter 11.

III

Fund-Raising Fundamentals

11

On the Campaign Trail

Conducting and Managing Campaigns

Military, Political, and
Fund-Raising Campaigns

I suppose the campaign organization is a little like a military organization. Maybe that's why it is called a "campaign." But in the military you can coerce people to do what you want. In a fund-raising campaign you don't threaten and you don't coerce. But you motivate aplenty! People have to believe in what they are fighting for. And they've got to be rewarded and recognized just like a foot soldier. Everybody has to feel like his or her contribution counts. If the solicitors and the planners don't, how are they gonna get the donors to feel that way?

A fund-raising campaign is no different from a political campaign. You need both a strong structure and an attractive product. Without these, there's no way you're going to get the commitments you need in order to succeed. Campaigning is hard business. If you're playing to win, you have to play hard.

Both of these quotes are from experienced professional fundraisers who have developed reputations for success. Both stress the nature of the organization of the fund-raising effort. Fund-raising campaigns are the focus of this chapter, specifically those aimed at increasing endowment funds, generating bequests, or supporting ongoing activities or new developments.

BUILDING THE CAMPAIGN STRUCTURE

No campaign is likely to meet its target unless it has one and unless it has the resources to accomplish its goal. In the first part of this chapter, I will focus attention on how campaigns are organized. Equal attention is given to what motivates both the solicitor and the donor. In the second half, I will turn attention to what I think are win strategies for common forms of campaigns—those conducted by mail and on the telephone. I conclude by examining the relationships between these and other fund-raising approaches and suggest one new medium for the twenty-first century—the Internet.

From the Horse's Mouth

First, I want to share some additional quotes with you. Like many others in this volume, they come from experienced fund-raisers, some who work at the grassroots level and others who work with the community's elite. They are stated as practice principles. Look them over. How do they articulate with your own sense of good (and ethical) fund-raising?

> To win at horse racing, you not only need horses that can run, you have to have that will run. It's the same with solicitors and donors. They've got to have the motivation, or they won't contribute to their utmost.

> Don't build a campaign around the hope of finding a sugar daddy who will bail the organization out. Broaden the base of the fund-raising effort to include large, medium, and small givers.

> Some people just want to give gifts and be left alone. But most want to know that others like themselves are also involved, and they want others to know they are involved. Develop a network of givers. Let them relate to each other and encourage each other to contribute more.

Let donors know that they and their contributions are needed. But don't build a fund-raising effort exclusively on guilt. Involve people in the sharing of the responsibility.

Treat all donors as prospects, but recognize that all prospects are not necessarily donors. Just because someone contributed money or other goods in previous years does not mean that he or she is going to be willing to contribute this year.

Contributors rarely reach their maximums. Most people can give more and/or can be induced to solicit others.

Don't ignore persons who have been irritated by a solicitation or by-pass those who refuse to contribute at this time. Build on their concerns, establish relationships, and cultivate them for the next round.

Although campaigns and events may be seasonal, fund-raising strategies should be planned the year round. They should be articulated not only with the organization's service programs, but also with its supportive public relations and community education activities.

Reward those who are involved in the fund-raising effort. Although involvement itself may be a reward, the benefits of participation may be insufficient to overcome the costs in time and emotional energy. Recognition is the best reward. Show people you care because they care. And always thank people for whatever they do, big or small.

Boost, don't boast. Involve people in the cause; a concern for a population in need; a commitment to a service program. Don't push yourself or your organization.

Keep these quotes in mind as you read this chapter and begin the planning of a campaign or other fund-raising activities.

Designing the Campaign:
Some Preliminary Considerations

It is not enough to decide to run a fund-raising campaign or even to decide on the kind of campaign it is to be—bricks-and-mortar, developmental, and so on. Each campaign must have clearly defined goals. Before beginning the campaign, do some preliminary idea inventorying with others whose involvement is crucial to the campaign's success. Begin by examining the goals of the campaign. Are they to raise money and nothing more, or do they also include energizing one or more of the organization's publics, increasing public awareness, or building a cadre of volunteers who might become involved in other aspects of the agency's program? How are these goals to be translated into operational objectives?

Goals and objectives should be clarified by key members of the organization's staff in collaboration with lay leaders who have a stake in the organization and who may be required to take primary responsibility for aspects of the campaign. Put the goals on paper. Determine which ones are compatible and which ones may divert energies from other organizational commitments. Assume, for the moment, that the major goal is to raise money for the organization. How much money? What is your target goal in terms of dollars? Is that sum to be reached this year or is the target to be reached over a 2-, 3-, or 5-year period?

Who is to be involved in the campaign process—which lay leaders and which of the agency's paid staff? Should outsiders, experts in fund-raising, be involved in campaign planning and management? Which publics are to be targeted for involvement as solicitors and as donors? Look at your completed matrix exercise from Chapter 2. Have all the appropriate publics been identified? Consider the following:

- geographic scope: neighborhood, community, state, and national;
- demographic characteristics of givers: age, gender, income level or employment, social position, education, race, ethnicity, and religion;
- functional characteristics: alumni (or former users of agency services), persons with problems in common (e.g., hemophiliacs or parents of children with developmental disabilities), and professional interests (lawyers, physicians, retired business people, etc.);
- psychographic characteristics: sense of identity or belonging, energy, and prestige.

Once you have made preliminary decisions on these issues, it is time to begin designing and building your campaign structure.

How a Campaign Structure Might Look

Most campaigns have a number of structural elements in common. Although no two campaigns are structurally identical, what follows is a description of a structure and a process that are relatively representative. For example, most have a campaign cabinet that operates independently of the sponsoring organization or the agency that is to benefit from the campaign's fund-raising efforts. A general chairperson will work with a small steering committee, often made up of the chairs of the cabinet's subcommittees or task forces. Typically, task forces may be assigned to

1. Solicitation of initial or special gifts
2. General solicitation
3. Prospect development
4. Public relations
5. Various administrative functions

Experienced campaign managers suggest that 20% to 25% of the funds to be raised during a given year be solicited from a pacesetter group during the early phases of the campaign, perhaps even before it has been officially kicked off. These funds are referred to as initial gifts. It is the responsibility of the initial or special gifts group to solicit persons who have regularly pledged the largest sums in previous years. Special gifts can continue to be solicited from individuals or business firms throughout the campaign.

Pacesetters need not be the wealthiest members of the community. They must, however, have confidence in both the persons soliciting and the organization if they are to be willing to put their money on the line. They must believe that the funds contributed will achieve what the organization has promised and that other donors will be induced by their examples to contribute sufficient sums to reach the targeted goal. Like all donors, pacesetters may require some recognition for their contributions. Although some prefer to remain anonymous, others may appreciate having their names appear on campaign stationery. This has the added strategic value of legitimizing the organization in the eyes of new or potential donors.

The general solicitation committee will aim its efforts at these other donors—those who give medium- and smaller-sized gifts. Depending on the scope of the campaign, the general solicitation committee may be divided further into a number of groups, each with its own captain. These groups may be organized around different categories of publics—for example, corporations, individuals who give medium-sized gifts, and so on—or they may be organized around peer groups—for example, doctors, lawyers, other professionals, small business owners, corporate executives, homemakers, and so on.

Households may be divided geographically by neighborhood or by size or they may be divided according to certain characteristics along ethnic and religious lines. A special category may include former consumers of an agency's services, such as families that have adopted children, persons who have used a hospital's services, parents of young men and women at a university, or alumni. Review the geographic, demographic, functional, or psychographic characteristics previously discussed when determining how general solicitations should be targeted.

The prospects committee locates individuals who should be added to the list of those to be solicited. A good way to begin a prospect list is to ask for names from board and committee members of the organization, current and former givers, former recipients of service, even agency partners. You may recall the story from Chapter 8 of the fire fighters who were close to parents of schoolchildren who had visited the fire station. Would campaign literature distributed by the fire fighters generate a parents' list from which the burn center could use to solicit donations? Lists require continual updating as new prospects are identified. Names may be coded according to size of gift anticipated and the history of the prospective donor's relationship to the agency.

The public relations committee is not concerned with fund-raising, per se, but with setting the scene for effective fund-raising. It may issue periodic press releases, arrange for feature newspaper articles, and work with the radio and local television people interpreting the campaign and the services it is intended to finance. Typical public relations activities include arranging for the following:

- orchestrated letter-writing campaigns to the local newspaper;
- printed handouts, posters, bulletins, and the like;
- special articles or features for the general press or the house organs of business corporations, unions, churches, and civic associations;
- displays in public places such as shopping centers and concert halls;
- speakers who present information to community groups prior to their solicitation.

The necessary supportive services without which the campaign could not proceed are provided by an administration committee that might be assigned to recruiting and training solicitors, auditing, clerical assistance, preparation of reports on the campaign, or monitoring the campaign structure and the activities of its component units.

MANAGING THE CAMPAIGN

People Who Make the Campaign Work

If to win at horse racing you need horses that will run, the same is true of campaign workers. Numbers are not enough. They need the competence, the skill, and the motivation to win. Like donors to the campaign, solicitors and others must be convinced of the importance of the endeavor and that the efforts put in will pay off. Like any other human service endeavor, however, campaigns can be slow in starting, and the results can be disappointing.

Good leadership can do much to overcome difficulties. Some leaders have developed their capacities to solve problems or to motivate others during the course of many previous campaigns. Others may start fresh with your organization, drawing on professional and occupational skills or on volunteer experiences with other organizations. If you are the campaign staffer, you may want a balanced leadership group composed of persons who have been trained through your organization and others who were recruited or borrowed from other organizations and who can bring relevant experiences to the campaign.

New solicitors and other volunteers will need some instruction. Even old-timers need refresher courses and pep talks. The following activities might be considered:

- orientation sessions that include written and spoken materials and that introduce the worker to the procedures to be used, the campaign structure and its key actors, the targets to be reached, and the purposes for which funds will be used;
- campaign literature that is designed for solicitors or other volunteers and other literature that can be mailed or given to prospective donors;
- solicitor training, which may include films and role play and practice experiences;
- On-the-job supervision and coaching, which may include observation of more experienced solicitors followed by joint solicitations and eventually solo flights;
- small group feedback sessions at which solicitors and others can be informed of how the campaign is faring and get reinforcement from sharing experiences with others.

Most volunteers need ongoing support and recognition. Many will need to get over inhibitions about requesting funds; others will need to become more realistic about what can be achieved. They may be thinking too high or too low. With sufficient commitment, they can go beyond their own expectations. Some organizations have routine ways of recognizing outstanding solicitors. These include awards and special recognition ceremonies, prizes, feature articles in the organization's newsletter or in the general press, and so on.

Getting Off to the Right Start and Ending on Time

All campaigns have beginnings and ends. Few campaigns can succeed without well-planned and carefully monitored timetables. The following events might belong on your timetable:

- meetings of the governing board, steering committees, and other committees;
- recruitment, orientation, training, and practice sessions for solicitors;
- placement of news releases and spot announcements in the news and entertainment media;
- mailing of information packets, solicitation letters, and other printed materials;
- special events, such as kickoff campaign meetings, ongoing support sessions, and award dinners;

- administrative follow-through and follow-up, such as thank-you letters and follow-up calls to persons who have made pledges but have not sent in their checks;
- interim and final reports.

These events must be paced properly so that there is sufficient time between steps to permit people to complete the required tasks. A well-designed timetable accommodates to various peak periods in which volunteers are expected to put in the bulk of their time. The timetable can be drawn up in a variety of ways. Chapter 14 describes several types of timetables, including PERT networks, Gantt charts, and time frames. Which system would work best for your campaign? Whatever system you use, it should not only help you to plan the campaign but also be used to determine whether or not your campaign is on schedule and the extent to which targeted goals have been met. If you are off schedule, readjustment of the time frame or a heavy push may be required to get you back on the timetable.

Fund-Raising Cycle

Rosso et al. (1991) describe the fund-raising cycle, a loop of activities and checkpoints that should occur on a regular basis. For example, all the activities that are normally thought of as being connected to a campaign (gift solicitation, volunteer recruitment and activation, design of a communications plan, and selecting a fund-raising vehicle) should become routinized and associated with other annual rhythms in the organization.

Identifying Prospective Donors

Ways of determining which publics to target for a fund-raising campaign have already been discussed. Some organizations, however, may not be able to develop lists of their own. It is possible to get lists of prospects from other sources. The fund-raising consultants in your community may be able to direct you to the appropriate list. You can locate them in the *Directory of Members* of the American Association of Fund Raising Counselors, described at the end of this chapter.

Also, there are a number of list brokers available in most metropolitan communities. They can either design or locate the appropriate list for you. For example, there are lists of music lovers, people who buy diet books or classical records, attorneys, business executives, psychiatric nurses, members of certain clubs, alumni of universities and colleges, and contributors to other organizations.

You may not need to go to a list broker. Your local librarian may be able to help you locate the appropriate reference book in which you will uncover lists of lists. You will recall that *Standard & Poor's Register, Dun & Bradstreet's,* and the *Directory of Directors* publish lists of companies nationwide, arranged geographically, with designations of the kinds of business they perform. Such lists can be used to locate industries that may have interests that complement those of your organization. *Thomas's Register of American Manufacturers* indicates the kinds of products produced by most manufacturing concerns in this country. *Moody's Industrial Manual* lists corporations, the names of their offices, plant locations, the names of trustees, and the names of corporations' attorneys and accountants.

Let your fingers do the walking. Consider the telephone directory or the local newspaper. Telephone directories frequently list professionals in the community by occupation in the Yellow Pages. Some cities publish a reverse telephone directory that can be purchased directly from the telephone company by any subscriber. In this type of directory, streets are listed alphabetically by neighborhood; house numbers are then given, and then the names of residents in each of the buildings, with their telephone numbers. This is an excellent source for a neighborhood canvassing program, and it permits you to target specific neighborhoods in the community.

Local newspapers are too often ignored. Staff members or volunteers might be assigned the task of clipping feature articles on wealthy people, those with special interests or life experiences, obituaries, birth announcements, and, as one professional fund-raiser told me, even robberies, which sometimes include the size of the home and provide a clue to the donor's interests.

Building Relationships, Building Trust

I'm no activist and I don't volunteer all that much, but I do appreciate my friends who do. Frankly, I probably wouldn't have given so much if it weren't for Hal and Betsy. They always seem to know what is needed and when. When Hal calls me at work, or Betsy stops by, it is likely to be about some new community need. I know they are here to solicit me, but frankly, I don't mind. I know they are both generous, and they never put on the pressure. They always make it feel as if they are giving me an opportunity to do something good that I might not have thought of on my own. And I appreciate it.

Big Givers Do Not Always Give Big

At one time or another, we have probably all had fantasies of a big giver bailing us or our organization out of a bind we may have found ourselves in. Big givers, however, like heroes, are made and not born. It may take a long time to cultivate a donor. A donor's gift can grow over time. In most communities and with most issues, there are some persons who will be able and willing to contribute handsomely. Some—a few—may seek you out directly or through an intermediary such as a tax attorney or a trust officer. You can locate the potential contributor through the same third parties or check with colleagues in the human services. They may know of someone who is not interested in their organization but who may be interested in yours.

Big givers may not be interested in any involvement with your organization beyond their financial gifts. Others will want to be involved in the campaign at a level that is commensurate with their gifts. Be careful not to move people up the leadership structure unless they have paid their dues in more than money alone; it is easy to demoralize other committee volunteers who may have worked painstakingly into positions of leadership.

The Solicitor's Pitch

The solicitor's pitch should emphasize those features in the agency's program or campaign objectives that the prospect is most likely to be interested in—those things the prospect values, such as religious concerns, the survival of an ethnic group, caring for needy children, fairness for the elderly, opportunities for the donor's children to attend college, the survival of a species, or the cleanup of the environment. The prospect may wish to know how the money given is to be used, what proportion of the budget raised will be allocated to one or another aspect of the program, and perhaps how much is being used for the administration of the campaign.

It may be even more important to indicate who else is being solicited and, without disclosing confidences, the average size of peer contributions. If the prospective donor contributed the previous year, it may be helpful to recall the amount and to indicate the general target for upgrading contributions this year. If the solicited individual gave a minimal amount in previous years, it may be time to try to upgrade the gift to a more adequate sum.

Most fund-raisers agree that it is not wise to try to move people up (increase the size of their gifts) too rapidly. A solicitor might try one of the following approaches:

"Last year you gave ten dollars, this year we'd like you to put aside fifty cents a week. It's not necessary for you to give the full amount all at once; you can pay off your pledge in quarterly payments."

"I'd like to see you move up to what I'm giving. Last year I gave five hundred dollars, but I know it's not easy to make that jump from a hundred dollars all at once. Why not consider two hundred dollars this year, and perhaps moving to three or four hundred next year?"

"Your gift is so close to what our pacesetters give, why not consider jumping from seven hundred and fifty to one thousand dollars? I know it's a strain in today's economy, but your previous gifts clearly show your commitment, and you are a well-respected member of our community. You really should be among the pacesetters. You've given so much in other ways."

Quoting the tax advantage of giving is no small motivator. Make certain that donors get receipts they can use for tax purposes, but remember that tax receipts do not substitute for acknowledgments. Donors should receive thank-you letters, even if these are not personalized. A personal phone call or a handwritten note, however, in particular to a donor who has made a large initial pledge or who has made a large jump from previous years, may be essential to maintaining that level of giving or to raising it in the future.

Most solicitors do not come to a campaign ready to make the pitch successfully. They may need training and practice in reaching individual or organizational prospects. Solicitor training frequently includes the use of films, role play, and coaching by an experienced solicitor. Coaching may include going along and observing an experienced worker or listening to a telephone solicitation conversation. Because the information can be overwhelming, you should consider providing manuals, information booklets, and question-and-answer sheets for solicitors. Working together in teams often provides the necessary support for solicitors to keep going when the going gets rough. It also permits them to learn from each other about how to be effective and how to be realistic about their own accomplishments. Many solicitors also need periodic inspirational talks. They need to be recognized for their efforts. Some organizations use prizes or special inducements to maintain high solicitor motivation. They recognize successful solicitors at banquets and other end-of-campaign functions, through newsletters that go to other campaign workers, and even through press and other public relations releases.

Solicitors often go directly to people's homes or offices. They also work by telephone. The United Jewish Appeal (UJA) tends to approach pacesetters and others who give medium-sized gifts in person, but it uses telephone solicitation to reach others who are not able, ready, or willing to make larger contributions. To make life more bearable for solicitors, most UJA campaigns sponsor a Super Sunday in which telephone solicitors work 1½- to 2-hour shifts. Each shift is preceded by a brief training session.

Coffee is available at these sessions and so is consultation and help when a solicitor has a particularly difficult prospect on the phone. Solicitor and donor prospects may be matched by organizational membership, previous associations, professional identity, neighborhoods, and so on. Telephone solicitors get support from each other. A snack or lunch may be served by other volunteers. Those solicitors who have gotten donors to make significant increases in their pledges may get special recognition, a novelty prize, or the like.

REACHING PEOPLE BY PHONE, MAIL, AND THE INTERNET

Telemarketing Has Reached Epidemic Proportions

Phone campaigns are hardly limited to Super Sundays or other one-day events. "Telemarketing is a public health problem," a colleague complained to us. "It's reached epidemic proportions." She was referring to the literally dozens of calls she received every

month, many of them from copycat organizations. "I get them from
the alumni associations from the two schools I graduated from and
my husband gets them from three. Then there are environmental
associations, health research funds, food banks, services for the blind,
Bosnia relief, you name it.

"I hate the intrusion into my time," she continued, "but the thing
I hate the most is that most times I get a sales pitch that shows the
caller has no idea of who I am, and probably even less about the
charity he's representing. I would almost rather get a call from one
of those computerized telemarketing services. At least I wouldn't
have to hang up on a live person."

So with all the bad vibes on phone solicitations, why use them?
Because for some kinds of campaigns, they are cost-efficient.

Calls are often made by volunteers. The telephone is an efficient
way of getting last year's donors to commit to this year's pledge (and
maybe to increase it) and to hook new donors. Investing some time
in the phone call and into solicitor training can have some real payoff,
even for organizations whose requests are copied by competitors and
scam agents.

A Call From the Cops

I don't usually give to people or organizations I don't know about.
And I rarely respond positively to phone solicitation. But last year I
did give to one. The call came from a member of the Policeman's Benevolent Society. Now I've heard about scams from sound-alike police
groups and I was wary. And I always hang up with some indignation
when the solicitor just spouts a prepared pitch without ever letting up
or giving me a chance to respond. But this caller was different.

He told me his name and explained that he had been on the force for
27 years. Then he proceeded to ask me about my experiences with
police officers. We got into a brief conversation in which he seemed
about as interested in me as he was trying to get me to be interested
in the society. Before making his pitch, he asked if we had a fax machine at home. We do. He faxed me some material that allayed my fears
of being suckered into anything. Then he called me back and clinched
my pledge.

I don't know if this makes me sound gullible, but it gave me some pause to think. I realized that I'm not really a very educated donor. I give when I trust the knowledge and integrity of the people who solicit me.

Many experts agree that telemarketing works best when it is combined with direct mail. This is perhaps most effective when focusing on renewals. In this case, the renewal letter is generally sent first, with a follow-up call coming within a few days. Unlike the offensive telemarketing in which the caller reads from a fixed script, the follow-up call—much like the call from the police officer described in the vignette—is interactive. In some campaigns, the "ask" call is separated from the "information" call. The latter may be made some time, perhaps 8 or 9 months, after the last donation. It is intended to share progress with the donor and to get his or her feedback. The ask call comes later, reminding the donor of the earlier conversation and last year's gift.

Although these calls have the feel of informality and some degree of spontaneity, they are not necessarily unplanned. Typically, they will follow a script that includes

- reminders of the information received earlier or previous telephone conversation;
- an overview or restatement of the major needs being addressed;
- tips on the amount of a gift that would be appropriate (and the rationale for it), which may include a request to upgrade—for example,

   "Last year your gift was $100. This year our donors are being asked to make a modest 20% increase to help us accommodate to the cut in government funds, and to match our 20% cut in administrative expenditures";

- confirmation of the amount pledged, agreement on how the payment is to be made (by check, credit card, etc.) or method of billing (and confirmation of correct mailing address);
- Thank-you in a flattering but not overly effusive tone.

The conversation should be followed up by a second thank-you in the form of a note with the solicitor's name (if appropriate), a confirmation of the pledge, and a return payment envelope or pledge card if payment over time is expected. In some campaigns, renewal letters are unconnected to a telephone call. In others, they precede the call. Whatever the case, the following tips are fairly standard:

- state, from the onset, that this is a renewal request (a request to renew the commitment made previously);
- describe the victories achieved or obstacles overcome last year (donors like to be associated with a winning team);
- indicate how this year's renewal will benefit the program or what would be lost if the fund-raising goal were not reached;
- ask for an upgraded amount.

Letters to Read and Letters to Throw Away

Everyone likes to get fan mail, but no one likes junk mail. People also like to learn something new and most have a need to belong, in the sense of being part of something larger than themselves. Letter campaigns build on just such insights—this is what makes the first impression in any fund-raising letter so important. Let us start with the way in which the reader is to be greeted. Wherever possible, the reader should be addressed by name so that it seems that at least someone was interested enough to locate him or her. With word-processing equipment, it is relatively easy to insert a recipient's name on an otherwise printed letter. If that is not possible, the reader should be identified as a member of a group or collectivity with which you know he or she is identified. Typical openings include "Dear Colleague," "Congregant," "Community Elder," and "Fellow Alumnus."

The opener, the first sentence, counts for more than almost any other part of the letter. It should be just what its title implies, an eye opener, an interest opener, and a commitment opener. Successful political campaign managers know that the first 10 seconds after a letter has been opened are the most important. If the reader's interest has not been aroused in those 10 seconds, the letter is likely to wind up in the wastebasket. That interest can best be aroused if it focuses on you, the reader, instead of me, the writer. Consider the following openings:

- You, as a mother, will . . .
- Because you are an adoptive parent . . .
- Whenever you see an elderly person, do you . . .

Instead of beginning with information about your organization, speak to the person's interests so that when you begin to talk about what your organization does or how its clients and others might be helped it will strike a responsive chord. For example, if the list you use for one batch of letters is composed of people who have received services at the county hospital, the opener might begin, "When you recently used the services of the county hospital. . . ." A list generated from the local newspaper might begin with, "When your children were married at. . . ." The point is to begin with who the person is.

If you are not sure about the person or if your list is of a more general nature, you might begin with a personal interest story. For example,

A little girl cried last night. She was hungry. Her father, too let down from months of unemployment, never came home to say good night.

The letter could then go on to indicate that the little girl will get less than one third of the nutrients required for her to grow into a healthy adult.

I recently received a letter that began,

Did anyone help you through school when you needed a helping hand? Why not take advantage of a tax break while ensuring that a needy student will be able to earn the same degree you did from XWZ University?

That second sentence was a beauty. It identified me, it stroked my guilt while assuming I was sure to be helpful, and it offered me a tax break to boot!

The rest of the letter should focus on that part of your organization's services most likely to generate the greatest human interest. Whatever you write, it should be accurate and true to the facts. Just as important, it should project a feeling of authenticity. It has to be

believable and sincere. It should speak about concrete services and
not about abstracts.

The closing sentence or paragraph should be punchy, straightfor-
ward, and forthright. It should spell out what is expected from the
reader, but it should never apologize for asking. Be clear about what
you are asking, and provide the prospective donor with a number of
guidelines for the choices he or she might make. For example, you
might want to spell out the range or size of gifts. You might even
include a checklist. It is not unusual to include a list of specific sums,
with boxes that donors can check. You should tell the potential giver
how to pay—by check, through Visa or MasterCard, or followed by
a later billing.

Whatever you write, use plain English, simple words, short sentences, and, especially, short paragraphs. Indent those paragraphs
that you want to single out for special attention or have them printed
in a different typeface or color. Tell your story in all the detail that
you think it needs, but get to the bottom line relatively early. Nothing
is as annoying as waiting to find out what the writer is asking of you
and scanning ahead to find the bottom line only to discover that it is
obscured by detail. Sometimes the bottom line can be located on a
separate enclosure, a brochure, a gift list, or a return mailing card or
envelope.

Honest Abe

How long should the letter be? I have a preference for short letters
with long enclosures rather than long letters with short enclosures.
This is a matter of judgment-based trial and error, however, and also,
to a certain extent, a matter of personal taste. When Lincoln was
asked how long a lecture should be, his answer was informative,
although today we might call it sexist: He said, "Like a woman's
skirt . . . it should be long enough to cover the ground, but short
enough to be interesting."

One of the more interesting and convincing parts of a letter is the
signature. I do not know about you, but I am more likely to give if
someone I respect, or if someone I want to be associated with, has
asked me to give. Also, I always look for names of other persons who

have given or who are supporting the campaign. The promise of being affiliated with a group that I want to belong to or with people whom I respect is an important inducement. These names are often found on the letterhead or on a list of sponsors.

Although what the copy (the content) of the letter says and how it is conveyed are most important, the style and format are also of great consequence. An organization struggling for survival and appealing to moderate-income publics would do well not to use a slick typeface or expensive paper. Nevertheless, there are advantages to using a distinctive style. The stationery, properly designed, will convey the type of program or service you are promoting. It may include a photograph, a recognizable logo, or a sketch of the program or the clients it aims to serve. Color, changes in the typeface or typewriter element, indentations, and checklists help to relieve the monotony of a long letter.

Also consider the envelope. Properly designed, it may wind up on the desk or the kitchen table instead of in the wastebasket. It may even be opened!

I have found that just as important as format and content is conveying a respect for the reader's judgment. Remember, the reader is being asked to make a contribution. The reader should also have the opportunity to make a choice—to give or not to give is the simplest choice. Other choices should include more than the size of the gift or its timing. They can also include what the gift should be used for. Some readers will prefer to make their gifts for a summer camp, whereas others might prefer theirs to be used for a family life education program or a scholarship fund. Provide choices whenever possible.

Tip: Between 1980 and 1987, the volume of nonprofit third-class mail more than doubled, whereas the cost of postage and production tripled! To succeed in this competitive market, you need an edge.

Why not ask potential donors what would turn them on?

SOME DESIGN TIPS

Tip 1: Get the letter opened by
— promising a reward for doing so (gift item, visible mailing labels, etc.);
— provoking curiosity (e.g., "Inside: How racism will reduce your child's earning ability and what you can do about it!").

Tip 2: Make the first sentence strong by
— keeping the message simple;
— appealing equally to intelligence and emotion (emotional appeals have been overdone—like violence on TV, they deaden the senses).

Tip 3: Use a "sound-bite" paragraph before you even write the salutation (generally a boxed-in summary of the ask or a scenario of the situation that necessitates the campaign).

Tip 4: Target your message properly by
— tailoring letters to different segments of your donor market (an appeal to doctors to address hunger needs might be different than a general appeal and might include endorsements by other well-known or locally respected physicians);
— respecting donor intelligence and recognizing that this is one of scores of other appeals, all worthy, but spelling out how this appeal is different, more urgent, or more directly relevant to the donor's interests or all three;
— informing the donor by providing information he or she may be able to use elsewhere—for example,

"When someone tells you that welfare benefits promote dependency, what you can tell them is. . . ."

"Five little-known facts about hearing loss. . . ."

Tip 5: Weave in the extras that can make a difference, such as
— how previous gifts were used;
— a scenario indicating how the organization's program makes a difference;
— an honest admission of the program's limits—for example,
"Your contribution won't help us stop the destruction of the rain forest. But it can help delay its devastating effect and build public support for. . . ."

Annual Reports and Newsletters in the Campaign

In addition to letters, many of which include pledge or solicitation cards, your organization may also wish to mail annual reports to prospective donors, to other persons important to the organization, and, of course, to people who have already contributed. Whatever else it contains, make sure the annual report clearly specifies the organization's name and address, its board members, and the time period covered.

Include information on the source of support, the purpose of the work the organization does, and how long it has been involved in that kind of work. Indicate who does the work (if professionals, what type, and if volunteers, who). If the organization raised funds from a variety of sources during the previous years, what were the sources and how much was raised from each? On what was the money spent? How has the program been modified to meet current needs? What are the future directions the organization is considering or has chosen to take? Who currently uses the organization's services and who will use those services if the plan for future directions is put into effect because of successful fund-raising efforts? Finally, how will the average citizen (presumably, there are many of these among the readers of the report) benefit from these programs and services?

Annual reports, like letters, can be used to awaken interest. They should be written in tangible, human terms. They should be graphic, not only in design but also in the imagery that the words evoke.

Some organizations use more than one version of the annual report. Although each covers approximately the same material, each is targeted to a specific audience. If a single annual report is used, but mailed out to a number of different audiences, different cover letters might tailor it to each of those publics. For some publics, a summary report with the information about where to obtain a longer report may be all that is necessary.

Tips on Tap (More Good Ideas From the Experts!)

Brick-and-mortar experts suggest that the campaign should not start until 25% of the needed funds are already in the bank or on pledge cards. This means reaching the pacesetters and generating the special gifts early. They also suggest that the campaign not assume an average gift from each of the prospective donors. The prospects should be divided into pacesetters, second-level gift givers, third-level gift givers, and perhaps even fourth-level givers.

Approximately one fourth of the total should be raised from the pacesetters, most of it before the campaign is officially kicked off. These may make up only 5% to 10% of all donors. Approximately one third should be raised from the second-level givers, who generally make up almost half of those who contribute. The rest should be raised from third-level givers, who will make up as much as 40% or 45% of those who contribute. Fourth-level givers, if you decide to try to reach them, may be persons who have not previously been actively involved in the organization or who are not members of it but who may be committed to the idea of an expanded service facility.

Bequest campaigns also require special approaches. Typically, the bequest program will include the following ingredients:

1. A bequest committee or task group that plans and manages the program

2. A booklet or other descriptive material that spells out details of the bequest program—how it will be used and for what purpose, the types of gifts that might be given, how the gift will be built on, how taxes favor the individual who gives or his or her trust or other beneficiaries, and other useful information

3. Development of a list of prospective givers and others who might be appropriate solicitors

4. A set of procedures used to canvass that list and to target certain individuals at the appropriate time

Development funds are generally earmarked for new or special programs that the agency hopes to establish in the future or for ongoing programs that require expansion or modification. All but special events require lists of actual and prospective donors. They may also require door-to-door interactions, letters, the targeted use of annual reports, and related public relations activities. In lieu of a campaign cabinet, it may have a development council made up of staff, board of trustees members, and others. In some organizations, the council coordinates and manages all the organization's fund-raising activities, making sure that grant seeking, campaigns, and other events all do their share in the resource development process.

Homing in on the Home Page

You may be surprised that, thus far, no mention has been made of the potential of electronic means to complement or substitute for some of the means described previously. I was surprised that, to date, so little use has been made of the World Wide Web or electronic mail. Agencies and nonprofits have begun to use the Web to make information available on their programs and services. Even community-wide organizations have used the Web. For example, universities (and their schools or departments), libraries, community arts programs, and social agencies have created *Web pages*—Web sites from which information can be sought on programs and services.

A home page could be followed by a contents list that directs the user to information on programs, budgets, board members, staff, and the status of the campaign. Information can be presented in text form, as still photos or illustrations, or as film clips and brief videos with both action and sound. In metropolitan Detroit, a consortium of child welfare agencies and the United Community Services (as the United Way agency is called) are working on putting program information on-line for member agencies. There may only be one more step before information is also available to prospective donors. In Austin, Texas, all the Jewish communal service organizations are connected to a Web page, and a newcomer can easily find out what services are available. The Jewish Federation may also find it a useful tool to inform donors about how their gifts support community and program development.

Universities are using the Internet for "distance learning"—that is, to provide information and even whole courses to students far from the campus. Some professional associations and for-profit firms are using electronic mail to target specific professional groups such as attorneys and personnel managers with information useful to them.

As other nonprofits, including ethnic, religious, and special-interest groups, begin to use the Internet for communication purposes, they may also find it to be a useful addition to telemarketing and letter campaigns and to other means of serving target groups with information of use to them but that could also benefit the campaign. For example, sending information on bequests and deferred giving programs to attorneys could initiate collaborations between them and your organization.

I imagine that there will be a great deal more information on this topic in future editions of this book. Why not share some of your experiences with the author and other readers? Drop a letter to me at the University of Michigan or you can reach me via electronic mail at alauffer@umich.edu.

SOURCES OF INFORMATION ON FUND-RAISING

There are a number of nonprofit organizations that can help your nonprofit in its fund-raising efforts. A number publish journals, tip sheets, books, and manuals. Others provide technical assistance and consultation. Some are primarily local, whereas others are national in scope (see Wagner, 1992, for other names and address).

University-Based Centers That Offer Workshops and Courses

These are mostly local in focus, although some publish materials that are disseminated broadly. A number are affiliated with degree granting programs. Only a few examples, representing different sections of the country, are given here.

1. Center for the Study of Philanthropy
   Graduate School and University Center
   City University of New York
   33 W. 42nd Street
   New York, NY 10036

2. Center for the Study of Philanthropy and Voluntarism
   Institute of Policy Sciences and Public Affairs
   Duke University
   4875 Duke Station
   Durham, NC 27706

3. Indiana University Center on Philanthropy/The Fund Raising School, Indiana University and Purdue University at Indianapolis
   550 W. North Street
   Indianapolis, IN 46202

4. Institute for Nonprofit Organization Management
   College of Professional Studies
   University of San Francisco
   2130 Fulton Street
   San Francisco, CA 94117

Nonuniversity Organizations That Offer Publications, Information, and Technical Assistance

These organizations publish useful guides, conduct workshops, maintain publicly available databases, provide technical assistance or all of these.

1. Council on Foundations
   1828 L Street, NW Ste. 300
   Washington, D.C. 20036

2. The Fund Raising Center
   287 McPherson Avenue
   Toronto, Ontario M4V 1A4

3. Independent Sector
   1828 L Street NW Ste: 1200
   Washington, D.C. 29936

4. KRC Development Council
   212 Elm Street
   New Canaan, CT 06840

5. National Charities Information Bureau
   19 Union Square West
   New York, NY 10003

6. National Council on Philanthropy
   650 Fifth Avenue
   New York, NY 10019

7. Nonprofit Management Association
   1508 Harvard
   Santa Monica, CA 90404

8. The Society for Nonprofit Organizations
6314 Odana Road
Madison, WI 53719

9. The Taft Group
12300 Twinbrook Parkway
Rockville, MD 20852

REVIEW

Campaigns tend to have their own structures, often composed of a cabinet, a steering committee, and a number of working groups or task forces. Solicitors often train or work in groups under the leadership of a team captain. Campaign leaders and workers both need ongoing training and support. Campaigns may target certain individuals for large gifts or otherwise segment the populations at which they aim—for example, by occupational groups or by services received.

Two specialized and ubiquitous types of campaigns—telemarketing and letter writing—were discussed in detail. Both are likely to turn many prospective donors off because of their intrusiveness. Because mailings and phone calls are cast broadly, however, they tend to generate significant income when properly designed and targeted. Techniques for generating interest were described—most hit a sympathy chord or respond to significant concerns of the prospective donor. Finally, the potential uses of the Internet were explored.

REFERENCES

Rosso, H., & Associates. (1991). *Achieving excellence in fund raising: A comprehensive guide to principles, strategies, and methods.* San Francisco: Jossey-Bass.
Wagner, L. (1992, October). Fund-raising research: Prospecting for gold. *Fund Raising Management, 21*(8), 36-43.

SUGGESTIONS FOR FURTHER READING

Adams-Chau, L. L. (1988). *The professional's guide to fund raising, corporate giving, and philanthropy: People give to people.* New York: Quorum.
Ashton, D. (1991). *The complete guide to planned giving.* Cambridge, MA: JLA.
Bailey, T. (1988). *The fund raiser's guide to successful campaigns.* New York: McGraw-Hill.

Bendixen, M. A. (1992, February). Planned gifts on a shoestring budget. *Fund Raising Management, 22*(12), 40-42.

Brody, R. (1988). *Fund-raising events: Strategies and programs for success.* New York: Human Sciences.

California Community Foundation. (1990). *Resources for your nonprofit organization: A how to do it manual.* Los Angeles: Author.

Dolenick, S. (Ed.). (1987). *Fundraising for nonprofit institutions.* Greenwich, CT: JAI.

Edles, P. L. (1993). *Fundraising: Hands-on tactics for nonprofit groups.* New York: McGraw-Hill.

Flanagan, J. (1991). *Successful fundraising: A complete handbook for volunteers and professionals.* Chicago: Contemporary Books.

Garrison, J. R. (1990, February). A new twist to cause marketing. *Fund Raising Management, 20*(12), 40-44.

Greenfield, J. M. (1991). *Fund-raising: Evaluating and managing the fund development process.* New York: John Wiley.

Greenfield, J. M. (1991). *Taking fund raising seriously, advancing the profession and practice of raising money.* San Francisco: Jossey-Bass.

Greer, C. (1996, August 11). Make pennies count. *Parade.*

Gurin, M. (1991). *Advancing beyond the techniques in fund raising.* Rockville, MD: Fund Raising Institute.

Hall, H. (1993, February 23). Direct-mail fund raising bounces back. *Chronicle of Philanthropy,* 29-33.

Heetland, D. (1992, September). How to build a major gifts program. *Fund Raising Management, 21*(7), 54-57.

Hopkins, B. R. (1991). *The law of fund-raising.* New York: John Wiley.

Klein, K. (1991, August). Getting started in planned giving. *Grassroots Fundraising Journal,* 3-6.

Klein, K. (1991, October). Beyond the bequest: Other kinds of planned giving. *Grassroots Fundraising Journal,* 3-8.

Kling, P. F. (1993). Planned giving and annual giving can cooperate. *Fund Raising Management, 22*(12), 53-54.

Krit, R. L. (1991). *The fund-raising handbook.* Glenview, IL: Scott, Foresman.

Kuniholm, R. (1995). *The complete book of model fund-raising letters.* Engelwood Cliffs, NJ: Prentice Hall.

Lindahl, W. E. (1992). *Strategic planning for fundraising: How to bring in more money using strategic resource allocation.* San Francisco: Jossey-Bass.

Nicholas, J. (1990). *Changing demographics—Fund raising in the 1990s.* Chicago: Bonus Books.

Taft Group, The. (1996). *Practical guide to planned giving.* Rockville, MD: Author.

Young, J. (1989). *Fundraising for non-profit groups.* North Vancouver, BC: Self-Council Press.

12

Writing the Proposal

As a Blueprint for Action

Integrity and Intent

We're not in the fast-buck business. We're in it for the long haul. Intent, integrity, and successful grant seeking go hand in hand. A proposal should be a plan for action. It should offer clear and precise projections about strategies, activities, schedules, and end results. If a project is intended to have a specific impact, that impact should be measurable, and the writer should indicate how it is to be measured. I never promise more than I know my agency can produce. I know that this is different than the "give the funders what they want and they'll give you what you want" school of thought, but I've seen that approach backfire more than once.

For two reasons. First, even if you get the grant, a poor design doesn't leave you with a clear idea of what to do with it. Second, it speaks badly about your integrity. The words in our proposal are important, but so is the reputation of the person and the organization that has prepared it. The proposal is as much about integrity as it is about intent.

PROPOSALS AS STATEMENTS OF INTENT

Proposals are statements of intent—plans of action that can and will be implemented if sufficient resources are available. They are also intended to be persuasive—that is, intended to induce others to act in concert with you and your organization.

The chapter begins with an outline of what goes into a standard full-length proposal—the title and cover pages, narrative, budget, time frame, and appendix. Then, detailed attention is given to both the cover and the narrative. The title page(s)—generally no more than one or two pages—identifies your organization, what it proposes to do, over what period of time, and at what costs. The narrative section is often much more detailed. It spells out the problem addressed, goals pursued, and what the grant seeker intends to do to achieve them. The budget, time frame, and appendices are discussed in Chapters 13 and 14.

Although all three chapters are written primarily for the grant seeker, the principles presented are equally relevant for allocation requests to one's own board of directors, appropriation requests to government bureaus and legislatures, or other written proposals that request support for specific actions.

ANATOMY OF A PROPOSAL

How Grant Proposals Are Structured

Although there are no standard proposal formats that serve equally well with all funders, the following components are relatively common:

1. Title page and abstract
2. Project narrative
3. Budget
4. Time frame
5. Appendix or other supportive materials.
6. Cover letter

The format and length of each section may depend as much or more on the funder as on the logic of the proposal itself. Sponsors may use different titles for each section or list them in different order. Most federal grant programs have very specific guidelines, as do state agencies that award purchase-of-service contracts and many foundation and corporate funders. Any significant variation from the funder's instructions is likely to generate a rejection or a no response.

For example, some federal grants give detailed instructions on what to include in each section and how long it should be. If an applicant omits a section or uses more than 10 single-spaced pages for the total, the proposal will not be read. A grants officer with the Administration on Aging stated, "We get between 10 and 30 submissions for each one we can fund. We reason that if proposal writers can't read the simplest of our instructions, they're not likely to address the priority issues we've identified. By screening out the ones that don't follow the format, we can give serious attention to those that do."

TITLE PAGES

Many governmental funding agencies provide forms for the title page. Some sponsors provide an outline of required information. Follow the instructions to the letter. Proposals with incomplete title pages may not be accepted. If neither are provided, include the following information on a title page of your own design:

1. Title of the project
2. Type of grant or Funder Priority Area
3. Name and address of your organization
4. Proof of nonprofit status (e.g., tax identification number)
5. Name and signature of the project director or the legally and fiscally responsible individual or both
6. Submitted to (name of funding source)
7. Proposed project dates
8. Dollars requested for this fiscal year and over the life of the project
9. Date of submission

Some funders require a one-paragraph abstract or a table of contents or both. Although others do not, I find it helpful to include a page of my own design that includes both (unless this is not permitted). For example, I like to add a second title page that includes

    10. A 200-word abstract in the upper half
    11. Boxed-in table of contents in the lower half

What goes into most of these items should be self-evident. A few words about Items 1, 2, 10, and 11, however, may be helpful.

Titles count! I mean that in more ways than one. Funders often limit you to the number of words or characters you may use. That may be frustrating, but these limits are actually helpful: They force you to tell the reader what your project is about in very few words. The following are a few examples:

Counseling Abusive Partners

Helping Older Men Stay at Home

Tapping Untapped Resources Now: A Community Partnership

Each of these can be turned into acronyms making them not only easy to remember but also focusing attention on a major theme of the project. For example,

"We can put a *CAP* on family violence by *c*ounseling *a*busive *p*artners."

"*Project HOMe* is about *h*elping *o*lder *me*n stay at home for as long as they're able."

"The Community Partnership is committed to *TURN*ing around the process of economic and social decline."

I find it useful to include "action verbs" in the title (and in the acronym if that does not stretch a term beyond recognition). The following are a few action verb acronyms I have seen in proposals. What do you think they might stand for?

Examples of Acronyms as Action Verbs

ACT	GROW	LAND	QUE	VEER
ADD	GUARD	LEAD	QUOTE	VOICE
BREW	HAND	MATCH	RESTORE	WAIT
BARTER	HOLD-UP	MOLD	RUN	WISH
CALL	IMAGE	NAME	SAVE	YEARN
CAMP	INVOLVE	NET	SOW	YIELD
DELIVER	JAM	OPEN	TIP	
DRAFT	JOIN	OUT-DO	TRAIN	
FILL	KEEP	PASS	UNDO	
FEED	KNOW	PULL	UPDATE	

Although acronyms are certainly not essential, they are effective ways of communicating who you are to both the sponsor and other key publics. I know that some grants officers think acronyms are corny, but they do remember them. Make sure, however, the acronym tells the story accurately. Also be careful about changing names. There is an apocryphal story told in grant circles about when People United to Recover Social Entitlements (PURSE) changed its name to Community United to Recover Social Entitlements.

Types of Grants

There are different types of grants, and some sponsors may be interested in some but not in others. For example, some sponsors (e.g., the Kresge Foundation) are specifically interested in contributing to capital campaigns. Others may fund demonstration projects, medical research, or scholarships. Sponsors need to know what kind of grant you are applying for. You need to know what types they will entertain.

TYPES OF GRANTS

Capital funds for
    Construction
    Equipment purchase
    Land acquisition
    Renovation

Enabling funds to serve as
  Challenge grant (to induce others to give)
  Matching funds (meeting the requirement of another funding source)
Start-up funds in support of a
  Demonstration (or pilot) project
  Planning grant (prior to submitting a second-level proposal)
  Seed funds (to get something started that may attract other funds)
General purpose funds such as
  Endowment (principal to be invested and income to be used for support)
  Operating funds (covers costs of operating a particular program)
  Organization support (supports the agency, not a specific project)
Special project funding for
  Conferences
  Consultation (to the agency)
  Dissemination (of materials, ideas, and innovations)
  Evaluation
  Publication
  Research
  Scholarships
  Training

Abstract

Typically, abstracts are no longer than 200 words. They summarize the objectives and significance of the project, the procedures to be followed in carrying it out, and the plans for evaluating results or making the results available to others. Reviewers use them (a) for a quick overview and (b) as the basis for summaries of the grants it has made that the sponsor might distribute. Abstracts need not include data already provided elsewhere on your title pages (e.g., duration, budget, address, etc.).

If you can answer the following questions, you should have a pretty clear idea of what goes into the abstract:

If I wanted the reviewers to have a quick fix on what my proposal is all about, what (in addition to the other title page information) do they need to know?

If I wanted the funder to inform others about my project, what would I want them to include (in one paragraph or less)?

Table of Contents

If a proposal narrative is longer than five pages or if it has a long appendix or both, I find it useful to include a table of contents, generally on the second page and just below the abstract. The table might be boxed in. It should include the titles of each section of the narrative, the budget, the time frame, and each of the groups of items in the appendices. For example, it would be appropriate to list a "Letters of Support" section of the appendices but not each letter individually.

Formatting the Title Page

In general, your format should either follow the sponsor's instructions or appear relatively familiar to reviewers by using common fonts and spacing (Figure 12.1). In most cases, photos or eye-catching graphics are not recommended. Your simple formatting techniques, however, can help to distinguish your document. For example, consider the use of

- lined or shaded borders;
- larger or boldface type for some or all components;
- shading over sections you want to emphasize, such as the project title or time frame;
- an agency or project logo (or print it all on agency stationary).

Take care that the format does not overshadow the content or in any other way suggest you place style over substance. The idea is to be simple and accessible, yet somewhat distinctive. Things not to use on your cover title page include

- color, embossing, ribbons, scented paper, or other extraneous materials;
- multiple or fancy fonts that are difficult to read;
- expensive paper or very heavy stock.

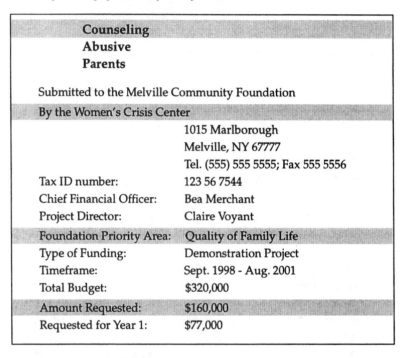

Counseling	
Abusive	
Parents	
Submitted to the Melville Community Foundation	
By the Women's Crisis Center	
	1015 Marlborough
	Melville, NY 67777
	Tel. (555) 555 5555; Fax 555 5556
Tax ID number:	123 56 7544
Chief Financial Officer:	Bea Merchant
Project Director:	Claire Voyant
Foundation Priority Area:	Quality of Family Life
Type of Funding:	Demonstration Project
Timeframe:	Sept. 1998 - Aug. 2001
Total Budget:	$320,000
Amount Requested:	$160,000
Requested for Year 1:	$77,000

Figure 12.1. Sample Title Page

NARRATIVE SECTION

If you have become adept at writing grant applications to one sponsor, do not assume the format you are using will be acceptable to another. For example, some sponsors expect the abstract, time frame, or the budget or all three to be part of the narrative instead of in their own separate sections. Typically, however, the narrative section includes

- an introduction;
- a statement of the problem to be addressed;

- the goals and objectives to be reached;
- the methods—activities or operations to be conducted or both;
- staffing patterns and project leadership;
- evaluation issues to be addressed and how;
- the capacities of your organization to conduct the program.

Some sponsors may also want you to include sections about

- the project's significance (in relation to sponsor priorities);
- its potential for replication or dissemination of the experience;
- the extent of community support for the program;
- plans for continuation beyond the funding period.

Keep your narrative to a reasonable length. Reviewers have a hard time dealing with more than 15 pages and usually prefer a document that is no more than 10 pages long. Many foundations and corporations may even limit you to 5 or fewer pages. If you do not have enough space, and the sponsor allows it, use the appendix for details and supplementary materials. If the appendix is very long, and if it is attached to the narrative, the whole package may appear overwhelming. Consider stapling the appendix separately and printing it on off-white, gray, or ivory paper to set it off from the white paper used for the rest of the document.

Many funders request narrative information in an order that differs from that which I presented previously. For example, most federal agencies require information about your organization to appear first in the narrative. That means including your "capacity statement" in your introduction. Research proposals may follow a different format from that of a demonstration project. Proposals for capital expenditures certainly will. Any of the suggested categories can be collapsed or regrouped if this fits the funder's requirements. For example, "significance" and "replication" can go under a single heading, and concerns about "continuation funding" might be handled in your explanation for the current budget request.

If you are unsure about what to include or where, and if the funder has not provided specific guidelines in writing, it is often helpful to ask the grants program officer (or other appropriate staffer). When no one is available, try to locate examples of previously funded proposals.

Introduction Section of the Narrative

This section may actually include two kinds of introductions: to the project and to your organization. If you have already written an abstract and if you are including a capacity statement elsewhere, the introduction will be very brief. The following are two examples:

Example 1: The Women's Crisis Center has a long history of protecting women and children in Tri-County, who have been victims of domestic violence. Now, in response to a challenge grant from the CarCorporation, we want to extend services to the partners of those who have been victimized by violence. That's the reason we are proposing CAP—the Counseling Abusive Partners project.

Example 2: The Foundation has a long history of addressing the consequences of domestic violence. That's why we think you'll be interested in CAP—Counseling Abusive Partners. The Women's Crisis Center, which for fifteen years has been the central address in the Tri-County area for victims of domestic violence, now proposes to refocus some of its efforts on preventive measures, so as to head off the violence before it erupts.

If you are using an acronym in your title, use it in a lead-in sentence—for example, for either of the previous examples:

CAP is about *counseling abusive partners!*

It's time to put a CAP on family violence.

Some funders expect the introduction to include a full capacity statement. In this case, it is not necessary to include an organizational history and capacity statement near the end of the narrative. This section should

- establish the identity and purpose of the applicant organization;
- briefly describe its mission or primary organizational goals;
- present the organization's credentials to do this kind of work;
- lead directly to the problem statement, which follows.

There are two ways in which you can establish the organization's credentials and capacity: (a) provide a brief history, emphasizing its experience with programs such as the one you are proposing that provide the context against which this project emerges, or (b) focus on the organization's distinctive identity, practice orientation, or philosophy. If the agency orientation is feminist and the funder is known for its support of feminist organizations, then an emphasis on philosophy and practice orientation makes sense. If feminism is regarded as neutral or suspect by the sponsor, then an emphasis on your agency's track record in dealing with a growing social issue should be given priority.

Tip: The principle is to build from strength, but strength is often in the eye of the beholder.

What if your organization does not have credentials? What if it needs this grant precisely because it is trying to establish the capability of acting on a problem? In this case, your strength may be in your weakness. The following example demonstrates one for way you to address a weakness:

For 12 years, since it first opened the Domestic Violence Shelter, the Women's Crisis Center has focused its attention on women and children who are the principal victims of domestic violence. We were so caught up in the need to address real-life crises that we were barely able to see that such crises could be prevented, or that the perpetrators of violence were victims in their own right. There's another side of the violence equation that needs to be addressed and we need help in addressing it.

Here's what we've achieved to date:

_____

_____

Here's what we need help in achieving over the next three years:

_____

_____

TIPS FOR THE SECTION OF THE INTRODUCTION DEALING WITH YOUR ORGANIZATION

Most organizations have "boilerplate" statements that describe their missions, provide a brief history, and describe major product lines and service constituencies. This statement may be found in an annual report or appear in proposals to other funders.

Tip 1: Do not use it as is. Tailor it to this proposal and to the funder's interests.

Tip 2: Boost the organization and what it wants to do. Do not boast about the organization. There is a difference.

Tip 3: Be honest about your track record. If it is weak, you can add some credibility by demonstrating how you will use consultation or help from other organizations or both to build capacity. Put major emphasis on the severity of the problem to be addressed (and the lack of other community resources to deal with it), bolstering your rationale for tackling it.

Statement of the Problem

This section is sometimes also called "needs assessment," although the two terms—problems and needs—are conceptually distinct. Conditions become problems when they are judged (by someone or some collectivity) to be harmful or negative (for someone or some collectivity). Facts are not problems, but problems are often defined when facts are interpreted as being problematic and that usually does not happen until those doing the defining also think the situation can be improved.

For example, an infant mortality rate of 20 per 1,000 births would hardly be defined as problematic in some developing countries. It could be very problematic in any American city. Thus, problem definition is relative. Those who might be induced to working on a problem have to agree that one exists and that something can be done to either eliminate or reduce the problem or ameliorate the condition that leads to it.

The statement of the problem is used to induce funders and other key publics to see the problem the same way you do and that something should be done about it. It should also reinforce the notion that your organization is well suited to deal with it. The problem statement should

- stake out the dimensions of the problem your project is intended to address;
- describe the problem's severity and who is directly and indirectly affected by it;
- explain your conceptual understanding about its causes or the consequences of not dealing with it.

This provides a rationale for the intervention strategy you will be proposing. The following is an example:

The Problem   The rate of infant mortality in Coretown is twice that of the greater metropolitan area. It is nearly four times as high for children born to unwed teen mothers. Of those infants who survive their first month, half are likely to be of low birth weight, at risk of mental retardation, and prone to frequent childhood diseases.

Who Is Affected

Directly   All three are tragic for the mothers involved and their children and place increased burdens on immediate and extended family members who already suffer from poverty and inadequate housing.

Indirectly   The social costs to the community are equally high. Every premature birth costs the county and other government health agencies 87 times as much as a healthy birth carried to term. Developmentally disabled children cost the schools in the area $11,356 per year plus other services, in contrast with an average per pupil cost of $5,640.

Concepts   The severity of the problem and its attendant costs are detailed in a report by Professor O'Brian at State University (see Appendix B: "Special Report on Prematurity"). The report also demonstrates a direct relationship between the nutritional and health levels of the birth mother throughout the first 6 months of pregnancy and the incidence of low birth weight.

Previously, I noted that this section is sometimes called "needs assessment" but that needs and problems are not identical. For those programs that are to be delivered as services, it is often helpful to translate problems into needs. People have needs (for nutrition, education, counseling services, and family recreational activities), and services or products are often developed to "meet" or address those needs.

The following are potential sources of information on problems and needs:

- published studies;
- agency-conducted needs assessments;
- market studies (e.g., Black & Decker's focus group sessions);
- priorities determined in public forums (e.g., neighborhood meetings, interagency planning sessions, public hearings, etc.);
- expert opinion (e.g., publications, results of consultations, etc.).

TIPS FOR THE PROBLEM DESCRIPTION

Tip 1: If you write this section properly, the reader should be able to anticipate your proposed solution. Keep your description limited and be concrete. Write only about those aspects of the problem or need that your organization is prepared to act on. Use the statement to provide a grounding for what comes later in the proposal, including (a) your claim's importance and the uniqueness of your approach and (b) a baseline against which outcome evaluations might be conducted.

Tip 2:   Provide both data and explanation. Facts without explanation are meaningless. Explanations without data are frivolous. If you need more room than permitted for either, consider using the appendices and footnotes. Documentation is required by many government and foundation funders.

Tip 3:   If you will be referring to the work of other agencies dealing with the same kind of problem later on, use this section to introduce this to them. For example, you might write that "these data are consistent with the findings of the Minnesota project, in which. . . ."

Tip 4:   Make the problem description interesting and engaging. Write in human terms if possible, staying away from dry academic language.

Goals and Objectives

Kettner, Moroney, and Martin (1990) use an "if-then" approach for moving from a problem definition to a working hypothesis that, in turn, can lead to hierarchy of goals and objectives. The following is an example of a working hypothesis:

> If the high rate of infant mortality is related to low birth weight (for which there is ample empirical verification), and if low birth weight is, at least partially, the result of ill health, poor living conditions, and malnutrition, then an intervention that addresses health, housing, nutrition, and should increase birth weight and reduce the incidence of infant mortality.

You could include this hypothesis in your proposal as a transition between the problem description and the statement of goals and objectives. Alternatively, you might go directly to the goals and objectives. Previously, I mentioned a hierarchy. For proposal purposes, I tend to use the term goal almost interchangeably with ultimate objective, which is distinguished from intermediate and immediate outcome objectives and from process objectives. This may seem very formidable, but it is quite simple when you learn to distinguish between them.

Goals. I like to think of the goal as the "end toward which a journey tends." Because goal statements should give direction to the enterprise and energize it, they are often written in relatively general terms, pointing to directions that most everyone can agree we should be moving toward. "Most everyone" means the potential funder, your agency staff, the other organizations with which you must collaborate, consumers, and other key publics. For example, the goal (ultimate objective) of a nutrition program for unwed pregnant teens might be to "reduce the incidence of infant mortality."

This goal becomes an *ultimate outcome objective* (what you are aiming for) when it is made more specific by referring to a (a) time frame, (b) target of change, and (c) more specific baseline and outcome measures. For example,

> The program's ultimate objective is to reduce the incidence of infant mortality over a 3-year period for children born of teen mothers in the Coretown area, from its current rate of 37 per 10,000 births to the Metro-area norm of 19 per 10,000.

The advantage of writing the outcome objective in more specific terms is that it gives you a concrete target to aim for and provides baseline information by which you (and others) can measure your achievements. This can also be a disadvantage. If you do not want to be held to a specific target, you might want to substitute a more general outcome for "19/10,000" (e.g., "to a rate more closely approximating the Metro-area norm"). The ultimate objective does not provide enough information to justify what you will be saying about the project's intervention approaches in the rest of the narrative. That is why it is often helpful to include intermediate and immediate objectives.

Intermediate and Immediate Objectives. An intermediate objective might be to "reduce the incidence of premature birth" and the immediate objectives might be to "improve the nutritional status of pregnant teens," "reduce their levels of infectious disease, accident, and trauma," and "improve their living conditions."

If we were to state all three in some hierarchy, they might look appear
as follows:

Ultimate	1	To reduce infant mortality
Intermediate	1.1	Reduce premature births
Immediate	1.11	Improve nutrition
	1.12	Reduce infectious disease, accident, and trauma
	1.13	Improve living conditions

Assuming that your agency deals only with nutritional issues, the
following goal statement might be written in the proposal as follows:

> Over a 3-year period, infant mortality will be brought down from the
> current rate of 37 deaths per 100,000 births in Coretown, to one
> approximating the norm for the Metro area. To achieve that goal, the
> number of premature births will be cut in half over the same period.
> We can achieve this by improving the nutritional status of 80% of all
> at-risk pregnant teens.

This statement provides the three levels of outcome objectives, but it
does not detail the means by which you expect to reach these outcomes. Those are generally called process objectives. The following
are three process objectives taken from Kettner et al. (1990):

1.111　To complete a nutritional assessment using the XYZ Nutritional
Scale on all women within 1 week of their entering the program;

1.112　To provide all women in the program with a 6-week nutrition
education program to be offered during their first 6 months in the
program;

1.113　To provide detailed nutritional plans for all women assessed to
have nutritional problems, within 1 week of that assessment.

Note that the three process objectives all flow from Immediate Objective 1.11 because the agency submitting the proposal provides
nutritional services but does not deal with other health and environmental issues.

Process objectives lay the groundwork for the next section of the
narrative—the description of the methods, activities, and operations
to be conducted. Many proposals state the objectives incorrectly,
focusing on what the program will do rather than on what it is
intended to achieve. Examples of poor start-up phrases for objectives

include "to extend availability of camping program to . . . ," "to assure continuity of . . . ," and "to utilize volunteers in. . . ." These are processes rather than outcome objectives and are increasingly suspect by reviewers who want to know what you intend to accomplish before asking you how you intend to do it.

TIPS ON GOALS AND OBJECTIVES

Tip 1: A properly designed statement of objectives will accomplish several goals. It will establish the criteria against which your project can be evaluated and provide a base from which to design your intervention approaches.

Tip 2: Keep the objectives relatively uncluttered by excessive verbiage.

Tip 3: Make sure that the statement of objectives flows directly from the problem statement. If it does not, consider rewriting it or reframing the description of the problem.

Tip 4: Design the objectives so that the process objectives lead directly to the program's activities, to be described next.

Tip 5: When listing multiple objectives, do so in order from the more general to the more specific (i.e., from the ultimate to the immediate or to the process objectives). These can be presented in narrative or hierarchical format.

Tip 6: Keep this section relatively short—usually no more than half a page. Use action verbs that can help you move from process objectives to activities in the next section. Examples include

adopt	describe	gather	label
arrest	discriminate	grade	lengthen
assess	delete	group	link
break down	differentiate	hypothesize	measure
build	drop	identify	modify
categorize	evaluate	improve	motivate
classify	extrapolate	increase	
collaborate	forecast	isolate	
complete	freeze	join	

Using Concepts in Both the Problem and Goals Sections

An if-then approach is the easiest way to bring concepts into the
problem and goals sections and then to move on to program activities. What if you do not have a good set of concepts? The following
vignette describes an approach used by an experienced program
developer.

Two by Two

I draw on the literature to put the problem in a more conceptual
framework. Isolated facts have to be explained, or else one's rationale
for action stands on very tenuous grounds. If I am not well grounded
in an area, what I do is search the literature for concepts that I can use
to understand the problem. For example, I've recently become interested in the relationship between teen violence in my community and
the extent to which violent teens appear to be alienated from their
community institutions. So I hit the library in search of recent studies
on alienation and identity to find some appropriate concepts that
could provide some rationale for an intervention.

There are times when I just don't know where to look so I may just fall
back on a sort of trick I've developed that helps me get alternative
insights into the causes of a problem. Suppose I'm concerned with
getting more elderly people to take advantage of a particular service
agency's program. I might begin by jotting down on one piece of paper
all the reasons why older people might not be taking advantage of the
program. Is it because they don't know of its existence? Is it because
the agency is located inconveniently or the hours make it impossible
for potential clients to take advantage of the service? Do clients feel
the agency staff is condescending or unresponsive to their interests?
Do they distrust that agency or the kind of service it gives because of
previous experience?

Then I make a similar inventory of possible reasons that the agency is
not currently serving this population. Is it because agency staff don't
understand the needs of older people or of a particular ethnic minority
among the aged? Is the technology they're using inappropriate to this
population? Are there insufficient numbers of staff people available?
Next I try to match one of the problems on the agency side with one
of the problems on the consumer or client side. I'll draw up a 2 by 2
table (Figure 12.2).

	+ (No Fear)	– (Fear)
+ (Appropriate)	(1) + +	(2) + –
– (Not Appropriate)	(3) – +	(4) –

(Agency's Technology — vertical label on left)

Figure 12.2. Client's Mistrust or Fear of Agency's Technology

If, on analysis, I find that the agency's technology is appropriate and the clients neither mistrust nor fear it, as indicated in Box 1 in Figure 12.2, then I know that's not the reason they're not making use of the service. On the other hand, the technology may be appropriate but the clients may fear it (Figure 12.2, Box 2). In this case, I know that part of the solution is related to consumer education or more effective outreach by the agency.

What if the facts show that there is no consumer anxiety, but the agency's services are nevertheless inappropriate (Figure 12.2, Box 3)? In this case, the appropriate action might be to get consumers to help educate the agency staff about what a particular client group really needs, or to put some pressure on that agency to change its procedures. It may also be important to create some staff training or development activities. But what if the agency's technology is bad and clients mistrust the agency (Figure 12.2, Box 4)? Some planners make the mistake of trying to move directly from Box 4 to Box 2, and then to Box 1.

Generally, I try to create the same 2 x 2 boxes for every logical combination of service blockages from both the agency perspective and the client perspective. Sometimes I find it useful to combine them all into a single larger table. When that's done, I suggest a strategy or set of strategies for dealing with the problem. I can now define the problem in operational terms. It's possible for me to list alternative intervention strategies and then select the best course of action. In my proposal, I give reasons for my selection. More than likely, the reasons will have to do with feasibility; that is, with what can be accomplished in view of available resources, support at the community level, the time available, and the political or sociological constraints limiting our possible interventions.

Methods (Activities and Operations)

The grant writer has moved us to the next section of the narrative: that which is often called the "methods" section—appropriately enough for research projects, but a bit awkward for service or action projects. It might be more appropriate to call this section

- program;
- activities;
- procedures;
- intervention approach.

This is the part of the proposal that receives the greatest scrutiny by some reviewers because it describes what you will be doing and demonstrates whether or not you have thought your program through. For example, if you were to actually develop the nutrition program for pregnant teens, this is the section to describe

Components of the program, for example,
        6-Week "healthy babies" course
        Recruiting and risk-screening program
        Individual and group counseling
        "Neighborhood mentor" program
        "Participating groceries" program

Recruitment: which teens, how many, and from where

Follow-up and supportive services: volunteer program (including recruitment training and supervision of volunteers)

Although some proposals describe location, administrative arrangements, and staffing, here they appear under their own headings in other proposals. Coley and Scheinberg (in press) suggest that all or some of the following issues might be appropriately addressed under project activities:

• location (geographic) site and facilities;
• location (administrative);
• scope of work to be conducted (e.g., counseling, training, or outreach);
• staffing;
• interagency collaborations;
• community involvement;
• client participation.

TIPS ON METHODS

Tip 1: Space permitting, do not just list the major activity (e.g., Meals-on-Wheels for the elderly). Also state which elderly, and for how long, and at what costs. In addition, provide some of the program components:

— where meals will be prepared;
— how they will be delivered (if by volunteers, how they will be recruited and assigned);
— special features (how they can be ordered, relationship to other home help services, etc.).

Tip 2: Relate the program directly to the problem, the goal statement, and your conceptual framework. For example, if you were to identify poor self-esteem as a major contributing factor to poor school performance, make sure that esteem enhancement is an essential component of your intervention.

Tip 3: Use concrete examples. Be graphic. Consider using graphs to show how the program will work. Flowcharts are quick and easy ways to depict the procedures that a program will follow (see discussion of "chart software" in Chapter 15).

Tip 4: It often helps to divide this section into subsections, particularly if you can group the project's tasks into specific categories. Common components of service include

— recruitment, screening, and intake;
— assessment, diagnosis, and problem definition;
— program or case planning;
— implementation of the program and case plan;
— monitoring;
— outcome or satisfaction evaluation;
— termination and follow-up.

SPECIAL NOTE: I can almost hear some of you thinking, "Whoa! My project does not lend itself to such systematic presentation and my expected sponsor would not know how to read it. Besides, if I'm that specific about outcomes, I set myself up for failure."

In many cases, you would be absolutely correct. So relax a bit. Truth be told, many of the methods used in the human services and in cultural programs are poorly understood by sponsors. The fact is that although we believe they do some good (e.g., after-school music programs, drug abuse counseling, or mounting a new museum exhibit), we can easily demonstrate a direct relationship between our methods and activities and the desired outcome. We do what we do because we know how, others expect us to, or we think it will work better and receive more support than some other way. The key to getting a sponsor to want to fund it is to be "credible" about your aims and about how you will achieve them. In the absence of more robust practice concepts, you may have to describe what you will be doing in more detail, that this is state-of-the-art practice (or an innovative experiment), and that a reasonable number of people will be served. Testimonials by satisfied consumers, experts, and other community actors may have to substitute for methodological rigor.

Administrative Location and Staffing

Sponsors will also want to know where the project fits administratively. The following are a few issues you may have to address:

- To whom is the project director responsible? Who does the director supervise?

- Is it part of another department, linked to services in other organizations, semidetached, or independent?
- Will the project have an advisory committee or a policy board? Is the group to be elected or appointed? Will members be representative of staff, other agencies, consumers, experts, board members, or various age or ethnic populations?
- How much authority will it have?
- Is there anything different about the management procedures to be used?

In general, you will not need much more detail than provided in the examples below. That is not always the case, however. Your expected sponsor may require more information.

Example 1: The "men's groups" project will be administered under the Center's Community Programs Division, along with other outreach, counseling, and community education services. Because of its newness, it will have a special community advisory committee, representative of industry sponsors, consumer advocates, and outside experts. For example Prof. Charles Mockle, internationally known for his research on male batterers, has already agreed to serve. A complete list of the other members is found in Appendix D.

Example 2: The program will be lodged administratively at County Hospital. However, its offices and service sites are found in the Northside Medical Center. Staff will be on loan from the following institutions:

St. Joseph Mercy Hospital — Nutritionist staff

Northside — Health care counselors

Northside — Medical personnel

County Hospital — Project Director

All three institutions share a history of collaboration. Staff salaries will be paid for via subcontracting. These arrangements make it possible to build on local capacity and expertise, avoid the costs of service duplication, and increase the possibility of continuity beyond the project period by securing the involvement of the major relevant institutions.

This may also be a good place to describe the staffing of the project. You will want to give brief job descriptions for all the key professional staff. If you are to use consultants, indicate for what purposes and to what extent they will be involved in the project. If you know who the persons will be who will perform each of the staff roles (e.g., the project director, associate director, assistant director, administrative assistant, and senior researcher), indicate their names and briefly discuss their specific qualifications. This may include previous work or their other supportive or complementary roles within your organization or agency.

If you do not know who will be assigned key roles, include something about how they will be recruited and selected and the required qualifications for each position. More detailed information on the staff may be located in the appendix. It might include either (a) abbreviated resumes on all professional staff persons to be involved in some significant fashion or (b) descriptions of desired qualifications, if they are yet to be hired. I find it useful to employ a simplified job description built from a number of task statements. These use the following "mapping sentence" to specify all the major tasks to be performed by key actors.

SAMPLE TASK STATEMENTS

Mapping Sentence	Sample 1	Sample 2
Who	The butler	The outreach coordinator
Does or will do what	laces	organizes
To whom or what	Mrs. Scarlett's tea	community focus group meetings
With what or how	with arsenic	in collaboration with churches, PTOs, and local associations
For what purpose	to do her in	so as to assess needs for after school activities
Under whose direction, auspices, supervision	at the behest of the upstairs maid.	under the guidelines provided by the partnership advisory council.

The narrative is not the place to list all the tasks to be performed by all the actors, but it is a good place to explain who will be responsible for performance or supervision of the major clusters of tasks. For example, you might write a brief job description for the outreach worker as follows:

The outreach worker will <u>organize</u> focus groups, <u>recruit</u> and <u>train</u> volunteers, and <u>coordinate</u> publicity for the program, in collaboration with relevant community groups and under the guidelines set by the partnership advisory committee.

Note that I underlined the action verbs (for this discussion and not to suggest that they should be underlined in the proposal narrative). These should be consistent with the major action verbs you used to describe project activities. In this way, the reviewer can easily connect what is to be done with who is responsible for doing it.

TIPS ON JOB DESCRIPTIONS

Tip 1: In addition to describing what the key staffers or community volunteers or both will be doing, make sure you also describe what you expect from a consultant if you have included one in the program narrative or the budget.

Tip 2: Some funders may want to know how much weight (percentage of time) will be allocated to each cluster of tasks. The intake worker's responsibilities include intake and screening (40%), responding to phone inquiries (15%), and referring clients to appropriate service departments in the agency or to collateral providers (25%) and related administrative tasks (20%).

Thus far, you have defined the position and described the major responsibilities associated with it. Funders may also want to know something about qualifications required for each of the key staff members, such as knowledge and skills, education and experience, and personal qualifications (e.g., empathy and the ability to speak Spanish). Only qualifications directly related to performance of the job may be included.

Evaluation

Mention "evaluation" to many novice proposal writers and you push the panic button. No wonder. The very term evokes an image of someone looking at what you did and what you are doing. Most of us do not like to be evaluated, even if we are doing the job ourselves. That is not what this evaluation is about, however. This is not evaluation of the staff: It is evaluation of what the program has been able to achieve and how it has gone about trying to do it. Program staff are understandably nervous about this, too, because it takes technical skill to do a proper evaluation. Staff hired to manage theater programs, provide outreach educational services to the disabled, or set up substance abuse counseling services may know plenty about what they do but not how to evaluate it. Now that you have gulped for air, and admitted your discomfort with this topic, we will look at what evaluation is all about.

Both the project's operations and its outcomes should be evaluated. *Formative* evaluation looks at what you are doing, often as you are doing it. Its purpose is to make adjustments and improvements in operations. It is a monitoring activity that makes it possible to engage in one or more "mid-course corrections," in effect reformulating parts of the program.

The following are some examples of process questions:

- Did all women complete the assessment instrument within a week of entering the program?
- Were all the women in the program offered the opportunity of attending the 6-week nutritional training course? How many enrolled, for which sessions? How many completed the program? What were the average number of sessions attended?

The evaluation of outcomes relates directly to the objectives you established for the project. For that reason, it is often referred to as summative. For example, the following are summative questions that related to the process, immediate, and intermediate objectives discussed previously:

- What proportion of the at-risk pregnant teens were enrolled in the nutrition program?
- Was the nutrition level of those enrolled improved? By how much?
- Did the incidence of premature births decrease among those enrolled? By how much?

In addition to finding out how well the project worked, funders may also be interested in knowing whether, given both costs and benefits, it should have been conducted at all. An important question, especially for demonstration projects, is "Were the goals or procedures to achieve them appropriate or realistic?" This is often referred to as impact evaluation. Costs and benefits are weighed and the question is asked about whether the project may not have been worth doing (i.e., was there enough bang for the buck?).

There is also a fourth approach to evaluation. Its focus is on consumer satisfaction—that is, the extent to which the consumer feels that the program or intervention helped and was delivered appropriately. These are more than "satisfaction" measures, often focusing on program quality.

If the funder expects a detailed evaluation plan in the proposal, consider including information on the following:

- the questions to be answered and uses (purpose) to which answers will be put;
- how the evaluation will be conducted (methods and time frame);
- by whom it will be conducted;
- data collection methods, sources of information, and sampling plan (if relevant);
- data analysis methods (and who will be involved);
- staffing plan for evaluation (including involvement of insiders and outsiders);
- uses of steering committee or involvement of key stakeholder publics;
- reporting procedures;
- budget for the evaluation.

Funders may require that the evaluation be done by an external evaluator on the assumption that an outsider is likely to be more objective and competent in evaluation methodology. Agency staff sometimes prefer to do their own evaluation because they assume that it can be done at a lower cost internally, that program staff are likely to better understand the issues, or that researchers are not as likely to understand some of the nuances of what is really happening. Therefore, when do you hire an outside evaluator and when do you do the evaluation internally? Answer: You may not have a choice. The sponsor may decide.

EVALUATION DESIGN TIPS

Tip 1: If you hire an outside evaluator, consider appointing a staff and board evaluation advisory committees so as to ensure ongoing dialogue between the evaluator and those who will use the results.

Tip 2: If the evaluation is done internally, hire an outside consultant so as to ensure that it is as objective and comprehensive as possible. When programs are repeated often, staff develop vested interests in doing "what we've always done." Outsiders can challenge vested interests with less discomfort.

Tip 3: Whether employing inside or outside evaluators, involve them in the program design and in writing the proposal. Evaluators can help sharpen up both objectives and operations by the kinds of questions they ask. Involving them early can help avoid communication problems later on.

Tip 4: It may not be enough to list the questions to be asked by the evaluator. Like the program itself, the evaluation must be planned, with its own objectives and methods and its own beginning, middle, and end.

Tip 5: If it uses all four, the evaluation plan should differentiate between formative, summative, impact, and quality measures.

Tip 6: Give as much attention to the evaluator's task assignments and qualifications as to any of the other top staff positions.

The following is another tip: Some government agencies and foundations may engage in their own processes of review and evaluation intended, by them, to make certain that they are making the right decisions. For example, they may be interested in tracking the general progress of each grant they make, assessing the extent to which they are successful in maintaining grant receiver accountability, increasing the knowledge base for similar interventions by other organizations, and so on. If you know that a potential sponsor is concerned about these issues, show how your evaluation process can contribute to their understanding.

Also, funders are notorious for demanding evaluation and underfunding it. The best way to deal with this is to start the process early and to build the evaluation questions right into your program design.

Organizational Capability Statement

Chances are that you have already covered organizational capacity in your introductory statement, part of which introduces your organization and its track record. If not, go over the instructions for that section and apply relevant suggestions to the capability section.

Significance, Replication and Dissemination, Community Support, and Continuation

You may also have covered these issues elsewhere. Funders are not likely to require specific sections of the narrative to deal explicitly with all four. They may well use these, however, as criteria for determining whether or not to support the project. If they have to hunt hard for the answers, the proposal may not "score" as well as it deserves.

Significance

Ask whether or not it would make a difference to anyone if this project were to not take place. You might be able to answer affirmatively if

- there is clearly a significant problem or need to be addressed;
- the methods to be employed are innovative or the program has special features that distinguish it from others;
- the approach has great promise of transferability to other settings or decreasing intervention costs;
- the consequences of nonaction would clearly be more costly than the cost of the project.

TIPS ON EMPHASIZING
PROJECT SIGNIFICANCE

Tip 1: The program's significance should be framed as closely as possible to the funder's interests. For purposes of the proposal, the project is not significant if the sponsor does not think it is.

Tip 2: Use buzzwords that are important to the funder, without resorting to cliches. The following are examples of buzzwords that work for different sponsors:

Multicultural environment	In collaboration with
Empowerment	Shared resources
Self-determination	Assurance of quality
Responsible	Accountable

Tip 3: Connect what you say here with what you said before or what will follow. In other words, do not surprise the reviewer with claims of significance. The project's significance should be visible throughout the narrative.

Replication and Dissemination

When sponsors think a project is significant, they may also be interested in drawing lessons from it that can be applied to other settings. Some funders provide support only on condition that the project design includes a plan for dissemination. This is especially true if they are funding a pilot with the intention of testing whether or not it should or could be replicated elsewhere. In this case, dissemination may actually be a component of the methods section. In addition to funder requirements, there are several other reasons to consider dissemination of your experience, including

1. Your experience can help others by demonstrating what works and what does not.
2. Sharing your experience may also result in getting feedback from others and in getting reciprocal information on other successful programs. You can learn from both.

3. It rarely hurts to receive recognition for the work your organization is doing. Dissemination increases appreciation of your program and often translates into additional support from current and potential funding sources.

DISSEMINATION TIPS

Tip 1: If you plan to do any, be sure to include dissemination in your budget. You do not want to wind up getting a myriad of requests for information, consultation, or reports if you have neither the staffing nor the time to respond.

Tip 2: Like other communication efforts, dissemination requires careful targeting. Determine who you want to communicate with and the best way of disseminating information. Consider using the following:

Journal and newspaper articles	Consultation
Professional meetings and conferences	Training seminars and courses
Newsletters and concept or working papers	Consortium arrangements with other organizations
Books and manuals	Public appearances, speaking on radio or TV, or community meetings
Internet sites and conferences	Demonstration workshops

Tip 3: Do not neglect internal dissemination. The success of your project may depend on the support of other departments in your organization, community advisory groups, or your organization's board.

Community Support

Many funders require some evidence of community or local support for the project or for the organization in which it will be lodged. The chapters on government, foundation, and private-sector funding were replete with examples of projects that require multiple organizational involvement. The term collaboration, one experienced grant writer tells us, "seems to be as common as prepositions and conjunctions." That may overstate the case slightly but perhaps not by much, especially when grants are intended to seed programs that are intended to operate independently at the end of the grant period.

Sponsors often insist on evidence of community support and collaboration because both are likely to demonstrate

- the sharing of resources or responsibility;
- legitimacy and acceptance of the program or project;
- the likelihood of continuation beyond the funding period.

TIPS ON DEMONSTRATING SUPPORT

Tip 1: Include letters of support from key stakeholders such as collaborating organizations, other committed resource providers, members and consumers, administrators, and local federations responsible for services planning or coordination.

Tip 2: When funding is designed to enable interorganizational collaboration or when such collaboration is essential to the project design, include charts and other descriptors of the working relationships in the appropriate locations in the narrative or expand on these in the appendix or both.

Continuation

Often, funders provide money to initiate a new service on the assumption that the recipient agency intends to continue the program beyond the initial grant. The following are a few questions that reviewers generally want answers to:

1. If the program is to be continued and new financial resources will be needed, from where will they come? From outside sources such as fees for service or other grants? From reallocation of the agency's internal budget?
2. Is there a plan for securing continuation funding? If so, whose responsibility is it to implement the plan, when does the search for funding begin, and when should some new funding kick in?

3. What will happen if external funding is not available? Will internal funds be redirected from other programs? Is the use of noncash resources a possibility?

4. If this is a pilot project, and if it proves successful, is it to be folded into ongoing agency operations, transferred elsewhere, or transformed into a separate organization with its own board and funding source? How is this to be decided and when, and how is the transformation to take place?

TIPS ON CONTINUATION

Tip 1: If this is a multiyear project, show increasing amounts of external income in each successive year. For example, the first year might include 25% in matching or internally generated funds; the second year 40%; the third and final year 60%.

Tip 2: If possible, include letters of commitment from other organizations to collaborate with or contribute to the program after the initial grant period. If not, include these in continuing grant applications (e.g., for the second and subsequent years of funding).

Even when a commitment to continuation is not specifically required, it is often helpful if the proposal demonstrates the applicant's concern for the future. This is particularly true when the absence of continued funding might jeopardize the client population through sudden termination of services.

REVIEW

Full-length proposals are generally divided into the following sections: (a) the title and cover pages, (b) the project narrative, (c) a time frame, (d) the budget, and (e) the appendix. The cover pages generally include (a) one page that specifies the title of the project, its type, the name and address of the organization in which it will be lodged, the name and address of project director or the organization's chief operating or financial officer or all three, budget and dollar amount requested, and proposed project period, and (b) a second page with a 200-word abstract and (for projects with 5 or more pages of narrative) a table of contents. The bulk of the chapter dealt with components of the narrative. These include (a) the introduction; (b) the problem statement; (c) listing of goals and objectives, (d) a methods section (e.g., activities, procedures, and location); (e) staffing and administrative arrangements; (f) evaluation; (g) organizational capacities; and (h) descriptions of the project's significance, plans for dissemination or replication, and continuation.

REFERENCES

Coley, S. M., & Scheinberg, C. A. (in press). *Proposal writing* (2nd ed.). Thousand Oaks, CA: Sage.
Kettner, P. M., Moroney, R. M., & Martin, L. L. (1990). *Designing and managing programs: An effectiveness-based approach.* Newbury Park, CA: Sage.

SUGGESTIONS FOR FURTHER READING

Bauer, D. G. (1988). *The "how-to" grants manual.* New York: Macmillan.
Belcher, J. C., & Jacobsen, J. M. (Eds.). (1992). *From idea to funded project: Grant proposals that work.* Phoenix, AZ: Oryx Press.
Ezell, S. (Ed.). (1986). *The proposal writer's swipe file.* Washington, DC: Taft Corporation.
Geever, J. C., & McNeil, P. (1993). *The Foundation Center's guide to proposal writing.* New York: The Foundation Center.
Geller, R. E. (1988). *Plain talk about grants.* Sacramento: California State Library Foundation.
Gilpatrick, L. (1989). *Grants for nonprofit organizations: A guide to funding and grant writing.* New York: Praeger.
Hall, M. (1988). *Getting funded: A complete guide to proposal writing.* Portland, OR: Continuing Education.
Herman, J. L., Morris, L. L., & Fitz-Gibbon, C. T. (1987). *Evaluator's handbook.* Newbury Park, CA: Sage.
Kaplan, H. M., & Ryan, R. (1997). *Grant proposal development.* Thousand Oaks, CA: Sage.
Lauffer, A. (1982). *Assessment tools* [See chapters on environmental mapping and on functional job analysis]. Beverly Hills, CA: Sage.
Lauffer, A. (1984a). *Strategic marketing for not-for-profit organizations: Program and resource development* [See Chapters 4 and 12]. New York: Free Press.
Lauffer, A. (1984b). *Grantsmanship and Fund Raising.* Beverly Hills, CA: Sage.
Lefferts, R. (1990). *Getting a grant in the 1990s.* Englewood Cliffs, NJ: Prentice Hall.
Locke, L. L., & Spirduso, W. W. (1987). *Proposals that work.* Newbury Park, CA: Sage.
Martin, L. (1993). *Total quality management in the human services.* Newbury Park, CA: Sage.

Meador, R. (1985). *Guidelines for writing proposals.* Chelsea, MI: Lewis.

Morris, L. L., & Fitz-Gibbon, C. T. (1978). *How to deal with goals and objectives.* Beverly Hills, CA: Sage.

Pecora, P. J., & Austin, M. J. (1987). *Managing human service personnel.* Newbury Park, CA: Sage.

Pequegnat, W., & Stover, E. (1995). *How to write a successful research grant application.* New York: Plenum.

Reif-Lehrer, L. (1989). *Writing a successful grant application.* New York: Jones & Barlett.

Ries, J. B., & Leukefeld, C. G. (1997). *Applying for research funding* (2nd ed.). Thousand Oaks, CA: Sage.

Rossi, P. H., & Freeman, H. E. (1994). *Evaluation: A systematic approach* (5th ed.). Thousand Oaks: CA: Sage.

APPLICATION FOR FEDERAL ASSISTANCE

2. DATE SUBMITTED	Applicant Identifier

1. TYPE OF SUBMISSION:

Application	Preapplication
☐ Construction	☐ Construction
☐ Non-Construction	☐ Non-Construction

3. DATE RECEIVED BY STATE	State Application Identifier
4. DATE RECEIVED BY FEDERAL AGENCY	Federal Identifier

5. APPLICANT INFORMATION

Legal Name:

Organizational Unit:

Address (give city, county, state, and zip code):

Name and telephone number of the person to be contacted on matters involving this application (give area code)

6. EMPLOYER IDENTIFICATION NUMBER (EIN):

☐☐ − ☐☐☐☐☐☐☐

7. TYPE OF APPLICANT: (enter appropriate letter in box) ☐

A State	H Independent School Dist.
B County	I State Controlled Institution of Higher Learning
C Municipal	J Private University
D Township	K Indian Tribe
E Interstate	L Individual
F Intermunicipal	M Profit Organization
G Special District	N Other (Specify) _____

8. TYPE OF APPLICATION:

☐ New   ☐ Continuation   ☐ Revision

If Revision, enter appropriate letter(s) in box(es): ☐ ☐

A Increase Award   B. Decrease Award   C. Increase Duration

D Decrease Duration   Other (specify):

9. NAME OF FEDERAL AGENCY:

10. CATALOG OF FEDERAL DOMESTIC ASSISTANCE NUMBER:

☐☐ − ☐☐☐

TITLE:

11. DESCRIPTIVE TITLE OF APPLICANTS PROJECT:

12. AREAS AFFECTED BY PROJECT (cities, counties, states, etc.)

13. PROPOSED PROJECT:		14. CONGRESSIONAL DISTRICTS OF:	
Start Date	Ending Date	a. Applicant	b. Project
			....

15. ESTIMATED FUNDING:

a Federal	$		.00
b Applicant	$		.00
c State	$		.00
d Local	$		.00
e Other	$		.00
f Program Income	$		.00
g TOTAL	$		.00

16. IS APPLICATION SUBJECT TO REVIEW BY STATE EXECUTIVE ORDER 12372 PROCESS?

a. ☐ YES THIS PREAPPLICATION/APPLICATION WAS MADE AVAILABLE TO THE STATE EXECUTIVE ORDER 12372 PROCESS FOR REVIEW ON

DATE _____

b. NO ☐ PROGRAM IS NOT COVERED BY E.O. 12372

☐ OR PROGRAM HAS NOT BEEN SELECTED BY STATE FOR REVIEW

17. IS THE APPLICANT DELINQUENT ON ANY FEDERAL DEBT?

☐ Yes   If "Yes," attach an explanation.   ☐ No

18. TO THE BEST OF MY KNOWLEDGE AND BELIEF, ALL DATA IN THIS APPLICATION/PREAPPLICATION ARE TRUE AND CORRECT. THE DOCUMENT HAS BEEN DULY AUTHORIZED BY THE GOVERNING BODY OF THE APPLICANT AND THE APPLICANT WILL COMPLY WITH THE ATTACHED ASSURANCES IF THE ASSISTANCE IS AWARDED

a Typed Name of Authorized Representative	b Title	c Telephone number
d Signature of Authorized Representative		e Date Signed

Standard Form 424 (REV 4-88)
Prescribed by OMB Circular A-102

Sample Government Application Title Page

13

Drawing Up the Budget

Expressing the Narrative in Numbers

Too Much and Too Late!

When I got to the budget part of my proposal, I thought I was over the hump. Was I ever wrong! By the time I had costed out what we intended to do, it totaled $256,000. The funder's average grant for last year was under $80,000. Not much chance that we could get what we needed for the project.

And there was just no way we could trim what we were planning to do without so emasculating the program as to make it relatively worthless. I should have started with the budget, then figured out what we could do with the limitations imposed.

The program planner learned his lesson too late. He also learned the wrong lesson, however. A $256,000 budget may have been perfectly appropriate, given the scope of the work projected. There is no reason, however, that the total amount should have been sought from a single funder. It is increasingly common for budgets to show income from several sources, including the grant-seeking organization itself.

THE BUDGET AS STATEMENT OF INTENT

Properly designed, the budget can be the section of your proposal that clinches the deal by convincing funders you know what you are about and that an investment in your program is a dollar well spent. Poorly designed, the budget can sink it. That is because, like the overall proposal, the budget is a statement of intent. It indicates, in dollar terms, what you expect to do and to achieve and how much will be invested in each component of the program and when. This makes it both a program and a fiscal document.

The chapter begins by describing the most common budget form, the line-item budget, and then contrasts it with performance and program budgets. All three are generally presented in tabular form, and I will discuss the mechanics of designing and presenting budget tables. Those familiar with budgets may want to skim most of that section, but you may not want to miss the discussions of indirect costs and cost sharing. Even experienced fund-raisers may find it useful to pay specific attention to the discussion of why the budget can be your Achilles' heel instead of the deal clincher! I have asked some government, foundation, and private-sector funders to share their perspectives on this topic with you.

Three Kinds of Budgets: A Brief Overview

Each of the three types of budgets has its own advantages and disadvantages. You are probably most familiar with the line-item budget, so called because it has a line for each item of expenditure. Budget lines list expenses just the way they are paid out. Typically, there are line items for personnel, operations, and indirect costs. Personnel lines show the costs associated with remuneration of the people who do the work. Personnel items can be in the form of salaries and wages, but they can also be designated as contract services (as when you contract out for the performance of certain tasks).

Nonpersonnel expenses include such items as rent, insurance, travel, supplies, and so on. Most human service agencies and many other nonprofits are highly labor intensive; therefore, the personnel section is likely to account for most of their expenditures. There are times, however, when the outlays for operations actually exceed those associated with personnel. Examples include the costs of mounting a museum exhibit, funding scholarships for a program, trainee or staff travel, or materials for free distribution to a client population. In these cases, such program expenses might be listed in their own section.

All these are the direct costs of doing business. Most programs, however, also have a number of "indirect" costs associated with them. This is the government term for what businesses usually call "overhead" and foundations are likely to call "administrative" costs. As this nomenclature suggests, these are costs that are not directly tagged to specific lines but reflect real costs incurred.

The performance budget projects the cost of performing units of work—for example, conducting a workshop, counseling clients, or managing a project. It reflects the work to be done by program category. A program budget goes one step further. It categorizes expenditures in relationship to the agency objectives or the objectives of a particular project. Administrative and maintenance costs are allocated to specific objectives, such as placing retrained workers on the job, getting a hard-to-place child adopted, completing a plan for staff and organizational development, or producing instructional materials. The examples in Table 13.1 may help you visualize the differences among these budgets.

Notice that the line-item budget tells you exactly what you expect to spend money on. For that reason, it is easy to monitor your expenditures. It is a good device for tracking the outflow of funds, but it has several disadvantages. First, by focusing on the expenditure of resources rather than on accomplishment, it does little to reflect the purpose of those expenditures. The budget is considered merely an accounting device. It is not very helpful in designing your program. The program or project, in fact, has to be designed fully before its objectives or activities are translated into budgetary terms. Because line-item budgets do not show enough about why each item is included, they generally require explanations that appear in a budget narrative following the tabular budget. These explanations (often referred to as justifications) are sometimes given in performance or program terms.

Table 13.1 Simplified Line-Item, Performance, and Program Budgets Compared

Line-Item Budget	$	Performance Budget	$	Performance Budget	$
Salaried personnel	40,000	Consultation on program design	13,000	Plan for staff development	23,000
Consultants	12,000	Staffing planning committee	6,000	Instructional materials design and distribution	41,000
Facilities	4,000	Design instructional materials	36,000		
Equipment	2,000	Printing	3,000		
Supplies	4,000	Administration	6,000		
Travel	2,000				
Total	64,000		64,000		64,000

LINE-ITEM BUDGET: A CLOSER LOOK

Because line-item budgets are most common, I will describe what goes into common items and then suggest what to consider in assigning a dollar value to each.

Personnel

The personnel line includes estimates of the salaries and wages that will be paid to all personnel employed by the project. Fringe benefits and employee pay are generally posted separately as two items on the budget document but may be combined as a single item. Personnel includes full- and part-time staff who perform professional, clerical, maintenance, and other supportive tasks. Indicate on your budget if personnel are to be full or part time. There may be personnel lines for consultants or contract services. People who perform these services are paid for their work but are not regular employees and do not receive fringe benefits.

For those who are employed by the organization, it is necessary to designate the proportion of their pay assigned to the project. The most common way of doing this is to specify their full-time equivalence (FTE) on the project. For example, a 0.5 FTE would indicate a half-time appointment (or half-time split among 2 or more people).

Five FTEs would indicate that the salaries sought cover the equivalence of 5 full-time employees in a particular category. In practice, there might be 10 half-time employees or 2 full- and 6 half-timers. From a budgetary perspective, there is no difference.

Consultation and Contract Services

These include services required by the project that its staff are unable to provide or that can be provided better or cheaper by outsiders. Such services may be performed by individuals or organizations with whom you contract (from the budget perspective, it does not matter which). Examples of consultants include

- staff developers or trainers;
- fund-raisers or proposal writers;
- reading specialists who assist your volunteer tutorial staff;
- experts in managing personnel practices or in staff recruitment.

Examples of other kinds of contract services include

- accounting;
- legal advice or representation;
- maintenance services;
- transportation (e.g., contract with Yellow Cab for regular transportation of seniors);
- clinicians who bill the organization on an hourly basis for the number of contact hours they spend with referred clients.

Anticipated fees, as well as expenses incurred by consultants in providing service (e.g., travel and per diem), may be posted as a single item on the budget document or broken down into cost estimates for each. The budget explanation is used to justify the costs involved.

Facilities

This line summarizes the costs associated with space required by the project to administer and perform its activities. Facilities may be leased, rented, purchased, or donated as an in-kind contribution. If space requires remodeling or renovation, these costs should also be distinguished as a line item on the budget document and the rationale for altering the site should be outlined in the budget justification. Few funders are likely to cover renovation or purchase costs for projects that are not expected to last more than 1 or 2 years. If space costs are minimal or absorbed by other agency operations, it may not be necessary to include a special line item for facilities. In this case, the costs involved may be lumped under "indirect" costs.

Equipment

The equipment line includes both office and program equipment such as furniture, computers and printers, copy and fax machines, audiovisual equipment, and other items that staff use in administering or carrying out activities. Equipment may be purchased (if the sponsor permits) or rented. An explanation of the need for costly pieces of equipment should appear in the budget justification. For relatively short projects—3 years or fewer—sponsors are more likely to cover the cost of leasing than of purchasing. It may be possible, however, to lease equipment that the agency can purchase for $1 or some minimal sum on completion of the project. Sometimes the sponsor will allow purchase of equipment for short projects if this is likely to save money and if the recipient organization agrees that the equipment will be used for bona fide nonprofit functions on completion of the project.

Consumable Supplies

Consumables generally refer to items that are used in day-to-day office operations, including

- office supplies (e.g., printing paper and cartridge, stationery, and lavatory supplies);
- less expensive office implements such as staplers and in-baskets;
- program supplies such as film, books, and other disposable items used in service programs;
- routine office-related telephone expenses;
- routine postage costs.

If the project is designed to make extensive programmatic use of the telephone, or make large mailings as part of its educational program, telephone and postage are likely to have lines of their own under "Program-Related Expenses." These are program rather than office consumables, which include estimates of the costs of monthly rental or charges for long-distance telephone calls and fees that might be charged for radio, television, and newspaper announcements. Printing and reproduction costs may be included here or may go into a special program or publications category.

Travel and Per Diem

This item includes estimates of the travel costs to be incurred by staff and volunteers within the local area and when going out of town on agency business. In some cases, it also includes travel expenses incurred by consumers participating in agency activities. Out-of-town expenses may include per diem expenses for room and board. Expenses for consultant travel and per diem may be included under either the consultant or the travel category of the budget document.

Reviewers usually want full explanations for out-of-town travel estimates. For example, if conference travel is involved, there generally has to be a good rationale for the trip. Even if the rationale is made in the body of the narrative, it may be necessary to repeat the essentials in narrative form right after the tabular presentation. Explanations for routine local expenses can be made right on the line. For example,

Home visits	5 workers, each driving 100 miles per month, @ $.31/mile, for 1 year	$1,860
Client transportation	Cab service: 170 trips/month $4.50/trip	765

Indirect Costs

These require prior agreement or understanding with the funder that overhead will be allowed and at what level. If your organization has had other grants or contracts from government agencies, chances are it already has a standard agreement with those agencies on how indirect costs will be calculated. Generally, this is an agreed-on percentage of either (a) the total budget (referred to as total direct costs [TDC]) or (b) the amount designated for total personnel costs (TPC). For example, government agencies sometimes arrive at a figure of 50% to 65% for TDC on university research projects but only 8% of salaries and wages for training grants. Why such a wide discrepancy? Research grants may include laboratories and equipment for which there are no other sources of funding. In contrast, most training grants are intended to cover the costs of faculty and other personnel. Because this is the primary business of the university, the government assumes that a lower indirect cost formula would not cause hardship to the institution.

Unlike government agencies, corporate funders are not likely to have a standard figure in mind, but because they themselves charge overhead whenever they do contract business, you should not find it difficult to point out the reasons you must do it also. If you can find out what they charge their clients (e.g., assume it is approximately 40% of TDC) and then budget slightly under that (e.g., 35% of TDC), chances are no one will question your estimate. Most foundations will also allow administrative costs of between 15% and 35%.

In mid-1996, the Federal Office of Management and Budget (OMB) issued one of its periodic updated versions of OMB Circular A-21, replacing the term indirect costs with two terms, *administrative costs* and *facilities costs*. Administrative costs are limited to 26% of all direct costs. Rules governing what can be charged to administration or facilities are expected to continue to change. Because these affect federal support, they are also likely to affect rules adapted by state and more proximate levels of government.

Unfortunately, some funders disallow indirect costs, however legitimate. If possible, your best bet may be to itemize all your expenditures, no matter how small. You generally are permitted to group some together (e.g., gardening and maintenance services). If an audit is conducted, you must be prepared to demonstrate that the amounts listed actually went into the organization's overall gardening budget.

If you have never put together a line-item budget, the sample in Table 13.2 and the following discussion may be helpful.

Table 13.2 Sample Line-Item Budget for a Training and Materials Development Project[a]

Line Item	Requested ($)	Donated ($)	Total ($)
Personnel			
Professional			
Director (0.125 FTE)		6,000	6,000
Associate Director for Curric (0.25 FTE)	10,000		10,000
Trainer/Evaluator (0.5 FTE)	18,000		18,000
Nonprofessional			
Receptionist/Secretary (0.5 FTE)		10,000	10,000
Maintenance (0.10 FTE)		2,000	2,000
Fringe benefits (30% of above)	8,400	5,400	13,800
Consultants			
Six consultants at $500 per day for 5 days	15,000		15,000
Travel and per diem (five trips/consultant)	6,000		6,000
Nonpersonnel			
Equipment			
Computer, printer, workstation purchase	3,500		3,500
Rent AV equipment as needed	1,500		1,500
Consumable supplies			
Office consumables	1,200		1,200
Telephone	800		800
Instructional materials	2,000	2,000	4,000
Software and instructional programs	4,000		4,000
Staff travel			
Mileage at $0.30 per mile for 2,000 miles	600		600
Four out-of-town trips @ $300 each	1,200		1,200
Facilities			
Rental of office space	1,200	1,200	2,400
Rental of conference facilities	800	2,000	2,800
Total direct costs	74,200	28,650	102,800
Indirect costs			
30% of total personnel costs	17,220	7,020	24,240
Total	91,420	35,670	127,040

a. The formula for calculating indirect cost was agreed to in advance by the sponsor.

DESIGNING THE LINE-ITEM BUDGET

Line-Item Tabular Categories—The Columns and the Rows

Budgets should be designed to communicate all necessary details to relevant audiences. If you are using a funder's guidelines, make sure that you follow those guidelines to the letter. If you are following the procedures used in your own organization, make sure you use the categories considered standard for other programs and departments.

Table 13.2 provides a somewhat simplified but fairly standard line-item presentation. Notice that there are three columns: one for the "total" budget (at the right, although it could have been the left-most column), one for the "requested" amount, and another for the "donated" amount. The Requested column specifies the amount requested from a particular source—for example, the United Foundation, the community mental health board, the city council, or Litton Industries. The Donated column refers to all other sources. The total budget sums up the Requested and Donated columns.

For different audiences, you may wish to use different categories. Instead of the requested category, a funder may prefer you use terms such as sponsor and to substitute "cost sharing" for "donated." If you have several sponsors, you might wish to divide the Requested column into one for each sponsor, although this can become unwieldy. Unless several funders have agreed in advance to collaborate and want the budget to reflect each of their contributions, it is general practice to combine all the donated or cost-sharing contributions (including your own agency's in-kind contributions) in a single column. The narrative explanation, rather than the line-item table, is the place to describe sources of income. Some potential sponsors may also want to know how much of what in the Donated column has already been committed. This, too, can be described in the budget narrative.

Should you be seeking funds primarily from your own organization's general fund (its regular operating budget) or other internal sources, the columns might include such designations as "general fund allocation," "client fees," and "parents appeal." Budgets are flexible tools. The categories you decide to use should be determined by what you hope to convey to the publics you are addressing. Unless the funder requests a great deal of detail, it is better not to crowd the tabular budget with too much information.

The tabular budget must include as much information as possible but no more than is needed. This may become clear when each of the line items are examined. I begin with personnel. The section on personnel generally includes three subsections: (a) salaries and wages, (b) fringe benefits, and (c) consultants and contract services. You might wish to subdivide salaries and wages further into "professional personnel" and "support staff." Indicating the specific salary allocated to a given staff member may be insufficient without designating the number of months that person will be working on the project or the percentage of work time allocated to that project. Assume that the project director's annual salary is $48,000 but he or she is assigned only quarter time to the project. Assume further that you are asking the funding source to cover the full 25% of his or her time allocated to the project for the entire 12 months. The following is how you could communicate this as a line item:

	Requested	Donated
Project director: .25 FTE at $48,000	12,000	

Suppose your project includes five caseworkers. The next line item might then read as follows:

	Requested	Donated
Caseworkers: 5 FTE at $30,000	120,000	30,000

In this case, the agency or some other donor is contributing 20% of the salaries from some other source. If one of those workers is already on staff, this might be part of the agency's in-kind or noncash contribution. Explain this in the budget justification. If you expect to be re-funded the next year, that explanation may be crucial. Some budget writers prefer to designate each item that is to be subsequently explained with an asterisk (*) or some other symbol, others prefer to use superscript numbers much as they might footnotes in a professional article, and still others prefer none of these designations, trusting that the reader will understand what is being communicated when reading the justification section.

If you expect salaries to change due to union contracts or annual merit increments during a given fiscal year, you will want to show this in the budget as well. Do so by designating that the project director will be paid for 3 months at the full-time rate of $48,000 and 9 months at $52,000. The adjusted sum would appear as a full-time rate of $51,000 during these 12 months. Other than the salary amount, this would have no bearing on the time invested. The director is still expected to be assigned quarter time to this project (0.25 FTE).

Determining Salary Levels and Other Costs

Assume you have decided what work needs to be done and how many people it will take to do the job. Each job is given a title. So far, so good; the trouble, however, is that you are not sure how much each person should be paid. What do you do? The first step is to find out what comparable programs, within your organization and outside, pay staff who have similar responsibilities. Is there a going rate for certain jobs? Pay rates on newly funded projects should neither exceed nor fall below those for comparable positions elsewhere.

If some or all of the staff to be assigned to the project are new, you will have to make some guesses about where, on a range of possible salaries, each might be placed. Assume for a moment that the salary for a caseworker ranges from $22,000 at entry level to $37,000 per year for those at the upper end of the scale. If your estimate of the average salary is too low, you will not be able to attract more experienced staff without exceeding your budget. If you start too high, your funders are likely to be suspicious, fearing that you are padding the budget. As a rule of thumb, it is helpful to divide the salary range into six segments.

In this case, if you employ $3,000 increments, you might arrive at the following salary levels: $22,000, $25,000, $28,000, $31,000, $34,000, and $37,000. Designate the average salary to be somewhere at the middle or just above the middle range—for example, $28,000 or $31,000. My preference is to go just above the midpoint to $31,000 instead of splitting the difference. Why just above the midpoint? Because funders will generally not question your selection of the higher figure, and because if you pick the lower or average figure you might be in trouble if more experienced staff are available.

The same thinking goes into estimating other costs. You may not know what the new Pentium computer is actually going to cost, but you can get some cost estimates and include the one which is a bit higher than the midpoint. That gives you some flexibility. If a new model becomes available (as it is bound to) when you are ready to make the purchase, that little extra may make it possible to purchase it.

308 FUND-RAISING FUNDAMENTALS

Fringe Benefits

Fringe benefits are generally calculated as a percentage of all salaries and wages. If you work for an established organization, chances are that the average is between 30% and 35% for all professional and support staff. The fringe package may also include voluntary contributions that are matched by the employer to cover (a) health, mental health, and dental health insurance programs; (b) an annuity or retirement fund; (c) life insurance; or (d) some other benefit program that is matched in part by the employer. Some organizations also provide what have come to be known as "perks." These may include payment to attend training programs, memberships in professional associations, access to agency services and facilities, subsidized rent, use of an agency vehicle, and so on. If your organization has already developed a fringe package, use the percentage allocation in your budget; otherwise, you will have to design a new one and justify it. The agency's comptroller or accountant will be able to advise you on which figure to use.

Consultant and Contract Services

These are services your staff does not have the competence to perform or that it is cheaper to contract for. Be especially careful to detail consultant and contract costs. Funders are likely to be suspicious if the fees you pay are high. Here again, you will have to check on the going rate. Recognizing that some consultants demand much higher fees than others, your agency may have to establish an upper limit beyond which it will not go.

Nonpersonnel Items

Examine the sample line-item budget in Table 13.2. Most of the nonpersonnel items are self-explanatory. Unusual items or costs must be explained in the budget justification. I discuss a few that might cause you some grief if they are not properly addressed. Whatever is requested for travel must be reflected in the program narrative. If part of that program includes a transportation service for the elderly or for other clients, in contrast with the travel costs anticipated for staff, you would not include those costs on this line.

Locate them on a separate line called transportation service under program expenditures.

Out-of-town travel for staff is probably one of the most vulnerable sections of the budget. If you have a regional or statewide project, and that project requires that your staff travel to sites throughout the area, this will generally be considered local in nature because it deals with your program's locality. Out-of-town travel refers to the trips outside of the locality in which the organization provides its services. The reasons for such travel might include participating in professional conferences, meeting with staff of comparable or sister projects in other parts of the country, attending staff training programs, and so on.

The designation, "other costs," may be used as a catchall for a variety of items, such as fire, theft, and liability insurance; dues to professional organizations; and items that do not seem to fit anywhere else. If, however, they are of central importance to the project, they should have their own category. Suppose you intend to design a series of how-to guides (or videotapes) for use in community education. This probably should have its own line, with a number of sub-items such as typesetting, printing, binding, addressing, and mailing.

Indirect Costs

This is one of the least understood aspects of the budgeting process. Although the direct costs (those that have been discussed so far) may be easy to identify, they may not be so easy to specify. For example, if the project in question is located in an existing agency, new office space and equipment may not be necessary. Accordingly, there may be no need to request line-item funds for space leasing, utilities, maintenance, and the like. These are costs typically incurred for common purposes in the operation of the total organization. The project does, however, use agency office space and equipment and the maintenance that goes with them. Such items can be legitimately charged to the project, but the exact costs involved may be difficult to ascertain. To reflect these real costs, you may be permitted to charge a percentage of all salaries and wages or of the total expenses as indirect costs. In this case, you would not list them elsewhere as line items.

Check with the funder about what is allowable. Do not overlook indirect costs. Without them, a project can end up costing the agency a great deal. Note that even if a funding agency will not pay indirect costs, it will often permit the grant recipient to use these in lieu of cost sharing. In this case, they would be listed under the Donated column.

Cost Sharing

When used this way, indirect costs become part of the applicant organization's cost-sharing contribution. Many government and foundation awards require some form of cost sharing or local match. They may even specify a specific amount or portion, as when a 25% or 50% local match is required. Any real cost to a project, whether direct or indirect, may generally be counted in cost sharing. Examples include consumer fees; third-party payments (e.g., insurance company payments); the income from a fund-raising campaign or endowment; or funds contributed by another funding source such as a local foundation, business corporation, civic association, or the United Way.

In some cases, the time contributed to a project by volunteers can also be used for cost-sharing purposes. This is a bit tricky, however. You will have to check with the sponsor to find out if this is permissible. When volunteer time is used, you will have to provide the actual dollar value of the time contributed before you can insert it under the Donated column. Follow the rules provided in Chapter 9 for assessing the value of noncash contributions. Coley and Scheinberg (in press) suggest that if in-kinds are extensively used for cost sharing, you should show the value of these donations in a column of their own. The following is an example of how a few lines of the budget might look:

	FTE	Requested	Agency In-Kind	Other Donated	Total Budget
Project director	1	8,000	22,000	6,000	36,000
Volunteer homemakers	3	—	60,000	—	60,000
Office supplies		—	—	8,000	8,000
Office equipment		—	4,000	—	—

In this example, one would calculate the relevant portions of the project director's fringe benefits under both the Agency In-Kind and Other Donated columns. There are no fringe benefits for volunteers, however. Although the agency might cover costs of work-related insurance or training expenses for volunteers, such outlays could appear on lines of their own or be grouped with other insurance and training costs. Some funders require extensive details on matching funds. Anything in the Other Donated column is subject to audit, just as requested funds are, and you may be asked to document staff and volunteer time actually allocated to the project.

You can describe in-kinds in the budget narrative or create a special table for them. The following is how it might look:

Sources of Matching Funds

Source	Cash Contribution	In-kind Contributions
Gifts	$50,000	
Fees	12,000	
Arlington Foundation Grant	84,000	
Beta Industries		12,000
Recipient agency (name) budget		30,000
Volunteer time		22,000

Details on In-Kind Match

Line item	Value	Source
Personnel	30,000	Recipient agency (name)
Volunteer time	22,000	Recipient agency
Computers	12,000	Beta Industries

If two or more funds share an agreed-on set of expenses proportionately (e.g., two of them each contribute 25% and a third contributes 50%), it is only necessary to indicate this via a footnote at the "total" line for "requested" funds. If each is contributing to different lines of the budget (e.g., one covers rent and equipment plus some supplies, and another covers staff, some supplies, and some travel), however, you may need separate columns for each.

Budgets Are Statements of Intent: Intents Change

As is the case with the entire proposal, budgets are subject to review and modification if original projections prove to be unfeasible. The budget, after all, is really the narrative written in dollar terms. Because they are numerical, however, sponsors may be slightly stricter about permitting you to change the budget than to change other aspects of the program. As a rule of thumb, you can expect that most funders permit minor adaptations in the budget without demanding prior approval. Permission is rarely required to make adaptations of 10%, more or less, on any given line item.

Thus, if the project director's salary turns out to be lower than you anticipated, but a caseworker's salary turns out to be somewhat higher, and all this does not exceed the 10% limit on each of the two lines, it will not be necessary for you to ask permission prior to hiring the persons in question. The funder, however, will expect you to report these changes in your quarterly (or howsoever frequent) expenditure reports. If there is no reporting requirement and you think there may be a question about reallocation decision, play it safe. Drop a note to the funder explaining the changes.

HOW FUNDERS LOOK AT BUDGETS

A Proper Budget Paves the Way for a Trouble-Free Audit

A properly designed budget can save you headaches if and when you get audited. An improperly designed budget may alert the funder to other problems in your proposal. To prepare for an audit, you will have to be able to account for your sources of income and your expenditures.

Getting Audited

Accounting refers to those ongoing activities involved in maintaining an updated and accurate record of the flow of income and expenses related to a project. Accounting is used to ascertain that income and expenses are in line with projections in the budget. The idea behind accounting is to make sure that money is not only spent as prescribed but also at a rate of expected or available income. Unless the rates of expenditure and income are in balance, or in favor of income rather than expenditure, the program may find itself in considerable trouble.

Audits are periodic examinations of the fiscal records involved to see whether income and expenditures go according to plan (the budget). The auditor considers whether the amounts expended on specified items were proper, whether the sources from which money was drawn were proper, whether the timing was appropriate, and whether documentation of each of these was correct. Audits may be conducted internally or externally. Internal audits are generally conducted by an accountant or other staff member within the organization itself. External audits may be conducted by the sponsor or funder or by an outside agent acting on behalf of the sponsor. Audits are sometimes conducted 2 or 3 years after a project has concluded its activities. Thus, it is important not only to maintain good records but also to keep them for a minimum of 3 to 5 years.

What Funders Look for

Table 13.3 is a "funder's checklist" compiled from interviews with a number of government, foundation, and private-sector grants officers. The insights expressed are not new, but some may be new to you.

Checklists have a way of sounding flat. The following are some tips provided by experienced proposal reviewers that may seem slightly more imperative.

Is the Budget Realistic?

I always look to see if the budget is realistic. If it is too low to accomplish what the writers propose, you can assume they have promised more than they can produce. If it appears too large for what they propose, I figure they may be trying to get us to carry costs that are normally carried in the agency's operating budget. These include costs not directly related to the project. I don't mean to suggest that such costs reflect a bit of larceny on the part of proposal writers. It may indicate sloppiness and nothing more. But short of some other compelling argument in favor of the proposal, that's often enough to give it a low ranking.

Table 13.3 Funder's Checklist

All budget items are justified in the text of the proposal, the narrative, and the budget justification. No important items have been left out of the budget.

Each figure is properly explained unless it is clearly self-explanatory.

The budget designates requested and donated sums or uses some other designation to convey what is required of the funder and of the recipient.

The budget is broken down into logical segments: personnel, nonpersonnel items, indirect costs, and so on.

Budget figures are realistic. For example, fringe benefits are not out of line and salaries are compatible with local standards. The costs are reasonable and made in relationship to concerns for efficiency.

Out of the ordinary costs (high telephone or travel costs) are fully explained in the budget justification.

The total size of the budget is appropriate to the project itself.

Line items represent not only reasonable estimates of current cost but also include estimates of future costs, taking into account inflation or changes in salary rates.

The proposal is tailored to the funder and follows the guidelines or procedures and forms required by the funder.

Figures total properly. The writers know their math.

Insufficient Explanation

Too many questions are left unanswered. The budget is not adequately explained or justified. It is not clearly tied to the program's objectives or operations. If I were to give grant writers two pieces of advice, it would be not to hide anything, and to be able to substantiate all their budget figures.

What Happens After the Project Period?

Unless it's a request for a one-time only expenditure, we tend to look for a description of how the organization plans to continue financing the program after our support is no longer available. Assurances that "We will seek for continued support from other community sources," just don't cut it. We want to know what the potential sources are and how and when they were or will be approached.

On a multiyear grant, asking for a decreasing amount each year, and showing an increasing proportion of cost sharing can be quite convincing. We want to invest in the future, not in the past. To put it simply:

Be realistic about future support and that requires making a realistic appraisal of your prospects. Don't ask for short-term funding when your future is in doubt.

Will Partial Funding Work?

Sometimes we just don't have the money to fund all that is asked for, and at other times we don't have sufficient confidence that an organization can pull off as complex or comprehensive a project as planned. Those are the reasons we sometimes suggest a small planning or start-up grant, or offer support for a pilot project. Rather than be disappointed, some project designers are actually relieved. From our perspective, planning grants make a lot of sense. We don't have to commit big dollars until we are sure that an agency can "cut the mustard."

Ask for What You Need

Ask for what you need to do the job described. Don't ask for retroactive funding. Don't ask for what you already have. And for heaven's sake, don't ask for a hand-out. Most funders aren't going to bail you out of a hole. They want you to do something they value.

REVIEW

The budget is a program and fiscal document. It can be used to plan services, anticipate cash income and outflow, and hold the organization accountable for what it sets out to do. It is not an immutable document, however, and should be adapted to changed circumstances or modified program objectives.

The most common budget categorizes all its expenditures into line items. These items are generally divided into two major sections: personnel and nonpersonnel. Personnel items may include salaries and wages for professional and other personnel, the fringe benefits they receive, and fees for outside contractors. Nonpersonnel items may include rental and leasing and related expenses, disposable office supplies, program supplies, and equipment. A number of programs or projects may also include travel and per diem expenses for staff, board members, trainees, and so on.

All line items must be consistent with the program narrative in a project plan or proposal (as when a project application is submitted to an outside funding source). Items may need to be explained further in a budget justification section that generally follows the tabular budget. This justification is generally couched in program or performance terms. Performance budgets describe the cost of performing certain program activities and generally relate to the functions or work of distinct operational units. Program budgets focus more directly on the purposes of an operation and the goals and objectives to be reached.

The accounting process is aimed at tracking funds into and out of an organization or program and checking on whether the rate of income is adequate to cover the rate of expenditures. The auditing process is used periodically to determine whether the expenditures are proper and according to plan.

SUGGESTIONS FOR FURTHER READING

Much of what you will need is found in the relevant chapters of books on proposal writing and the grants process listed at the end of Chapter 11. If you wish to read further, the following items should prove helpful:

Coley, S. M., & Scheinberg, C. A. (in press). *Proposal writing* (2nd ed.). Thousand Oaks, CA: Sage.

Garner, W. (1991). *Accounting and budgeting in public and nonprofit organizations.* San Francisco: Jossey-Bass.

Gross, M. J., Warshauer, W., Jr., & Larkin, R. F. (1991). *Financial accounting guide for not-for-profit organizations* (4th ed.). New York: John Wiley.

McKinney, J. B. (1986). *Effective financial management in public and nonprofit agencies.* New York: Quorum.

Shinn, L. J., & Sturgeon, S. M. (1990, September). Budgeting from ground zero. *Association Management, 42*(9), 45-48.

Vinter, R., & Kish, R. (1984). *Budgeting for not-for-profit organizations.* New York: Free Press.

14

Getting It Right

Timelines, Appendices, Formats,
Letters, and Letter Proposals

A Perfect "1"

The only thing that tops getting off to a good start is finishing well. Too many proposal writers blow it all on their ideas and ideals and don't give themselves enough time to edit, add supportive documents, or figure out when key events in their project are to take place. You can't leave out something essential and expect your proposal to net a high score. Leaving out the "0" in "10" doesn't leave you with a nine, it leaves you with a "1," a failing score in anyone's book.

Less Is More

It's not only leaving things out of a proposal that can kill the chances of getting funded; it's putting too much in. I have a tendency to overwrite. This can be a fatal flaw, especially when funders are very specific on permissible length. For example, some foundations require that you complete a three- or four-page questionnaire. That's it! Others may require a two-page letter proposal. You have to say it all in their format.

Getting it right takes more than good intentions and good ideas. This chapter begins with conclusions, by describing two items that generally appear after the main body of the full-length proposal—the timeline and the appendices. Timelines are used to demonstrate that the project staff know what is to be done by when and by whom. Timelines can also be used to summarize and integrate other proposal components. The appendices include supplementary documents used to support or flesh out the narrative. The twin challenges of formatting and final editing are described, and suggestions are made for what should be included in your transmittal letter.

The bulk of this and the preceding two chapters deals with full-length proposals. Many sponsors, however, require only short proposals. The final section of this chapter focuses on questionnaire and letter proposals and discusses the preproposal "concept paper."

TIMELINES AND APPENDICES

Timelines

Timelines Are Money

They say that "time is money." True enough. But in project proposals, "timelines are money" or should be.

That may seem to be a curious claim. It may be, however, the most important guide to successful proposal writing you will glean from this book. The inclusion of a timeline gives evidence of serious planning on the part of the applicant agency. That can be very important to the potential funder. It also makes it possible for you to get a running start if you do get funding because you will have thought through the timing of all the project's major events or activities or both. You may be thinking, "OK, OK. We can save some money by doing our planning in advance, and we won't waste time trying to figure out what to do first. But is this really all that convincing to a potential funder?"

Probably not. But wait! There's more. I will share it with you at the end of this section.

Timelines (sometimes called timetables, time frames, or time-charts) are best represented in chart form. The chart might be a half page to several pages long, depending on the amount of detail provided, the complexity of the project, or the expectations of the funder. In chart form, the timeline provides a visual summary of what you intend to do and by when.

Timelines depict

- the time needed to perform activities in some desired order;
- the major events or milestones that must be achieved to conclude the project successfully;
- a combination of activities and events.

Probably the best known activity timeline is the Gantt chart, and the standard for milestone timelines is the Program and Evaluation Review Technique (PERT) or "critical path" chart. I will describe each briefly. Before I do, I want to show you a "chartlike" timetable.

Desk Calendar Timetable

It uses a very simple format—one based on the monthly desk calendar. Mary Hall (1979) uses this approach in her "Timetable for Proposal Development" (Table 14.1). I include it for two reasons. First, most of us are accustomed to working with calendars and may find this approach more intuitive. I tend to think of it as a "Half and Half" model—half narrative and half calendar—rather than a true timeline. It allows us to design a brief overview of all the project-relevant activities that must be performed and events that must take place during predetermined time frames (e.g., weeks or months). That is the second reason to call it the Half and Half model—half event and half activity.

For example, in her notations for August, Hall (1979) refers to "Review and clearance sought as necessary from local and state agencies." That would be an activity because doing a review and

Table 14.1   Timetable for Proposal Development

Month	Activity
March	Idea identified. Preliminary discussions held with colleagues in local agency to determine their interest; contact made with colleagues in other communities or states to determine the regional or national significance of the idea. Preliminary discussion held with agency administrators.
April	Needs assessment instituted. Inquiries submitted to national information systems to determine if similar idea has already been tried, to get names of communities or agencies with related experience and to identify related research. Statistical data collected to support statement of need.
May	Various approaches to implement idea discussed. Best approach chosen after contacts made with other local agencies, state agencies, etc. Approval to proceed with development of project obtained from administrators. Project director or program developer selected and other staff to be involved in proposal preparation. First draft of ideas in project form developed and discussed with agency administrators, potential population to be served, and other groups necessary to local support.
June	Potential funding sources identified and preliminary outline sent to determine their interest in the project and to acquire necessary application information.
July	Project idea modified by input received during previous months. Another inquiry to potential funding sources may be warranted. Second draft completed and circulated for review to agency administrators and any local or state group involved in a clearance procedure.
August	Funding source chosen. Final draft prepared based on source's forms or requirements. Official clearance received from local administrators. Review and clearance sought as necessary from any local or state agencies.
September	Proposal submitted to funding source. Receipt card with processing number received in return.
December to February	Approval or rejection received. In either case comments of reviewers should be sought.
March	Authorization for expenditure received.
April	Recruitment of personnel. Modifications started on facilities, if necessary.
May-June	Plans developed for staff training. Materials prepared.
July	Personnel salaried and project started. Staff training initiated. Detailed management plan outlined. Assignments and responsibilities clarified.
October	Refunding application prepared and submitted.

SOURCE: Mary Hall, *Developing Skills in Proposal Writing*. Eugene: University of Oregon Continuing Education Publications, 1979.

seeking clearance takes time and activities take time. What the chart tells us is that these activities should take place in August before the event, "Official clearance received," occurs. From the project staff's perspective, that is an event—something that occurs after a preceding activity and before another set of activities can take place. It is a point in time that does not require staff action or energy. The fact that both events and activities are listed in the same time frame is one advantage of the Half and Half model. This is also a disadvantage, however, for several reasons. First, this format makes it difficult to distinguish between points in time and what it takes to get from one to the other. Second, the format leaves little space to indicate who is responsible for each activity. Perhaps most important, it uses months as timeline dividers, whereas in most projects some activities are likely to extend over several months (e.g., recruiting children for day camp) or to reoccur again and again (e.g., admitting clients to substance abuse clinic).

Event-Oriented Timelines

The Milestone chart is, perhaps, the simplest of all event-oriented timelines, whereas the PERT chart is the most complicated. For this reason, you might want to reserve the former for relatively simple projects or brief proposals and the latter for more complex projects or very detailed proposals. A milestone event is a key point in time—one in which several activities conclude or a new set of activities is launched. The example on the following page should be relatively self- explanatory.

As you can see, this chart provides a quick overview of the points in time when processes (activities) end or begin. It is easy to read and understand. The project activities leading to or following an event will have been described in the narrative section on methods or program approach. The timeline shows that you are aware of when the activities must be begun or concluded to make the program work and have assigned staff to relevant responsibilities.

A disadvantage is that it does not give much detail and leaves the description of activities—both what they are and how long they take—entirely to the narrative. Moreover, by calling each event a

Sample Milestone Chart

Project Title: Tutorial Project

Event	Staff Responsible	A	S	O	N	D	J	F	M	A	M	J	J
		Fall Term						*Spring Term*					
Staff management													
Volunteer tutor plan designed	Director, trainer, & evaluator	x											
Tutor recruitment completed	Director & trainer		x						x				
Training sessions begun	Trainer				x				x				
Tutor capacities assessed	Evaluator				x				x				
Training completed	Trainer				x				x				
Pupil recruitment	Director												
Materials disseminated			x				x						
Presentations made to teachers & PTO		x				x							
Assignment													
Pupil needs assessed	Evaluator				x				x				
Progress score charts created	Evaluator				x				x				
Pupil/tutor matches made	Director				x				x				
Tutorial work													
First tutorial sessions begun	Trainer				x				x				
First progress scores noted	Trainer					x				x			
Pupil/tutor relationships evaluated	Evaluator						x					x	

milestone, it does not distinguish between the start and finish of single activities and those that culminate or initiate a process that might include a chain of activities. PERT charts can accommodate both activities and events and distinguish between normal and milestone events.

PERT

Although designers might use different symbols, it is most common for events to be depicted as circles on the chart, whereas milestone events (completion of a project, a turning point, etc.) are sometimes shown as squares or circles within squares. The lines between circles and squares represent the time it takes to perform those activities leading up to an event.

For example, on the chart shown in Figure 14.1, 1, 2, 3, 4, and 5 are events, and 5 is a milestone event—the final event in a chain of events. It is at the right side of the PERT network because it follows the international charting convention of moving from left to right. Events that follow others are called successor events, whereas those that precede others are predecessor events. On the chart, 3 is a successor to 1 and a predecessor of 5, which means that it cannot occur until 1 is completed, nor can 5 occur prior to the completion of 3 (or, for that matter, 2 and 4 on the chart).

PERT's network approach, linking events and activities, is both its advantage and disadvantage. The advantage is that it permits you to see when the project might encounter a time problem because there are (a) too many activities or events scheduled to take place in the same period of time or (b) long periods of slack in which staff have few responsibilities.

The chart also allows specification of which staff members are responsible for various event and activity chains.

PERT charts are especially useful when deadlines are important and when you are aiming toward some major event, such as a conference or launching a new camp program. Their disadvantage is that they generally require listing the activities and events titles on accompanying pages. The chart itself does not have room to show

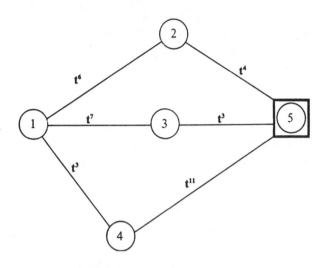

Figure 14.1. Sample PERT Network

both the complex network relationships and their designation. Thus, one cannot read the chart and understand it without comparing it with the accompanying lists.

Activity-Oriented Timelines

Because of the disadvantage of the PERT charts, some proposal writers prefer to use less sophisticated activity timelines. Less sophisticated does not mean less useful. They can be very useful in designating what is to be done and when. The best known of these are Gantt charts. Henry Gantt, a turn-of-the-century industrialist, was one of the early pioneers of scientific management. He found it helpful to both managers and workers to use bars or lines as a way of defining when something should be worked on and by what time it should be completed. As you can see from Figure 14.2, the chart provides for a set of dates posted at the top of the page (in weeks, months, or quarters). In the left-hand column, the major tasks (activities) to be accomplished are listed. Lines are then drawn on the chart to indicate start and finish dates for a task or activity complex.

	1st Quarter	2nd Quarter	3rd Quarter	4th Quarter
Staff				
Recruitment and Selection	———			
Training	——	——		
Advising Committee				
Appointed	—			
Meetings	—	—	—	—
Assessment				
Instrument Designed	———			
Survey Conducted		———		
Report Issues			—	
Block Checks				
Organizations				
Activities	————————			
Meetings		– –	– –	– –
Association Formed			——	
Conference				———
Evaluation				
Ongoing Monitoring	—————————————			
Evaluation Designed		———		
Evaluation Conducted			————	
Report Issued				——

Figure 14.2. Sample Gantt Chart

The activities are the same as those described in the Methods section of the proposal narrative—for example

- recruitment, screening, and intake;
- assessment, diagnosis, and problem definition;
- program or case planning;
- implementation of the program or case plan;
- monitoring;
- outcome or satisfaction evaluation;
- termination and follow-up.

Unlike the PERT chart, this approach does not depict a network of event and activity chains. Its advantage, however, is that it is highly intuitive. Activity lines show when they are to take place, and one can infer the location of events from the start and ending of each activity line.

Why "Timelines Are Money"

What is the "more" I had promised you in the first paragraph of this section? Here it is.

In the proposal narrative, you will already have described

- process objectives;
- program activities (which flow from them);
- job components for key staff (which include conduct of those activities);
- program evaluation (some of which focuses on activity performance);
- budgets (which may include costs for the performance or major groups of activities).

Now I have a sixth and final aspect that pulls all these functional categories together. Think from a reviewer's perspective. Wouldn't you be impressed if a proposal did the following?

1. Defined the project's outreach outcome and process goals
2. Indicated who would be doing what with relation to outreach
3. Provided a procedural outline
4. Described how outcomes and activities are to be monitored and evaluated
5. Defined what proportion of the overall budget would be consumed by outreach
6. Depicted the outreach and other activities on a timeline that shows what is to be done by when and by whom

This makes for a well-crafted and integrated proposal that is likely to stand out from most of the others received by the funder. If you can use your timeline to demonstrate the integration of all program components, chances are the proposal will be "on the money."

Chart-Design Software

Virtually any proposal can be improved by professional looking charts. Hand-drawn timelines and flowcharts look about as current as proposals written on manual typewriters with carbon copies. Fortunately, chart-design software programs are fairly easy to use and relatively inexpensive. Many of the better products on the market can also help you think through the steps or stages of a process, leading to improvements in overall program design. Give yourself enough time to practice with the program if you have not already had experience using it.

The programs in the following list all do more than you need for a project proposal. They are relatively easy to master, however, and you should be able to use only those components you are interested in. Unless otherwise indicated, these programs are for the personal computer and work in a Windows environment. Prices, manufactures' addresses, and detailed reviews are found in many popular computer magazines. The programs include the following:

1. ViSiO 3 and ViSiO SHAPES (Shapeware Corporation) include orgcharts, flowcharts, network designs, maps, project management software, and useful clip art. ViSiO 3's project management software creates easy to read Gantt charts and simple PERT-style charts. ViSiO SHAPES provides additional shapes for drop and drag drawing of virtually any kind of chart or map. A "connector tool" and other innovations make it easy to locate appropriate types and lengths of connections between shapes. Both programs mimic the bar menus of Microsoft Office and Lotus SmartSuite.

2. ManagePro (Avantos Performance Systems) is a project management tool that focuses on the people behind the project. Its Goal Planner section includes such standard tools as Gantt and PERT charts. The People/Team Planner is useful in assigning tasks and relating them to others on the staff. Because human service agencies are highly labor-intensive, managing paid and volunteer staff may be of major concern in project design. This software demonstrates staff activities graphically.

3. For more comprehensive (and costly) project scheduling and management programs, consider Microsoft Project version 4 for Windows (Microsoft Corp.), CA-SuperProject (Computer Associates International), Time Line 6 (Symantec Corp.), Sure Track (Primavera Sys-

tems), or Project Scheduler 6 for Windows version 1.5 (Scitor Corp). These can be used for more complex project planning and management than is necessary for most human service agency project and contract proposals. Agencies that routinely use these software programs as aids in planning and management, however, should have no difficulty in printing out proposal-relevant information.

4. Three popular and inexpensive flowchart programs for Windows include Flow Charting 4, an easy to edit program in which you can design your own shapes for specific applications (Paton and Paton), CorelFlow-2 (Corel Corp.), and ABC Graphics (Micrografx).

5. Useful Mac programs include (a) Microsoft Project 4 for the Mac (see Windows description), and (b) TeamFlow 3.1 (CFM Inc.), which focuses on tasks to be performed and people who perform them, including PERT and other planning and tracking systems.

Appendices

There are times when a chart may not fit in the body of the proposal but may be a useful addition to the appendices.

What the Appendices Are for and When to Include Them

The appendices include supplementary and supportive materials. Everything essential to the proposal should go into its body (cover pages, abstract, narrative, budget, and time frame). You can use appendices when

- the sponsor allows or even requires one (e.g., when letters of support or assurances of cooperation are required);
- funder-imposed page limits force you to leave important details out of the body of the proposal;
- the information included would be too detailed for the main body of the proposal.

What to Include

Include whatever you think will answer important questions for which there was insufficient space in the narrative or that would have been distracting if located there. Examples are found in the following chart.

INVENTORY OF USEFUL APPENDICES

- study reports that provide detail on the problem you intend to address;
- press clippings that highlight the severity of the problems or that recognize the agency's efforts to deal with it;
- journal articles, conference presentations, and concept papers that either provide the background for the project's conceptual rationale or demonstrate the organization's or staff's capabilities;
- pictures, graphs, charts, and other visuals that highlight and reinforce the points you have made;
- more details on components of the project design, such as evaluation or the budget;
- organizational charts;
- lists of agency board or project advisory group members;
- historic materials, including brief information on other current or recent projects undertaken by the applicant agency;
- resumes of key staff;
- budget details or alternative budget presentations (e.g., transformation of the line-item into a performance or program budget);
- assurances of cooperation;
- letters of support.

What you decide to include should reflect your best judgment of what the funder may find helpful. For example, a foundation may permit you only five pages, including the face sheet narrative and budget. These are the pages the board members will see when they make their allocations decisions. The grants officer, however, may need more information on the nature of the problem or conceptual framework that informs your intervention approach because he or she knows that the board may want assurances from the foundation staff that the problem you have described is genuine and the conceptual framework sound. In this case, the grants officer may request supportive documentation that only he or she may read. This explains why foundations sometimes ask for multiple copies of the core proposal (for board members of the review panel) and only one copy of appended supportive materials.

Two items often found in the appendix warrant special attention. Both are "credibility enhancers."

Letters of support often include

- commitments on the part of key community players or relevant organizations to be part of the program (e.g., school authorities in regard to a teen drug prevention program);
- endorsements by respected individuals (e.g., political leaders, experts in the field, heads of umbrella organizations such as the United Way or an Area Agency on Aging, other current or former funders, and potential consumers and clients);
- agreements by other funders to cover parts of the costs for this project or to provide continuation funding when the grant period is over.

Copies of consortium agreements are required when the grant is made to several recipient organizations that have agreed to work together on a project or several sponsors agree to fund different aspects of a single project. The written document provides evidence that such agreements exist. To have the force of law behind them, agreements should define

- which organizations are involved;
- what responsibility each has agreed to undertake, when, and for how long;
- how the budget for the project is to be shared;
- the administrative arrangements and project location (e.g., where will the project be housed, who handles the financial obligations, etc.).

EDITING AND FORMATTING

Check the Writing and Spelling

A great deal of the good work that goes into proposal writing can be undone by sloppy editing. It is hard to edit your own work, but if you have to, the following suggestion works well:

Read the proposal out loud with two colleagues following along silently. One should be focusing on spelling and grammar . . . that's your proofreader. The other should be listening for how it sounds.

Written language is sometimes stilted, and tends to have a lot of jargon as well as other high-falutin' verbiage. If the proposal sounds good to the listening ear, it's likely to "read" well. If not, you have some editing to do.

The following is a checklist of common writing problems:

- Pages have not been numbered (an absolute no-no!).
- Paragraphs are more than eight or nine lines long (six or seven reads better).
- Sentences are longer than two lines.
- Headings and subheadings are missing or inconsistent.
- Charts are messy, unclear, or unlabeled.
- Budget figures are missing or do not total up.
- The same information is located in more than one place.
- What you say on one page is contradicted on another.
- Essential information is left blank (e.g., names, addresses, and statistics).
- Names are misspelled.
- References are inaccurate.
- Appendices are missing.
- Assumptions are naive and unsupported (not documented).

The following are three words to avoid:

- hopefully" (use "we anticipate that" or "it is likely that");
- "might" or "may" (use "can" or "will");
- "could" (use "will").

Do use transition words linking thoughts and paragraphs together. Examples include

- precisely because;
- moreover;
- resulting in;
- accordingly;
- therefore;
- hence.

Use an active rather than passive voice:

Poor	Good
This proposal is being submitted by	We are submitting this proposal
Budget reports will be submitted by	_____ will submit budget reports

Make Sure the Proposal Looks Good

Proposal writers often spend so much time on design of the progıam, making sure the budget is reasonable (and balances) and maintaining contacts with collaborators and other funders, that the proposal's appearance gets short shrift. Mistake! The following are some guidelines I find helpful.

TIPS FOR PRESENTATION

Tip 1: If the funder tells you that the proposal must include sections on goals, program, and evaluation, use these categories in your headings. If the funder asks you to answer some questions, answer them using the language suggested in your titles. For example,

The Funder's Language	Your Title
Goal statement	The Goal: KIDS TEACHING KIDS
Unique aspects of the program	What Makes This Project Unique
Evaluation section	An Evaluation That Works!

This makes the narrative both accessible and familiar. Funders know what to expect in each section (it is what they wanted you to include) and are satisfied that you took their instructions seriously.

Tip 2: Even when the potential sponsor's expectations are vague, try to use familiar language, language the funder uses, and avoid jargon wherever possible! Some consultants even suggest you make your document look like documents produced by the funder, using familiar layouts, fonts, type sizes, and so on.

Tip 3: Some consultants, however, suggest that there must be something visual that sets your proposal apart from others. The following are some bad ideas:

- using colored or expensive paper stock;
- binding the proposal (makes it hard to photocopy);
- using fancy fonts or mixing families of fonts.

The following are some good ideas:

- including a table of contents (using level 1 headings only);
- selecting easy-to-read fonts;
- using white space to avoid overly dense presentations (e.g., this list uses white space to highlight the words);
- breaking up narratives with charts, illustrations, lists, and other techniques that help you communicate visually as well as syntactically;
- including something unexpected, such as a photo, a quote by a client, or part of a news clipping.

Tip 4: Pay attention to esthetics. This means using simple graphic design principles in your choice of typography, page layout, shading, and so on. Most sophisticated word processing programs make it possible to

Shade Your Headings

Box in sections using

- Bullets
1. Numbers

for emphasis, or use

BOLDFACE and *ITALICS*

INCREASING or decreasing Size

Take care not to either overuse any of these techniques or apply them inconsistently. Remember that aesthetics should be in the service of communication. An effective design helps

- reviewers find the information they need;
- structure ideas and hierarchies of importance;
- contribute both to the proposal's distinctiveness and to your organization's image.

Boldface is <u>more effective</u> than underlining when emphasis of headings is needed (because that is what newspapers and magazines use).

Take care, however, not to allow your graphics, tables, or other illustrations take over. Unusual graphics and tables are likely to draw away the reader's attention. The larger, the more attention. Two tips:

- Make sure the illustration complements or leads to the text—that is where you are making your case.
- Keep it large enough to be noticed or to provide emphasis but not so large that it detracts from your message.

COVER LETTERS

Unless the proposal is in the form of a "proposal letter" (see the following section), append a transmittal letter. It should include essentially what goes on the face-sheet or the abstract or both (see Chapter 12). This includes

- identifying information (who is submitting the proposal);
- what you are submitting or will be submitting under separate cover;
- the project's title and a one- to three-sentence overview of what it is about;
- the grant category or funder priority it addresses;
- the amount requested, over what period of time;
- who is available to answer questions.

Keep it to half a page or so.

BRIEF PROPOSALS AND CONCEPT PAPERS

The foregoing discussion assumes that you will be writing a full-length proposal. Some funders, however, require a brief concept paper before inviting a full-length proposal. Many others—smaller foundations, civic associations, and religious organizations—will not accept anything longer than one to four or five pages. These short proposals are generally referred to as "letter" and "questionnaire-type" proposals. You might be thinking, "Good, I can deal with two or three pages." Perhaps so, but you may find that it is often more difficult to say all that must be conveyed in very little space. Most of us are not gifted with the ability to write concisely.

Concept papers, questionnaire-type and letter proposals are described below. Then, I will walk you through the sections of the letter proposal and include a few writing and formatting tips.

Concept Papers

The concept paper can be thought of as a "preproposal" document. From the applicant's perspective, it is a way of introducing one's intentions so as to elicit interest or feedback on the part of a funding agency. To make sure it is not mistaken for a short proposal, the words "concept paper" rather than "proposal" should appear prominently at the beginning of the document. Government agencies, larger foundations, and corporate funders often encourage the submission of concept papers prior to requesting full-length proposals. They may even require it. If this is the case, they will be using it as a screening device to decide whom to invite to submit a full-length proposal. Concept papers used for screening purposes often have very precise instructions on what to include.

When instructions are not included, follow the general guidelines given under Letter Proposals. Attention to detail is as important as it is in the final draft of a more comprehensive document.

Proposal Questionnaires

For many funders—especially those without full-time grants officers or whose awards are relatively small (under $25,000)—neither a concept paper nor a full proposal are required. These funders appear to make it easier for applicants by providing them with a two-, three- or four-page questionnaire.

Tip: Answer only what the funder asks.

The questions are generally purposeful. If the funding organization wanted to know more, other questions would have been asked or more space for responses might have been given. Keep your answers to the point. Funding agencies, however, are not infallible and an outline that fits one project may not fit another. There may be insufficient space for some responses and too much for others. Moreover, it may be difficult to line your answers up properly if using a computer and printer.

In this case, it may make sense to retype the proposal questionnaire, filling in the answers as you go. If some answers take more space than originally provided, try to make others briefer. The overall length of the document should not be significantly different than the funder's original form. If you are unsure whether this will be acceptable, check first.

Letter Proposals

Letter proposals are generally of two types—all in the form of a letter, as the name implies, or a brief, one- to five-page proposal accompanied by a one- or two-paragraph cover letter. Finders generally do not allow appendices. They may not frown on your sending additional explanations, however, as long as (a) these are not appended to the letter or proposal document itself (so as not to make it appear longer than the permitted number of pages), and (b) all the required information is included in the letter proposal itself (so that the appendices could be ignored—as they probably will be).

The skeleton of a letter proposal is generally as follows:

Outline for Letter Proposal

Part	Content	Space or Location
I	Abstract	1-3 sentences that introduce and sum up what is to follow
II	Sponsor relevance	1-3 sentences
III	**Problem**	1 or 2 paragraphs
	Goals	1 paragraph
	Activities	1-3 paragraphs
	Evaluation	1 paragraph
IV	**Capability**	1 or 2 paragraphs
V	**Budget**	Quarter to half page
VI	**Closing**	1 paragraph

If appropriate, use the words in boldface as headings.

Some funders also permit you to add a one-page time frame that summarizes what you will be doing and by when.

The suggested number of paragraphs assumes you are permitted at least 3 pages. You may be allowed only 1½ or 2 pages, however. In this case, you may have to group Parts I and II, Part III, and then Parts IV and V each into single paragraphs, with Part VI taking up no more than one sentence.

The following pages provide some section-by-section tips and samples.

Abstract

The entire proposal should be explained in one or two sentences that explain (a) who you are (the organization's name or program location or both), (b) organizational capabilities, (c) program addressed and expected outcome, (d) how this fits the funder's interests, and (e) budget request. The order can be changed. The following two examples use two "mapping sentences" to convey this information. Look over the mapping sentences, which define what is to be included, and then the two examples that follow.

Mapping sentences:

(1) Who

(2) will do what

(3) to or for whom

(4) in order to

(5) at what costs

(6) over what period of time.

(7) How agency capabilities or special characteristics complement

(8) relationship to funder's interests.

Example 1: LaSed Services proposes creation of a Hispanic Parenting Center to serve low-income residents of the central city area, at a cost of $370,000 over 3 years. LaSed's long history of service to new Americans complements the foundation's commitment to multiculturalism.

Example 2:   Dr. Melvin Melba suggested we contact you. The Golden Years Institute, a division of County Hospital's Health Maintenance System, invites your participation in a $300,000 2-year demonstration program of cultural and social enrichment for senior citizens whose social isolation contributes to poor health. The program appears to be an ideal match to the Newtech Corporation's twin interests in the promotion of health and the cultural arts.

In the second example, someone who is known to the funder is mentioned, suggesting possible endorsement (be sure not to mention someone who will pan the project).

Relevance to the Funder (Substitute Actual Name)

Explain why you are approaching this funder. Build on what you stated in Part I.

To write this section, you will need a handle on the funder's recent funding history and on its aspirations. Large foundations are likely to provide such information in their annual reports and many government agencies include them in their application kits. Smaller and more local funding organizations, however, may not have these materials readily available. You may have to find out from a funding agency representative, a current or former grant recipient, foundation tax records, and so on. Try to find out what the funder really cares about. Is it the elderly, cultural programs, or health promotion? Or is it innovation? Is the funder only interested in financing sure winners (organizations with proven capacity) or is it seeking high-risk enterprises?

The following are a few sentence lead-ins with which you might start this section:

Our jointly shared commitment . . .

Since 1987, with passage of the _____ Act, the agency has funded _____. Today, when fewer funds are available, every dollar has to count. That's why . . .

For a congregation like yours, which has set standards of excellence in its family life education programs . . .

The following is an almost complete paragraph that speaks to a funder's style rather than to a population or problem commitment:

> Throughout the past decade, the company's involvement in the promotion of positive intergroup relations has been an inspiration to others. That's why we think you will be especially interested in (. . .). We are proposing an innovative approach to (. . .). This approach is not without risk, and that is precisely why we are suggesting it to the corporation. Your experience in supporting hi-tech industrial incubators is as important to us as the financial support we seek. We see this project as the first of a number of "social programs incubators"— projects in which community members can become "social entrepreneurs." Let me explain.

The Problem

If you have written Part II properly, you have already demonstrated that you are sensitive to the funder's interest. Do not stop there. The problem that your program or project addresses should be written with the sponsor's interest in mind. Remember, funders are likely to be interested in helping you do your business, only if by doing so they are doing their own business. As in longer proposals, you will need to be specific.

For example, it is not delinquency or violence that you are trying to solve but rather the problem of youth-on-youth violence in the schools (on the route to and from school). It is not the high incidence of infant mortality that you expect to tackle directly (although ultimately you hope to reduce its rate in your city) but rather the nutritional deficiencies that contribute to low birth weight, which in turn increases the high incidence of infant mortality.

Refer to "gaps." They are easy to understand and lend themselves to envisioning the difference between what is and what could or ought to be. Gaps should be explained in number or other values. The following are a few examples of how the problem statement might begin:

> The demographic revolution is what drives this project. The foundation's current report estimates that by 2006, the percentage of the elderly in this area will be 17%, in contrast with its current 12%. Yet

the services that exist today were designed in the seventies when only 8% of the population was over 65. Today, the average age of those we serve is 72. By 2006 it will be 77. In terms of home health care needs here is what we can expect:
    (FILL IN THE DATA)

If we don't take steps now, here is what we'll see:
    (FILL IN PROJECTIONS)

New Americans face (DESCRIBE CHALLENGES).

Current programs and services (DESCRIBE WHAT EXISTS).

This leaves many in need of (DESCRIBE).

Unless their economic needs are addressed, we can expect that (etc).

Goals

The goals section describes what you expect to accomplish in response to the problem. This does not mean what you intend to do (that comes next) but what you expect to achieve. You will need to define the extent to which you expect to reduce the problem or ameliorate the situation. For example,

> By the program's third year of operations, we expect to bring the reading scores of fifth graders in low-scoring classrooms from an average of 62% of the state standard to 85%. At least half the children will be at or beyond the average reading score in Michigan.

See also the discussion of goals and objectives in the previous chapter. This section can also lead to discussion of process objectives that, in effect, describe how the program will work.

Activities

This is the section to describe how you expect to achieve your goals as well as the conceptual framework that informs your approach. It is also the section to demonstrate how innovative your approach may be, how it builds on other experiences, or how it might have implications for programs. If the funder permits, you might also include some of these details in a one-page time frame attachment. For example,

> Two innovators distinguish our approach to reading-score improvement: (1) the use of computers; and (2) the involvement of learners in teaching each other. Thus, we will be using several kinds of motivators. The first comes from the fun and excitement of working the computers. The second comes from the ownership students have over their own learning speed (and style—computer programs allow students a choice of learning activities). More interesting, perhaps, is the extent to which we will be involving students in coaching their peers. We know, from the Oakdale studies, that . . .
>
> We think we can reach these goals by building on the Portland experience with unwed teen mothers [assume that the funder is familiar with the Portland project because it provided the funding and takes pride in its accomplishments]. However, it differs in one important respect (DESCRIBE). This has implications for other programs located in rural communities, because . . .

Evaluation

The evaluation section sums up how you will know how you did. If the goals section was well written, it should not be difficult to refer to outcome and process goals. In a letter proposal, there may be enough room only for the former. It is possible to include both, however, without taking up an excessive amount of space. For example,

> We'll have a preliminary indication of our success if we meet our enrollment targets of 120 low-income pregnant women from the catchment area in Year 1, and 240 by Year 2. We expect their nutritional quotient to rise from an average of _____ to _____ using the _____ Nutritional Scale, when measured six months after first enrollment.

The example also mentions a research instrument and methodology. Funders may also be concerned about whether the evaluation is to be conducted internally or by outside evaluators.

Capability

This section establishes your organization's credentials and capacity to do the project. This is the section in which you can demonstrate your unique capabilities to deal with the problem described. Funders are likely to be concerned about (a) the capability of the project's director, (b) the capacity of the organization within which it is placed, and (c) the credibility of the concept for the program and its approach. The first can be handled by a one- or two-sentence statement of her or his other experience, background, and achievements. If the project director has not yet been hired, you may need to say something about the agency or division director under whose supervision it will be conducted or the qualifications you will be looking for in a project director. For example,

> Sophia Rodriguez, a national authority on reading skills advancement, will serve as project director.

> The project will be located in the hospital's outreach department, headed by Dr. Sandy Wechstein, whose work with low-income mothers has attracted national attention (see *Time Magazine*, July 10, 1996). The project director is expected to have a master's degree in public health, nutrition, social work, or nursing, with at least 10 years of experience, half of which should be with low-income families.

Generally, a brief statement on the agency's history and reputation is all that is needed. Build on the positive. People feel safer when betting on a horse known to be a winner (or that someone else knows has the capacity to win). For example,

> LaSed has been serving the needs of low-income Hispanic families since 1954. It receives funding for its core programs from _____, _____, _____, _____, and _____. Its programs have served as models for agencies nationally.

> The Urban Ministry has recognized the All-Families agency for its outstanding work with the homeless. In 1978, when the problems of homelessness first received national attention, the center had already had 10 years experience with . . .

There are times, however, when lack of organizational capability may be the best reason to fund it. For example,

The problems of alcoholism on the reservation have never been effectively addressed. Until this year, the Tribal Council had been rife with dissension and tinged by scandal. But the recent tribal election promises to change all that. The reform group, currently holding the majority of seats on the council, has given the twin problems of alcoholism and joblessness its highest priority. A federal grant of $375,000 is pending a match from local sources. Thus, the foundation's grant of $100,000 will not only assure the receipt of government funds, but also help reinforce a new spirit of self-help and responsibility in the community.

Budget

Be precise about what you ask from the funder and what proportion of the overall budget this makes up. If appropriate, mention—as the previous example does—how this award is connected to other sources of funding. If there is room for a tabular budget, follow the guidelines in the previous chapter. If not, you may have to collapse categories and present the request in narrative form. For example,

Your grant of $120,000 over three years will help generate four times that amount in government grants, third-party payments, and the value of volunteer efforts. We are asking for funding in decreasing amounts: $50,500 in Year 1, $40,000 in Year 2, and $29,500 in the third year, after which we expect to be self-sufficient. The overall budget projects expenditures of $190,000 in the first year, $200,000 in the second, and $220,000 in the third.

Projected first-year expenditures are as follows: (a) Personnel ($90,000); (b) trainee costs for transportation and child care ($42,000); (c) nonpersonnel costs such as rent, office supplies, training materials ($32,000); overhead ($26,000). The first year's unit cost of $1,900 per trainee is somewhat high, reflecting start-up costs. By Year 2, it drops to $800/trainee, considerably less than comparable programs.

This description also promises independence after the grant period and breaks the costs down into yearly expenses and unit costs.

Closing

Define what you expect and connect the proposal back to the funder's interests and the problem addressed. For example,

> We know this is not the only way to address low reading scores and poor school performance, but we think it has more promise than others. We think our experience with this approach will complement the foundation's long-standing commitment to innovation and excellence. For the program to begin during the coming academic year, it would be helpful for us to hear from you by May 1. We know the brevity of this proposal may leave many questions unanswered. Please feel free to call me at _____ or our educational consultant, Dr. Sly Fox of the University of _____ at _____.

If the person who signs the letter is not someone who is likely to have name recognition or prestige with the funder, it sometimes is a good idea to "cc" someone who has. This could be someone who originally suggested you approach the funder and whose name you mention in the opening line of the proposal.

SUMMARY

All proposals require careful attention to details—all the details—including how much time it will take to complete a set of tasks. One excellent way of demonstrating good planning is to design a timetable that shows when activities are to be performed, by whom, and by when they will conclude. Time frames that include the same terminology as words you used previously to describe activities and events, or to justify budget expenditures, are especially impressive. Many proposals require supportive documents—letters of endorsement, survey results, and expert opinion. Because these are important but not necessarily essential, however, they often go into a packet of explanations or into an appendix.

Charts are especially good ways to summarize, focus attention, or integrate various components of the project. Careful attention to formatting can make or break a proposal. A few good formatting principles include making the proposal stand out from others, but maintain a style familiar to the reader, using headings and subheads; and keeping sentences, paragraphs, and lists short.

Some proposals and concept papers are, by design, short—limited to five pages or less by the prospective funder. A nine-point outline for a letter proposal that could be written in three to six paragraphs is provided.

REFERENCE

Hall, M. (1979). *Developing skills in proposal writing*. Eugene: University of Oregon Continuing Education Publications.

SUGGESTIONS FOR FURTHER READING

Refer to suggested readings in Chapter 12. The books by Coley and Scheinfeld (in press), Hall (1988), and Kaplan and Ryan (1997) are especially useful.

15

Before and After

*What to Do Before Writing the Proposal
and While You Are Waiting for Review
Results and How to Respond if You
Do or Do Not Get Funded*

What to Look Out for (View 1)

Things went according to clockwork. The NIMH panel did a preliminary review of our proposal. We passed the first hurdle. Dr. Milton,
one of the NIMH project officers, called and arranged to make a site
visit with one of the members of the external review panel. A visit was
scheduled for mid-April. I had five weeks to arrange things at our end.

I called representatives of the other agencies with whom we would
have to collaborate if we got funded, sent them copies of the proposal,
and invited them to one of the sessions during the site visit. One of
NIMH's evaluative criteria was the extent to which there was involvement and commitment by other service providers. The site visit went
beautifully (although one of the secretaries was a little nervous and
went overboard in preparing coffee and cake); beautifully until we got
to the afternoon meeting with the other agency people who represented collaborating institutions.

Sondra Kravel of the Child Guidance Clinic sat through the first half of the session reading the proposal; then she started asking questions, even suggesting improvements in the proposal. Well, that opened things up. Some of the other agency folks joined in, each trying to improve the proposal. They meant well, but . . .

You guessed it. We did not get funded. The reasons: Agency collaborators had not adequately been involved in project design and improvements were still possible. We could, if we wished, resubmit during the next funding cycle. Problem was, we would have to wait 6 months, and the staff we wanted to assign to the new project would not be able to wait that long to find out if they had jobs or not. What a bummer!

Truth is, we really had had all these discussions before, and all the agency folks had signed off on the proposal before we'd sent it off to DC. But that was 7 months earlier, and most of the participants, like Sondra, had forgotten.

What to Look for (View 2)

It's not easy to be a reviewer. Decisions are rarely cut and dry.

Sometimes even the best-written proposal from the most reputable source gets turned down if the proposal is weak on other foundation priorities. The foundation guidelines for reviewers emphasizes the importance of grantee capacity to do the job, but they also say that resources should be allocated where they're needed most, specifically identifying low-income neighborhoods and ethnic minorities that do not currently have easy access or entry into the service system. And they require accessibility of service to all those in need.

Recently, for example, we reviewed a poorly written proposal from an organization with a minimal track record for service delivery, which was originally established as a self-help group for immigrants from Cambodia. The proposal was to establish a multipurpose center for Cambodian refugees who are not currently receiving adequate services from anyone. We had a hard decision to make. The proposal clearly met the criterion for putting resources where the need is greatest, but by limiting services to Cambodian immigrants, we would be negating the principle of universal availability. Moreover, we were not convinced that the organization that had applied for the grant had or could develop the capacity to work up to our standards.

We have a couple of other policy statements, too. One is that social services should permit consumer choice and should allow for the protection of individuality and consumer participation in policy making. Now those are nice principles, but they're not always operable. If a good proposal comes in that doesn't include consumer participation in policy making, but does protect the consumers by providing them with a variety of grievance mechanisms, we're likely to fund it. Another project might come in that doesn't allow for grievance machinery and in fact threatens the principle of confidentiality simply because clients are involved in policy making. How do we choose?

TWO VIEWS OF REVIEWS

The two views expressed in the previous vignettes represent the perspectives of people standing in different places—one seeking funding and the other trying to make the best possible decision about awarding a grant. No matter how well prepared you are before you submit a proposal, there always seems to be something left undone. In addition to preparing the proposal (and yourself), you will need to consider preparing the potential sponsor and other key stakeholders in the program. Even when all the right preparations are made, reviewers may not find it easy to make the right choice. As the second vignette suggests, even when the review criteria are clear enough, they may be in conflict with each other. If this creates dilemmas for review panelists, one can imagine how much more so for the proposal writer. Can the proposal writer anticipate the difficulty and make it easier for reviewers to select their proposals for funding?

Proposal writers can prepare themselves, potential sponsors, and other relevant publics before writing and submitting the proposal. This chapter begins by describing this start-up process and then turns to those processes used in proposal review. Although the criteria used in determining whether or not to fund a project do sometimes contradict each other, a number of criteria will be examined that are almost always important to funders.

There are still things to do even after the proposal has been posted in the mail and you are waiting to get the review results, including making adjustments to the proposal and getting ready for start-up of the grant. If you do not get funded, there may be things you can do to get the proposal reconsidered and to increase the likelihood of its being funded at a later date or by a different sponsor. What if you do get funded? There are also processes to set in motion even before the project's scheduled start-up date.

GETTING STARTED: WHAT TO DO
BEFORE WRITING THE PROPOSAL

Getting started takes some preparation: (a) preparing yourself and your organization, (b) preparing sponsors, and (c) preparing others.

Preparing Yourself and Your Organization

You can prepare yourself by gathering relevant information on your own organization's needs and capacities, on funding opportunities, and on the proposal writing and submission process. If you have read Chapters 3 through 11, you already have a good idea of where and how to find out about potential sponsors. Your challenge now is to turn this general knowledge into more targeted and applicable information. To do that, consider using one or more of the techniques:

1. Create a clip file and data bank.
2. Use the Internet, the library, and other accessible information sources.
3. Talk to colleagues and others who have had experience with specific funders and with the grants or contracting processes.

These are not do-it-yourself tasks. They are best done with others who can share in the work and in the learning that comes from it. Fund-raising that is directly related to program development (e.g., grant seeking) works best when those who must live with the outcome are involved at every stage of the process.

Clip Files and Data Banks

So much program development time can be spent on chasing information that proposals are often late or are submitted before they are quite ready. You can save a good deal of grief if you and others in the organization regularly contribute to a clip file on potential funding sources, useful program ideas, and transferable proposal components. The file can be electronic or hard copy or both. The following are some categories others have found useful in organizing their files:

1. Files on funding sources and potential sponsors

   Relevant pages from the *catalogue of Federal Domestic Assistance*, state and local funding sources, and various directories on foundation and corporate giving

   Foundation annual reports and corporate reports of recent funding

   Proposal guidelines, requests for proposals, *Federal Register* program announcements, and applications

   News clippings about new funding priorities, grants to local agencies, new appointments to foundation boards, human interest stories on corporate executives and their concerns, and so on

2. Proposal forms and formats

   Samples of proposals that worked for others

   Proposal ideas you and your organization worked on before but that may not have resulted in a completed or funded project

   Good project ideas; reports on programs conducted elsewhere to borrow or find out more about

   Wish lists and priority statements that staff and board members have worked on

3. Proposal components that might be used or redrafted

   Agency capacity statements (fact sheets on the agency, its history and mission, and programs)

   Data on problems and needs and relevant study reports

   Staff profiles, resumes, and job descriptions

   Descriptions of collateral service providers and collaborative arrangements that already exist with them; descriptions of collaborations that take place elsewhere but that are potentially replicable

   Descriptions of related programs, policies, and activities

   Samples of evaluation approaches and how-to guides on evaluation

   Sample budgets, suggestions on how to design performance and program budgets, and benefits package information

Other income sources—actual and potential

Sample cover letters or letter proposals or both

Useful materials to include in an appendix (reprints, financial reports, news clippings, case histories, and letters of support—actual or in model form)

Graphs and charts that describe agency operations (flowcharts, Gantt charts, etc.) or that can be used as models for a proposal; chart software

4. Advocates and stakeholders—names and addresses of

Your board members

Program experts in academic and practice settings

Directors of other relevant programs and projects

Specialists in related issues (legal matters, budgets, and program evaluation)

Leaders of relevant civic associations and church and community groups

Using Libraries and Building Your Own

Although the clip file is tailored to your specific needs, you do not have to duplicate general information already available elsewhere. Libraries are extraordinary resources on grants and other fund-raising information. Directories and other guides to donors and funding sources were described in Part II. Most are available in those libraries linked to the Foundation Center's Cooperating Libraries system. Many "grants" librarians conduct workshops or provide consultation on how to connect with grant sources.

You can also build your own grants and fund-raising library or one that you share with other organizations that share space in your building or with which you collaborate on program-related activities. Check the library to preview books and journals you may want to purchase. Write for catalogs to those publishers such as Sage and Jossey-Bass that, as you may have noticed from the reading suggestions in previous chapters, carry many books on fund-raising and nonprofit management.

Some commercial distributors, such as NonProfit Partners (phone: 1-800-860-4490), include books from many publishers in their catalogs. This firm also distributes CD-ROMs with data on funding sources, newsletters that cover grants information, and other materials. In many regions of the country, nonprofits have organized Nonprofit Forums that distribute information on voluntarism, grants seeking, and government regulations. For example, the Michigan Nonprofit Forum distributes a monthly "MNF Member Mailing" in partnership with *Crain's Nonprofit News*. Is there something comparable in your state?

Accessing the Internet

For many, the Internet will soon become a primary source of information. If you are new at surfing the Internet, try the sets developed to accompany this book:

GRANTS, ETC.—A University of Michigan Web site for the human services and other nonprofits

URL = http://www.umich.edu/~alauffer/grantetc.html.

For a description of the Web site and other useful Internet addresses, see Appendix A.

Michigan COMNET—information sources for the human services

URL = http://comnet.org/

Comnet is the nonprofit and public service community's gateway to local and national resources on the Internet. Although there are many other sites through which you can access the same or comparable information, I do not think you will find better designed, more comprehensive, or more user-friendly sites.

GRANTS, ETC. was initially prepared by Anita Morse for students in a graduate-level course on grants, contracting, and fund-raising; is clearly indexed; and provides what is probably the easiest access to multiple funding sources on the Internet. More detailed information on this guide is found in Appendix A.

Networking Is With People, Too

Do not limit yourself to collecting and filing and libraries and the Internet. Get more information personally or via regular channels. Talk to colleagues who have worked on grant applications. Find board members and volunteers who know something about a local foundation's current interest.

Consultants Can Help

Because of the complexity and competitiveness of the fund-raising market, some agencies are paying for fund-raising counsel. Consultants and consultation services can help you design a fund-raising strategy, locate the appropriate funding source, and handle many writing and other communication chores. You can get lists of consultants and referrals from local affiliates of the following organizations:

National Society of Fund Raising Executives, 1101 King Street, Suite 3000, Alexandria, VA 22314; phone: (703) 684-0410

American Association of Fund Raising Counselors, 25 West 43rd Street, New York, NY 10036; phone: (212) 354-5799

Check also with national agencies that your organization may be affiliated with (e.g., the Child Welfare League of America), and local central agencies (e.g., the United Way) that can also provide you with names of consultants. To save both time and money, you will do well to develop screening criteria for use in determining who you want to interview and then who you will select to consult with you. The following are some common selection criteria:

- track record—success level in doing the work you need help with;
- years and relevance of experience and reputation for excellence;
- commitment to helping organizations such as yours, the field, and clientele you represent;
- ability to communicate and relate to the constituents you must consider.

Convene a committee to determine the criteria and the way in which you will screen prospective consultants. Use a five-point scale and other techniques similar to those used by proposal reviewers to screen prospective consultants. After you have narrowed down to two or three prospects,

- study the consultant's portfolio (sample proposals and other materials);
- hold interviews;
- check references;
- compare costs and fees.

Preparing Sponsors and Others

Preproposal Contacts

Preparing yourself and your organization is likely to result in many prepoposal contacts with prospective sponsors. You make an impression by the way in which you communicate requests for information and present materials that describe your organization and its interests. That impression is important if you are to cross the first hurdle—getting the information you need and then the help that you will find useful in moving your proposal from idea to funded project. In your contact with sponsors and others involved in the funding process, you may find yourself

- writing or calling for application guidelines and forms;
- asking for advice from previous grant and gift recipients or reviewers;
- contacting program or grants officers.

Application Guidelines

Each funding source has its own special requirements. In some cases, instructions on format and length will be quite detailed. In other cases, the funder will permit you considerable latitude. This may even vary with the kinds of projects a single funder supports. For example, research proposals are likely to require a significant review of the literature, a rigorous methodology section, and attention to its significance in light of previous research. Those oriented toward services will require documentation on the needs of those to be served or problems to be addressed. Training proposals are often required to demonstrate how participation will increase the quality of service programs.

Call or write for application forms and guidelines. Letters should be brief and addressed to a real person. If you do not find an appropriate name in some printed or Internet resource or get it from a colleague, call the funding source and ask. In your letter, you might include (a) a one- or two-sentence description of your organization and its interest and (b) a request for the organization's guidelines and application form, plus other relevant materials (e.g., examples of recently approved applications, list of current grantees, etc.).

Contacting Previous Grant Recipients

Check with current grant recipients and former reviewers for the funding agency. By now you know that fund-raising is extremely competitive. Therefore, you might ask, "Why would anyone want to share information on funders or successful fund-raising strategies?" For the same reasons you would. Nonprofit organizations are prone to sharing information that will benefit the general public or populations at risk. There may also be some direct benefit to sharing information. Funders increasingly require evidence of collaboration at the community level. An agency that has secured funding last year may be on the lookout for potential collaborators for the coming year.

The following is a beginning inventory of questions you might want to ask former grant recipients:

- Does the sponsor welcome contacts before the proposal is submitted?
- Will the sponsor want to see a concept paper or draft prior to the final proposal? How important is evidence of community support? Is it helpful to get outsiders to advocate with the sponsor?
- Did you receive the entire amount requested or was the budget modified?
- Knowing what you now know about the sponsor, would you have written your proposal differently?

If you call a former reviewer, ask the following questions:

- What kind of scoring system is used?
- What are the key issues you look for (criteria for funding)?
- What are the most common mistakes applicants make?
- How much time did you have to read each proposal?
- Was there any discussion between you and other reviewers?
- Is the peer review panel recommendation the final word? If not, who makes the final decision?

Preparing the Grants Program Officer

As you and your organization get to be better known, government and foundation officers may seek you out as often as you do them. When potential sponsors accept nonsolicited grant applications, however, getting known by the sponsor may be as important as gathering information on its funding priorities and processes. Many funders employ grants or program officers to perform some or all of the following tasks:

- soliciting submission of the best possible proposals;
- assisting proposal writers in their design efforts;
- screening out those submissions that do not meet the funder's criteria;
- managing the peer review process;
- assisting award recipients with their initial start-up activities;
- reviewing progress (periodic program reports and budgets) to assure accountability and to help grantees over the hurdles.

These activities are aimed at helping applicants to submit good proposals. If your first contact is by phone, be prepared to answer questions from the grants program officer in addition to asking your own questions. You will probably be asked about

- your organization and its location, mission, clientele, and history;
- your job and your role in the grant-seeking process;
- the kinds of support you seek.

Be ready to ask

- if the project fits within the funder's current priorities; if not,
- where the funder recommends sending it; or if it is close,
- how it should be modified to fit;
- what was the average size of awards given last year and what can be expected for this year;
- how many complete applications are submitted and how many are funded;
- if there are any unannounced programs you should be aware of;
- what kinds of issues are frequently overlooked by grant applicants and what kinds of mistakes do proposal writers often make.

Also ask if the grants officer would be willing to review a concept paper or preliminary draft if sent early enough and if he or she will send you copies of successful project proposals.

In a second contact or after sending a concept paper, be prepared to answer some of the following questions from grants officers:

- What difference do you think your project will make (for your constituents and for the field)?
- Is the project likely to have relevance beyond the client population, geographic area, or time frame in which it is located?
- Are these differences likely to be significant?
- Is your organization actually capable of doing the work you propose?
- What kinds of support for this program exists in your agency or community?

First contacts are likely to make impressions that carry over throughout the grant application process. Good impressions carry some weight, and they do take some preparation.

Preparing Others

Your success is not likely to depend solely on good communication between you and a sponsor. It will often depend on the buy-in and collaboration of other key publics. I have seen more than one award turned back because colleagues and board refused to accept it. I have also seen others subverted because clients and collateral agencies did not feel any ownership over the process.

GETTING REVIEWED

Review Panels and Procedures

Federal agencies often use external panelists to review research, training, or service-oriented proposals. Experts in their fields may be brought to Washington or some other central location to participate in rating proposals that have been prescreened by staff to weed out those that are inappropriate. Increasingly, the rating process is conducted electronically to lower costs, speed up the process, and broaden the range of inputs into decision making. A "rating sheet" may be used on which reviewers score different questions on a five-point scale, ranging from "very positive" to "very negative." The criteria used generally includes some or all of the following:

- *significance and relevance to funder's priorities:* importance of objectives, generalizability of impact, and compatibility with sponsor's mission or priorities;
- *scope of the work—procedures and program description:* completeness, precision and detail, knowledge of related work, overall design, and realistic timetable;
- *capacity:* qualifications of personnel, organizational track record, availability of nonfiscal resources, and appropriate facilities;
- *support:* evidence of support by relevant stakeholders (including funding, if required), likelihood of continued funding after the grant period or of effect on other relevant programs and populations;
- *cost:* appropriateness of budget items and costs assigned and efficiency of operations (how much it costs to achieve program objectives or to conduct program operations);
- *feasibility:* whether or not the work can be done as described and at the costs projected.
- *consistency, completeness, and clarity:* what is written in one part of the proposal is consistent with what is said elsewhere; all required components are complete; the proposal is easy to follow; and the formatting contributes to rather than contradicts the substance of the proposal.

Proposals that score the highest on each of the criteria are generally put in the "yes" pile, those that are clear rejects go into another, and those in between (or that score very highly on some criteria but poorly on others) go into a "maybe" pile. Be aware that some projects are approved pending funding. In government programs, approval is sometimes nullified by a cut in appropriations or a redirection of spending priorities. Panelists are sometimes convened as a group (face to face, by phone, or electronically) if there appears to be some anomaly in the scoring. For example, if six panelists feel a proposal should be funded, two are not sure, and one feels that it should not, efforts to resolve the differences may require some discussion.

State-level funding decisions are much more variable. The procedures may change from year to year or from agency to agency. Some use external panels, but most rely on staff decisions within the agency making the grants or contract awards. Some large state departmental decisions are subject to review by the governor's budget priorities committee or some other oversight group that is concerned with the level of government expenditure or with the equitable distribution of state funds. This can result in holding up, and sometimes rejecting, a proposal that has overcome all other hurdles.

Local government grants rarely go through an external review panel. Line staff in appropriate departments (e.g., recreation or housing) may be entrusted to issue contracts or grants. On some programs—for example, Empowerment Zone grants—a citizen's review board or council may be established by the mayor or the city council to review and approve submissions before they are passed on at the state level and then forwarded to a federal agency. This process can get extremely political, requiring the buy-in of many community actors. In such circumstances, the quality of the proposal may be only one of many factors to be taken into account in the funding decision.

Although large foundations have become increasingly professional in their grant-making processes, the vast majority of foundations are small and do not have professional staff. Many of the largest foundations in the United States are relatively young, and experience shows that it can take 5 or more years to create a set of workable procedures. Once in place, however, staff often screen proposals before sending them on to the board. For example, at the Mott Foundation, program officers can decide, within the limits of the budgets they have control over, whether to fund projects with price tags of $15,000 or less. Larger grant applications must be reviewed by the foundation's board of trustees or by a special review panel that deals with a particular sector of the foundation's work.

In the more professionally run foundations, program officers are expected to consult with those grant seekers who appear to be on the right track. A project officer at a major foundation stated, "I can't stop anyone from sending in a proposal, but I view it as my job to screen out inappropriate ones early, so that there is enough time to help other proposal writers to submit a fundable project design. Our trustees are busy people, and we don't want to waste their time by sending up a bunch of projects that won't fly."

Be aware, however, that smaller foundations may not employ staff at all. Funding decisions are made by the donor, by a member of the family, or by a trustee entrusted with such responsibility. The trustee, perhaps an attorney or a banker, may know little of the issues your proposal deals with. Some decisions are made by a panel of family members who are committed to following the intentions of the original donor. Knowing who makes the decisions and who influences the decision process may be as important as knowing the official criteria by which decisions are presumably made.

When corporation grants are made at headquarters, a panel of executive officers is often involved. Authority for local giving, however, may be delegated to branch managers or entrusted to a community relations officer. In many situations, the process continues to be very idiosyncratic, even though a number of major corporations have begun to share information on how they make funding decisions with each other. The intent is to make the process more routine and professional.

In contrast, the United Way and other well-established fund-raising and allocating bodies in the voluntary sector tend to have highly formalized review processes. These were described in Chapter 7. Staff members work closely with applicant organizations and guide lay committees organized into sector review panels in the decision-making process. In United Ways that operate traditionally, most of these decisions are focused on whether to increase or decrease allocations based on the previous year's experience. New applicants may be put through a particularly rough review process that examines not only the application itself but also the problem or population to which it is addressed and the capacity of the organization submitting the application to do the job specified. In some of the newer patterns described, however, United Ways make competitive grants rather than more traditional allocations, operating much more like community foundations or public agencies.

Church, mutual benefit association, and civic association members may not feel they have the capacities to make judgments about the applicant organization or how it has chosen to serve those in need. To minimize the risks associated with making the wrong decision, some rely on priority areas determined by their national bodies. At the local level, some churches may collaborate through an urban ministry or some other structure. A decision to pursue a new funding option may have to be ratified by the board or the entire membership at an open meeting.

Tip: The United States Department of Education's Horace Mann Learning Center for Continuing Education conducts occasional workshops for application reviewers. Participants receive a three-part manual. Module I is an introduction to the review process and the roles performed by different people. Module II walks you through the process of reading, analysis, and applying selection criteria. Module III focuses on technical aspects of the review process (scoring, writing comments, and participating on the review team). If you are interested in a copy, contact the Government Printing Office (Fax: 303 872-5051). Ask for document ED/OM91-6, "Reviewing Applications for Discretionary Grants and Cooperative Agreements: A Workbook for Applications Reviewers").

Why Proposals Are Rejected

Several years ago, in a review of some 605 disapproved research grant applications, the Public Health Service determined that rejections were made on the basis of the following shortcomings: the problem (58%), the approach (73%), the investigator (55%), and other reasons (16%). Of those proposals rejected because of the problem being investigated, more than half were determined to be of insufficient importance or unlikely to produce any useful information. Of those rejected because of the approach used, half were determined to include scientific procedures that were unsuited to the stated objective. More than a third described the approach to be used in so nebulous a manner as to preclude serious examination, and about one of six was judged to have a poorly thought-through design.

Project directors were rated low when they appeared to have inadequate experience, were unfamiliar with pertinent literature and methods, or because their published work did not inspire confidence. Others were rejected because of unrealistic requests for equipment or personnel, unfavorable institutional settings, and an assumption that the project director would devote insufficient time to the project. These are not that dissimilar from reasons given for turning down other kinds of applications.

TIPS FOR SCORING HIGH
IN THE REVIEW PROCESS

Tip 1: The key issues should be highlighted so as to make it possible for reviewers to be satisfied that all their conditions have been met and impressed by the way in which you propose to deal with them.

Tip 2: None of us are so experienced that we can always guess right about what reviewers are going to find. A good way to prepare for all kinds of eventualities is to go through a mock review process. Ask colleagues, friends, experts, and others to go through a simulated review process. Give them copies of the review criteria to be used by the funding agency.

If you want to know how some of the larger corporations and company foundations evaluate proposals, find a copy of The Conference Board's research report "Screening Requests for Corporate Contributions," first published in 1986 and updated periodically. The report includes case studies of how funding decisions are made, examples of review criteria, screening forms and formats, corporate grant-making policies, and form letters for company "turn-downs." You can write for the most recent copy to The Conference Board, 845 Third Avenue, New York, NY 10022; phone: (212) 759-0900.

For a brief overview of the issues you should address before writing your proposal and before submitting it to a funder, see

Appendix B. The list includes all the items that funders are likely to be concerned about when reviewing your proposal. You may find it a useful review of what was covered in Chapters 13 through 15.

Site Visits

I now focus on two issues touched on in the vignettes at the beginning of the chapter. As the applicant to NIMH learned, it is sometimes insufficient to say all the right things in the proposal itself. It may be as important, or more important, to get other people to corroborate your claims. In the example given, a well-designed proposal was rejected because the other key players did not understand the rules of the game. They fought over the ball when they should have been passing it to each other.

TIPS FOR DOING WELL DURING A SITE VISIT

Tip 1: Consider a "dress rehearsal" before being embarrassed by the review team.

Tip 2: Stay on schedule. It may look as if you have plenty of time, but you can fritter away precious minutes on extraneous information. If you are going on a tour of the agency and its programs, allow enough time for visitors and regulars (staff and clients) to talk to each other.

Tip 3: Emphasize the major points in your written materials, but do not repeat information ad nauseam, and do not include reams of new information. It may confuse reviewers and throw a monkey wrench into the proceedings.

Tip 4: Provide a structure (that is your edge) but do not control the entire process. Allow plenty of time for site visitors to ask questions. Prepare for those questions by asking the head of the site visit team what members are likely to want to know about. If appropriate, have written materials available. Better still, answer the question in advance by pointing to the answer on your tour of the facilities or program.

The funder quoted in the second vignette at the start of this chapter spoke of the importance of fitting a proposal to the purpose of the missions of the funding agency. Your support will come from others who are convinced that you are doing their work and doing it in the best manner possible.

WHAT TO DO WHILE YOU ARE WAITING

What should you do while you are waiting to find out if your application has been approved? Keep busy! There may be much more work to be done. The following are a few suggestions:

1. Update the proposal if necessary.
2. Promote the proposal or the ideas behind it among relevant publics.
3. Design a fall-back plan in case you do not get funded.
4. Gear up for operations in case you should get funded.

Update

It is not unusual, under the pressure of deadlines, for proposal writers to submit a less-than-perfect document. There are also times when circumstances change, and a modification in the narrative or the budget may be necessary. Funders often permit modest changes on receipt of an explanatory letter with supportive documents. This is almost always true if your materials get there before the review process takes place. For example, the results of a United Way survey may come in 2 weeks after you have submitted your proposal to a federal agency. If the UW data support your argument, summarize them and send them in with a note asking that the summary be appended. If financial support is confirmed from a source mentioned as a possibility in the proposal (e.g., a gift from a foundation or from a wealthy philanthropist), inform the potential grantor and modify the budget request accordingly. If new letters of endorsement or support arrive after you have mailed the proposal, send them in and ask that they be added to your file.

Promotions

Promotional activities during the period of review or just before can pay significant dividends. Some years ago, I submitted a grant application to a federal agency on behalf of the University of Michigan. The Michigan Department of Social Services was anxious for the university to get the grant. State officials, through telephone calls and visits to Washington, made it clear that the project was in the state's interest. Members of the congressional staff of one of the Michigan delegation also let the word out that Michigan voters were concerned that previous grants had gone to Illinois, Ohio, and Indiana. Michigan was next in line. A word of caution here: Informal influence, especially when well orchestrated, can be very effective, but it can also backfire if it is perceived as an organized campaign.

This may be less true at the local level, particularly when citizen support is active and vocal and when a case is made in noncontroversial terms. Local officials and citizens' task groups are going to listen to organized voters who know what they want and are willing to articulate their demands in ways that are not going to be insulting or that will not cause opposition or backlash from other quarters. When a proposal is submitted that deals with an issue that is poorly understood, press coverage of the issue is likely to help educate and sensitize decision makers in a way that even the best-phrased program design cannot.

A proposal submitted to the United Way or to a local corporation is likely to be received positively if officials are knowledgeable about the issues your project is designed to deal with. A call from a well-wishing booster telling officials about how effective your agency is and why he or she thinks your project should be funded is a "no-no." Worse, it is likely to backfire. Pressure of this kind may work in some settings, but it tends not to work in most grant programs. "Education" about an issue, however, is not perceived as pressure. The chief development officer at a community college confided to me, "We treat proposals to local funding sources much the way we do our other fund-raising campaigns. We're most successful when we combine an 'ask' with an educational program that appears unconnected to our institution. For example, for a year or more before we submitted the proposal to expand services to handicappers, we orchestrated news coverage about discrimination against disabled adults and about how the differently abled had overcome various disabilities through 'grit and education.'

"We also cosponsored several communitywide meetings and a conference on disabilities at the college. By the time we were ready to submit the proposal, there was a heightened awareness, locally, about the 'disabling prejudice that the differently abled suffer from.' The News ran several related stories during the few weeks after we'd submitted the proposal. None of these stories mentioned the proposal, and hardly referred to the college at all. A community awareness campaign rarely works if it appears to serve the interests of those conducting the campaign."

WHAT TO DO IF YOU DO OR
IF YOU DO NOT GET FUNDED

If You Do Not Get Funded

What should you do if the project does not get funded? The following are a few options:

- Seek alternative sources of funding.
- Substitute noncash for cash resources.
- Delay start-up or phase in slowly.
- Reallocate some funds from other operations.
- Collaborate with other organizations.
- Rethink your agency's priorities.
- Accept the inevitable and move on.
- Use this as an opportunity to build a relationship with the funder.
- Do all or most of the above.

Your choice of options will be easier if you have prepared a fallback position. If the organization is not able to do without the grant, your fallback position should include seeking alternative sources of funding; no need to wait to find out if the grant was approved. There is rarely any rule against soliciting support from more than a single source. Funders may ask you whether a similar proposal for support has been submitted elsewhere and may encourage you to do so. If they want to fund you, they will—even if other sponsors are also interested (and sometimes because other sponsors are interested). Always find out why the proposal was rejected. If the funder does not deal with the kinds of issues you proposed, find out if there is a more appropriate source of supply. If the proposal itself is wanting, find out how it might be improved, whether you can submit again, and when.

Not long ago, a proposal I had submitted to a relatively young foundation was turned down for what I later discovered had little to do with inadequacies in my proposal. The foundation had instituted a peer review process, but that process was poorly managed, and panelists found so much to disagree with among themselves that virtually every proposal that came before it was turned down at least once. Fortunately, I was asked to resubmit, with some specific suggestions for improvements. They appeared reasonable and I was able to address them all. The application was turned down again! Once more, however, I was invited to resubmit—this time with suggestions that contradicted some of those made after the first round.

Clearly, the panel wanted to fund me but did not have its own act together. This time, I explained that I could not do so, intimating that it was "not seemly for the University of Michigan's stature to strike out three times in a row." I would seek support elsewhere. I stated, "However, we will be happy to answer any questions the review panel might have." This was a way of saving face for both the foundation and for me. It was also a bit like playing chicken, but someone, I reasoned, had to blink first.

Principle: When you seem to be at an impasse, do not panic and do not quit. Find out what is going on beneath the surface, and then find a tactic that will get you and the sponsor back on track.

Tip: Use the rejection as an opportunity to build relationships that may pay off in the future. Indicate appreciation for the sponsors' consideration, reiterate shared interests, and suggest that you will contact them with a new or changed idea at the appropriate time.

If You Do Get Funded

Let's be wildly optimistic. Just to play it safe, you submitted similar proposals to more than one funder. All were for an AIDS education project. To a foundation in Chicago, which supports projects aimed at the gay community, you stressed the depth of the problem for male homosexuals. To the county health department, you stressed the public health aspects, and to a local foundation concerned with minorities, your figures stressed the extent of the problem among heterosexual African Americans.

Multiple submissions are increasingly common and so is cofunding. Funders often encourage applicants to seek support from multiple sources. It lowers both your risk and theirs. Multiple funding sources makes it possible for each sponsor to share the risk of investment with other funders. If you submit to more than one source, each proposal will have to be tailored to the interest of the funder to whom it is submitted. One-size-fits-all and unisex proposals do not make it very often. Indicate, in the narrative or in your cover letter, that funding is being sought elsewhere, and name the other two potential sponsors. These sponsors may want to negotiate among themselves over how much each will contribute to the overall budget.

Suppose you get multiple funding for a project! Could you just expand it by extending for another year, adding more staff or buying more equipment? Not without permission. The reason for this is that when you write a proposal, you are making a commitment to do a certain piece of work for a given level of support. If the level of support is increased beyond what you indicated was needed, you cannot ethically change your mind about what you now intend to do without informing the sponsors. Sponsors may well permit you to expand services in different areas, but it is their money and they have to make the decision. For example, in the AIDS education project, you may be permitted to expand the program for each of the populations you sought funds for. You may also, however, be required to consolidate your general administrative costs.

This is a matter for negotiation. It is a process you will have to engage in whenever the conditions around your program or agency change sufficiently to cause you to make a major change in what you propose to do. Now, let's be more realistic. Your proposal was funded but at a lower level than you had requested. What do you do? The following three options exist:

1. If the cuts are not too deep, cut back on some aspects of the project that are not essential or reduce the project's length.

2. If the cuts are deep, but it is possible to locate supplementary funds, go for it.

3. If the cuts are too deep for the project to succeed, or if the drain on your organization is likely to seriously affect other essential operations, you may have to turn the offer down. Explain the reason or ask if you can delay start-up pending your ability to find new sources of support elsewhere.

Sometimes it pays to accept less than is optimal for no reason other than to establish a relationship with a funder. This can also be a formula for failure, however. If it cannot be done for less than $100,000 and there is no way to generate more than half that amount, chances are you will not live up to the promises you have made.

Once you and the funder have decided that the project is a go (you received full funding or renegotiated an acceptable alternative), there is still much to do. The goal is to get a running start on Day 1 of the grant period. To avoid wasting start-up time, begin seeking staff and lining up needed facilities or equipment as soon as you get final word (or earlier if you feel confident of getting the award). You may not be able to hire staff before you have the grant award, but you can start the interviewing process early; you can also negotiate with appropriate persons in your organization for the reallocation of staff from other responsibilities.

Prepare Yourself for Project Management

Just as you prepared yourself to research and write a proposal, you may need some prep time to get ready to manage the project. I encourage use of some of the same tools you may have applied to program design. I refer specifically to some of the software packages described in Chapter 14. The following is what project management can do:

- perform timeline calculations;
- sort and extract data for use in reports to the funder and other publics;
- test various intervention strategies in terms of possible impact and cost;

- design alternative scenarios to explore the potential impact of your interventions;
- depict data in easy-to-read charts;
- create audiovisual displays for use in presentations.

Selecting and using the right software takes time. Why do it after start-up when there may be little learning time available?

What to Do After Start-Up of the Project

Program and project management are also the subjects of another book!

Ongoing contact with the sponsor from the start-up to the end of the project, however, is an essential component of the grants process. Many funders require careful accounting of what you are accomplishing and how close you are to your original design, timetable, and budget. Quarterly, semiannual, and final program and financial reports may be necessary. Put as much time and effort into these as you did for your original proposal. You may know that you are doing well, but the funder will need assurance as well. That assurance often requires documentation.

Tip: Just as you framed your proposal to articulate with the potential funder's interests, phrase your report with the sponsor's concerns (not your success) foremost in mind.

Do not limit your reporting to the sponsor alone. Sponsors are delighted when they get positive feedback on their projects from other sources. Your promotional efforts should not end when you get the grant. The following is a list of activities that will give your program more visibility and generate important contacts:

- Get articles in the local press.
- Present at professional conferences.
- Publish articles in professional journals.
- Give talks and demonstrations at community events.

- Consult with colleagues in other agencies.
- Make oral reports to your board and to colleagues in other departments.

WHAT HAPPENS IF YOUR OTHER FUND-RAISING ACTIVITIES ARE SUCCESSFUL OR IF THEY ARE NOT

Accountability to Individual Donors

How about other fund-raising activities? Do you have the same obligations to individual donors as to institutional funders? Yes, but they are not always worked out in the same way.

Donors, because they are individuals rather than organizations, are not likely to come up with a collective set of requirements, guidelines, or performance criteria by which to monitor the use of their gifts. The administrator of a family service agency explains in the following vignette.

No Action by Default

We can't just take the money and run. We have the same kinds of obligations to our individual donors as to the larger institutional funders with which we deal. When people contribute something to this agency, they are investing in a program, an idea, a service. We owe it to them to manage that investment honestly and competently. We have a reputation for quality service. We don't believe in defaulting on our clients. And we don't default on our investors either.

Well put—a sentiment shared by many professional fund-raisers and human service agency personnel. Just as a default in business is likely to reduce confidence in a firm and putting out faulty products is likely to turn off customers, a default with a provider public is likely to reduce confidence with other publics as well. Honest and competent investment of donated funds, however, is more than a short-term tactical concern. It is also an expression of the professional values of the practitioners in the human services and of those who manage those services. The colleague quoted in the previous vignette explained how he fulfills what he considers his professional obligations to the public in the following vignette.

Keeping the Faith

First of all, we never just ask for money when we fund-raise. We raise money for specific purposes: sending kids to camp; buying books and games for our volunteer tutors to bring to families in deprived neighborhoods; increasing the hours we can maintain a hot line. People know what they're giving for. Our door-to-door canvassers and other solicitors give prospective donors pledge cards on which they can not only indicate how much they wish to give, but how they want their gift allocated. We make it plain on the card that 20% of all donations goes to general agency programs and services. That generally gives us enough flexibility to do some reallocation if all the gifts bunch up in one or another program category.

Second, we send every donor a thank-you with a summary report on the campaign. A copy of his pledge card with the bill makes it possible for the donor to compare his gift with the collective gifts of others.

If we go over our target in some area, say, sending kids to camp, or if we set up a program but don't get enough takers for it, we may find money raised for a particular purpose has to be reallocated to some other program. Well, we inform the public in several ways. Donors who give over $50 or who have contributed small sums for several years get a summary quarterly report, so they know what's happening. It may sound like a lot of paperwork, but you would be surprised. Without any solicitation, we find that about 1 out of every 40 newsletters yields another contribution; enough to cover the cost of putting out the report plus some.

We also encourage open house days and invite donors to special meetings with the staff or board members. This not only is our way of saying thanks, but it nets us a big bonus in terms of volunteers. We often recruit future solicitors, committee members, and ultimately even board members from some of these contacts. When people make a contribution through us, they are making a contribution to kids and to their community, not just our agency. What they are saying is that they have faith in our stewardship of those funds. And we do the best we can to keep the faith.

Success Begets Success—Sometimes

Successful fund-raising efforts generally lead to other successes. They do not always follow directly, however. A colleague confided, "We had a great bike-athon in October. So we decided to do a walk-athon in the spring. It just didn't go over. Our volunteers were still tired out from the fall effort. I suspect we might have had less burnout had we tried a different fund-raising approach, but long-distance walking is just too similar to long-distance bike riding."

She was right on both counts: The events were too close to each other and too similar. There is always a temptation to repeat a success and that temptation need not be resisted; it just should not be succumbed to too frequently.

Unfortunately, fund-raising efforts do not always succeed. That too might be communicated to the public. The same colleague who spoke to me about keeping the faith stated, "One year we fell terribly short of our goal for tutorial materials. That's not something to cover up or to blame the public for. The fault is not theirs. We're the ones who didn't get the message across; so we try to do it after the campaign. I was very honest in a press release and indicated that 'despite an inadequate information program, the public has responded generously. Unfortunately, the sums raised leave 80 families unserved.' That generated a few belated gifts. More important, I used our lack of success in the following year's campaign. 'Let's not leave 80 families and 234 kids without the books they need to succeed' is the way our campaign letter opened."

The consequences of not meeting one's fund-raising goal can be serious for the agency itself in addition to those consumers who may be unserved or underserved. A neighborhood center director admitted, "We couldn't come up with the dollars we needed, so had to give up our option on the property we had worked 5 years to locate. Now I don't know when we'll be able to open up a new center."

On examination of her fund-raising efforts, it became clear that she and her campaign team had relied too heavily on a single solicitation strategy and had approached only a narrow segment of the public.

Tip: It sometimes helps to test several different approaches to see which ones work and then to discard those that do not. It can be pretty disastrous if you never do a test run and you put all your eggs into a single basket.

Talk about mixed metaphors! The point is important, however. Even the most successful fund-raising effort is no guarantee of continued support. Remember that a single gift, like a grant, is rarely a lifetime commitment. What happens when the gift is expended or when the grant period is over? What could happen if a 3-year grant is not funded after the second year because of a government cutback or a change in funding priorities? You will need a contingency plan that guarantees continuation.

Successful agencies generally do well at getting grants and raising funds in many ways and from multiple sources. Organizations that have been successful in raising funds and getting grants are considered to do well at other things too. A frequently heard lament is that, "If we only could get the money we need, we could do the things we have to." I suggest that "If we would only do the things we must, we could get the money we need."

Samuel Butler phrased it in a more ingenious way: He said, "A hen is an egg's way of making another egg."

REVIEW

Writing successful proposals requires good preparation: preparing yourself and preparing others—colleagues and board members, other service providers, local supporters, grants program officers— all those involved in supporting the program and its goals. Preparing yourself requires, among other things, getting the information you need. You will find some of it in the library and on the Internet, but much of it is available from colleagues, potential funders, and others who share some of your organization's concerns. Suggestions were made for how to communicate with sponsors and others on whom success in fund-raising and program development is dependent.

The point was also made that such contacts do not end when a proposal is transmitted to a funder. There is still much to do to: continue the promotional effort, prepare for a possible site visit, and deal with the consequences of a rejection. In the event your request is turned down, you still have several options, including seeking alternative funding sources or resubmitting and delaying project start-up. Suggestions were also given for how to respond to partial or inadequate funding and to the occasional embarrassment of riches when more than one funder allocates funds to different versions of the same proposal.

SUGGESTIONS FOR FURTHER READING

In addition to many of the resources mentioned in Chapter 12, consider the following:

Cannon, T. J. (1990). *No miracles for hire! How to get real value from your consultant*. New York: AMACOM.

Hombersley, B. (1989, December). Charities: Best advice at a price. *Accountancy, 104*(1156), 68-69.

Kibbe, B. (1992). *Succeeding with consultants: Self-assessment for the changing nonprofit*. New York: The Foundation Center.

Knutson, J., & Bitz, I. (1991). *Project management: How to plan and manage successful projects*. New York: AMACOM.

Moore, P. (Ed.). (1990). *Models for success: A look at (federal) grant-winning proposals*. Alexandria, VA: Capitol.

Public Management Institute. (n.d.). *Seven ways to contact corporate funding executives*. San Francisco: Author.

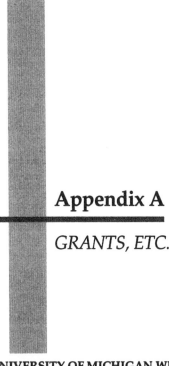

Appendix A

GRANTS, ETC.

**A UNIVERSITY OF MICHIGAN WEB SITE FOR
THE HUMAN SERVICES AND OTHER NONPROFITS**[1]

To reach the *Grants, Etc.* home page, use a graphical browser such as Netscape, Mosaic, or Microsoft Internet Explorer. Each has its own set of instructions. For example, on the Netscape Web page, you click the Open button on your tool bar and then type in the Uniform Resource Locator (URL) for *GRANTS, ETC.* at the University of Michigan.

You can read it via COMNET at

      URL = http://comnet.org/

and then click on

      GRANTS, ETC.

or directly via

      URL = http://www.umich.edu/~alauffer/grantetc.html.

Note that all URL addresses are case sensitive, so be sure to type in caps or in lowercase as shown in this guide.

GRANT AND FUND-RAISING INFORMATION RESOURCES ON THE INTERNET

Why the Internet

Information is the fund-raiser's primary resource. The Internet provides you access to the World Wide Web (WWW), a global network of information. Through the Web, you will be able to find out where the money is and how to access it. Every Web site is accessible through a home page, which serves as its front door and as an entryway through which to access other sites.

Moving Around the Internet

Once you have accessed a home page, such as *Grants, Etc.*, you can jump from one document or Web site to another by clicking on the underlined or otherwise highlighted words, phrases, or addresses. For example, if you need a *Primer on the Internet*, which is located at

URL = http://www.eit.com/goodies/www.guide/

click on the boldface words and you will move directly to the location. In the pages that follow, I will guide you to

- finding fund-raising resources on the Internet;
- accessing information sources on funding;
- exploring tax implications of fund-raising for donors and nonprofit organizations;
- locating other fund-raising resource sites on the Internet;
- learning about the Internet;
- starting up your own Web page.

FINDING FUND-RAISING RESOURCES ON THE INTERNET

1. *The Philanthropic Advisory Service* is a service of the Council of Better Business Bureau providing reports and an online complaint service for hundreds of nonprofit organizations that solicit nationally.

URL = http://www.igc.apc.org/cbbb/pas.html

2. *The Standards for Charitable Solicitations* from the Council of Better Business Bureaus are model standards for charitable organizations seeking donations. The standards emphasize voluntary disclosure of information by nonprofits that prospective donors should consider, such as organization activities, finances, fund-raising practices, and governance. An explanation of disclosure and reporting rules applicable to Section 501(c)(3) organizations under the Internal Revenue Code is provided.

URL = http://www.igc.apc.org/cbbb/pas/standard.html

ACCESSING INFORMATION SOURCES ON FUNDING

Charitable and Corporate Foundations

The Foundation Center—79 Fifth Avenue, New York, NY 10003-3076; phone: (212) 620-4230—provides library services nationwide through its national collections in New York and Washington, DC, field offices in Atlanta, Cleveland, and San Francisco, and more than 200 cooperating libraries in all 50 states and abroad. The center offers proposal writing seminars throughout the year (call 1-800-424-9836 for registration information) and publishes annual compilations on national foundation and corporate giving as well as individual publications geared toward funding for specific groups or interests. Membership in the Foundation Center Associate's Program entitles fundraisers and grant seekers to specialized search services, fund-raising materials, and current information on grant makers. The Foundation Center Web page includes information on the center, addresses of participating library locations, links to grant makers and government resources, a searchable database of its publications, *The Philanthropy Digest*, and information on the proposal development process.

URL = http://fdncenter.org

Government Grants and Contracts

1. *Grants and Contracts*, from the Documents Center, University of Michigan, includes links to resources of the federal government. You

will find the *Catalog of Federal Domestic Assistance*, a searchable database of federal government programs including grants, loans, scholarships, and other financial assistance. There are also links to the
Commerce Business Daily, the *Federal Register*, the GSA grants database, and other sources on government grants and contracts.

> URL = **http://www.lib.umich.edu/libhome/
> Documents.center/fedgen.html#grant**

2. *The Federal Web Locator Service* provides links to over 350 federal
government agency information sites, searchable by table of contents, keywords, or highlights of latest links.

> URL = **http://www.law.vill.edu/Fed-Agency/fedwebloc.html**

3. *The United States Government Manual* provides background information and contact names, addresses, and phone numbers of
government agencies and branches.

> URL = **http://www.gpo.ucop.edu/catalog/govman.html**

Private-Sector Giving

1. *The Securities and Exchange Commission* (SEC) home page is an
archive of corporate information. New users should start with *General Information: Retrieving Data*. Experienced users can use the hypertext link for the *Search the EDGAR Database* for keyword searching
by company name or a central index key (CIK), which SEC uses to
identify individual filers.

> URL = **http://www.sec.gov/edgarhp.htm**

2. *Involve:* Corporate Community Involvement is a project of the
American Leadership Forum that gives links to resources on how to
bring corporations into philanthropy and community giving. Titles
include *Winning Strategies for Corporate Community Involvement* and
Resource Guide for Corporate Community Involvement.

> URL = **http://www.alfsv.org/involve/**

Proposal Development

1. *The National Network of Grant Makers* (NNG) includes links to common grant application forms accepted by participating grant makers. Get the membership directory from the National Network of Grant Makers at 1117 Kettner Boulevard, Suite 110, San Diego, CA 92101; phone: (619) 231-1348. The *NNG Cover Letter* form asks for summary information on the requesting organization, type of request, organization mission, project or grant request, organizational budget, and funding need.

URL = http://fdncenter.org/fundproc/nngcover.html

2. The *NNG Application* form provides a standardized format for submissions of project proposals.

URL = http://fdncenter.org/fundproc/nngappl.html

3. The *NNG Budget* form categorizes total project expenditures and revenues for grant request into salaries, wages and fringe benefits, fees, travel, equipment, supplies, printing and copying, and telephone. Sources of revenues include government, foundations, corporations, earned income, United Way or other combined campaigns, individual corporations, membership income, in-kind support, and other support.

URL = http://fdncenter.org/fundproc/nngbudg.html

4. *A Proposal Writing Short Course* from the Foundation Center suggests the following: explain how the project fits into the mission of your agency; set forth the nature, timetable, anticipated outcomes, and staffing needs of the project; and detail the financial needs of the project. Components of a proposal include an executive summary, a statement of need, the project description, organization information, and conclusion. A proposal is usually no more than seven or eight pages in length plus appendices.

URL = http://fdncenter.org/fundproc/prop.html

EXPLORING TAX IMPLICATIONS OF FUND-RAISING
FOR DONORS AND NONPROFIT ORGANIZATIONS

1. *Foundations and Other Non-Profits*, by Louis H. Hamel, Jr., advises donors and fund-raisers about Internal Revenue Code requirements that nonprofit agencies must meet to qualify as a tax-exempt organization to which a donor may make a qualifying charitable deduction. Both the charitable organization and the donor are subject to reporting requirements under the Internal Revenue Code. Donors should be advised of the tax consequences of specific types of charitable donations.

> URL = http://www.haledorr.com/publications/trust/
> 1995_09_TrustNewsFoundation.html

2. *Charitable Deductions*, by Susan Valente Marandett, is a primer on estate and gift tax consequences of charitable deductions.

> URL = http://www.haledorr.com/publications/
> trust/1995_09_TrustNewsDeduction.html

3. *Name a Charity as Beneficiary*, by Michael Fey, explains the advantages of soliciting planned giving of annuities and other retirement funds from donors.

> URL = http://www.haledorr.com/publications/trust/
> 1995_09_TrustNewsRemainder.html

4. *Charitable Contributions of Securities*, by James A. Brink and William A. Caldwell, advises tax planners and charitable organizations that some donors may find it to be an advantageous tax strategy to donate securities to a charitable organization. Tax planners advise donors to give the charity decision-making power over disposal of the gift so that full benefit is received.

> URL = http://www.haledorr.com/publications/
> trust/1995_09_TrustNewsContrib.html

5. *Give Deferred Income to Charity*, by A. Silvana Giner, explains the tax planning strategies of charitable contributions.

URL = http://www.haledorr.com/publications/trust/
1995_09_TrustNewsIncome.html

6. *Charitable Planning* is a searchable database operated by the National Network of Estate Planners. Gift and estate planning is subject to both federal and state law. Features include a searchable database of financial planners organized by state and separate searchable databases on estate planning and charitable planning.

URL = http://www.netplanning.com/ch3.htm

7. *Tips on Tax Deductions for Charitable Contributions*, a publication of the Council on Better Business Bureaus, explains the difference between tax-exempt and tax-deductible organizations that solicit charitable contributions and how to find out an organization's status. IRS Publication 78, *Cumulative List of Organizations*, is an annual list of tax-exempt organizations to which a donor can make deductible charitable contributions. Information is included on deductibility limitations of donations to specific types of organizations that solicit donations and on specific types of gifts, such as volunteer services, goods and services, and gifts for which the donor receives any benefits in return.

URL = http://www.igc.apc.org/cbbb/pas/tipstax.html

8. *Taxes* from the Documents Center, University of Michigan, provides links to tax forms and the *Internal Revenue Code*.

URL = http://lib.umich.edu/libhome/Documents.center/
fedlgen.html#taxes

LOCATING OTHER FUND-RAISING
RESOURCES ON THE INTERNET

1. *Philanthropy Journal Online* is a meta-index of nonprofit organizations, nonprofit job opportunities, foundations, and corporate giving on the Web maintained by the *Philanthropy Journal of North Carolina*, a nonprofit newspaper for the nonprofit sector.

URL = http://www.philanthropy-journal.org

2. *Guide to Internet Resources for Non-Profit Service Organizations* is an encyclopedic guide to resources publicly available on the Internet organized by subject and searchable by keyword. It includes Gopher sites, WWW sites, and mailing lists.

> URL = http://www.sils.umich.edu/nesbeitt/nonprofits/
> nonprofits.html

3. *Libraries and Locations* from the Foundation Center gives the addresses of Center Libraries and is searchable by main, regional, state, and cooperating collection locations.

> URL = http://fdncenter.org

4. The Grantsmanship Center in Los Angeles provides information on training programs, publications, and information on *TGC Online*, a subscription service with comprehensive funding information accessible over the Internet.

> URL = http://www.tgci.com

5. *Federal Laws* from the Documents Center, University of Michigan, is a full-service site for access to federal laws, with links to recent public laws, the *United States Code*, the *Code of Federal Regulations*, and the *Federal Register*. These are essential resources for finding federal government grants, contracts, and assistance. For example, the *Internal Revenue Code* is Title 26 of the *United States Code*. The *Federal Register* is a daily publication of the federal government in which you will find legal notices of federal agency meetings, proposed and final rules and regulations of government agencies, and presidential documents. The *Code of Federal Regulations* is an annual subject compilation of final rules and regulations first published in the *Federal Register*. For example, the Internal Revenue Service implements the *Internal Revenue Code* in federal regulations contained in Title 26 of the *Code of Federal Regulations*.

> URL = http://www.lib.umich.edu/libhome/Documents.center/
> fedlaws.html

LEARNING ABOUT THE INTERNET

1. *Guide to Cyberspace*, by Kevin Hughes, introduces new Internet users to the history and terminology of the Internet such as hypertext links and URLs. Also included is information on how to obtain browser software for your computer.

URL = http://www.eit.com/goodies/www.guide/

2. *Frequently Asked Questions About the Web*, by North American Internet Service, answers questions about the Web. This includes information on obtaining browser software for your computer, authoring home pages, and using Web servers.

URL = http://www.boutell.com/faq/

3. *InfoSeek Search* permits subject searching on keywords of a search question to find useful document sources. It can also be accessed by opening the Net Search button on the Netscape toolbar.

URL = http://www.infoseek.com:80/Home

4. *Lycos* is an Internet search engine for WWW documents from the Carnegie Mellon University that allows searching on document titles and contents.

URL = http://lycos.cs.cmu.edu

5. *Argus Clearinghouse for Subject Oriented Internet Resource Guides* provides links to Web page guides organized by broad subject headings, such as health and medicine, social services, and social issues.

URL = http://www.clearinghouse.net/

6. *Local Public Library Web Page* provides public library Web sites in the United States with information on where to find Internet guide books, other "how-to" resources, and Internet access for community users.

URL = http://www.tiac.net/users/mpl/public.libraries.html

STARTING UP YOUR OWN WEB PAGE

1. *Creating Web Services:* Starting up and maintaining a Web page takes careful planning and a commitment of time and money. You can learn about hypertext markup language, the standard used for Web documents, from Netscape.

URL = http://home.netscape.com/assist/net_sites/index.html

2. *Michigan COMNET* is an example of a community server for social services agencies. It includes public service information, bulletin board services, and links to other resources for nonprofit organizations in southeastern Michigan and the metropolitan Detroit area.

URL = http://comnet.org

These URLs are up to date as of September, 1996. The following is a hint if the URL has been changed: Cut back the address to the basic stem address—for example,

URL = http://home.netscape.com

and look in the directory for what you want.

NOTE

1. The *GRANTS, ETC.* Web site was developed by Anita Morse of the University of Michigan's School of Information for a course taught by Armand Lauffer and has been expanded for community access.

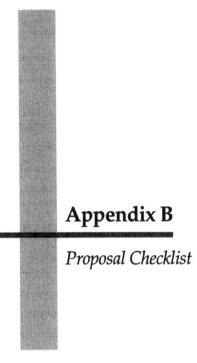

Appendix B

Proposal Checklist

TIPS FOR USE

To decide what to include in your proposal, use this checklist. Then, to make sure you have covered all the bases, use it again before sending the proposal to a potential sponsor. This is a generic list, so if the funder's guidelines indicate specific concerns, make sure these are addressed clearly in the proposal. Use the funder's language and, if appropriate, a writing style similar to that found in the sponsor's own literature. Keep your writing terse and interesting. Put supplementary information in an appendix. Use subtitles or other means to highlight what is important to the funder.

Proposal Sections and Components	*Comments*

Cover materials (may be 1 or 2 pages)

Face sheet

Project title   _____

Sponsoring agency name   _____

Address, fax, phone, e-mail   _____

Tax status   _____

Chief financial officer or director   _____

Contact person (if different)   _____

Overall time frame   _____

Current year or period (if different)   _____

Total budget   _____

Amount requested from funder   _____

Current year budget (if different)   _____

Amount requested from funder   _____

Cover page

Abstract—200 words, that includes

Problem addressed   _____

Goal or objectives sought or both   _____

Program approach or methods   _____

Evaluation approach or methods   _____

Organization capacity   _____

Significance or importance   _____

Table of contents (optional)

Headings for all major sections   _____

Time frame   _____

Budget   _____

Appendix   _____

Narrative

Agency or community capacity

Applicant agency   _____

Purpose or mission   _____

History   _____

Current programs   _____

Populations served   _____

Prior accomplishments or evidence
of qualifications or both   _____

Other relevant organizations,
constituencies, and services   _____

Problem statement

To the point, focused   _____

Well documented (who affected,
how much, how, and to what
severity)   _____

Causal or related factors   _____

Who cares or is affected   _____

Who was involved in identifying
and defining the problem   _____

Relevance to agency mission   _____

Relevance to community concerns   _____

Program goals and objectives

Goal

Shows direction and energizes   _____

Flows directly from problem   _____

Outcome objectives

Specifies what will happen to
whom or to what, by how much,
and by when   _____

Differentiates between ultimate,
intermediate, and immediate   _____

Flows directly from goals   _____

Process objectives

Specify what will be done to or for
whom or what, to what extent,
and when   _____

Lead to outcome objectives   _____

Measurable (if possible)   _____

Clearly define beneficiaries   _____

Program and activities

Activities to be performed   _____

Procedures or sequence of activities
(e.g., flowchart)   _____

Why these and not others   _____

How similar or different from other
programs   _____

How clients, members, and partici-
pants to be selected or recruited   _____

Administration

Structure

Where program is lodged   _____

Linkages to other departments or
organizations   _____

Staffing

Job description of major staff   _____

Tasks grouped functionally   _____

Qualifications for principal staff   _____

Monitoring and evaluation

Monitoring

Built-in feedback mechanisms   _____

Routine stock taking   _____

Involves relevant publics   _____

Relates to process objectives and
time frame   _____

How adjustments to be made   _____

Evaluation

Clear plan for evaluating achievement of outcome objectives _____

Who responsible (i.e., insiders
or outsiders and rationale) _____

Criteria for success _____

Processes for data gathering _____

Process for analysis of findings _____

Explains instruments _____

Reports to be made and to whom _____

Other issues

Significance

Importance (and to whom) _____

Relevance to funder's interests _____

Transferability _____

Builds on or departs from experience _____

Style of presentation

Jargon-free _____

Consistency (goals to objectives,
program, staffing, and evaluation) _____

Use of graphics (if appropriate) _____

Logic of presentation _____

Interesting and compelling _____

Clear _____

Neat _____

Nonnarrative Essentials
Time frame

Activities and milestones _____

All relevant items included _____

Constant with narrative _____

Uses complementary terminology
(tasks similar to those in job
description and process objectives;
achievements similar to outcome) _____

Graphics

Easy to follow   _____

Useful in monitoring   _____

Budget

Tabular (line-item) budget

Consistent with narrative   _____

Includes all items requested of
funder and expected from others   _____

Uses standard categories
(i.e., personnel or nonpersonnel
[travel, supplies, etc.])   _____

Uses reasonable or allowable costs   _____

Includes in-kinds (if permitted)   _____

Includes fringes and benefits   _____

Includes contract services   _____

Includes indirect costs
(if appropriate)   _____

Dollar figures all balance   _____

Justification or explanation

Justifies expenditures in functional
terms (or uses functional table)
that parallels achievement of
outcome or process objectives   _____

Explains unusual or high costs   _____

Explains sources of income to cover
costs beyond funder award   _____

Explains why some items and not
others are asked of funder   _____

Future and complementary funding

If appropriate, plan for continued
or operational funding beyond
the grant   _____

Includes letters of commitment
from other sources (if needed)   _____

Index

About the Author

Armand Lauffer is Professor of Social Work at the University of Michigan. He has written more than 20 volumes on resource development, social marketing, planning, and community organizing. He is founding coeditor of the *Sage Human Service Guides* and the *Sage Sourcebooks for the Human Services*. He is a frequent flyer who splits his time between Ann Arbor, Michigan, and Jerusalem—where he consults with government, municipal, and voluntary agencies. A partial list of his books includes *Strategic Marketing for Not-for-Profit Organizations; Understanding Your Social Agency; Careers, Colleagues and Conflicts; Social Planning at the Community Level; Doing Continuing Education and Staff Development; The Aim of the Game;* and *Assessment Tools. Grantsmanship and Fund Raising* (1984) was a Behavioral Science Book Club selection.